# A SAILOR'S GARLAND

A SAILOR'S GARLAND

SELECTED AND EDITED

BY

JOHN MASEFIELD

Granger Index Reprint Series

 BOOKS FOR LIBRARIES PRESS
FREEPORT, NEW YORK

Originally Published 1924
Reprinted 1969

Permission to include the preface
by John Masefield in this edition
has been granted by the Society of Authors
on behalf of the literary estate of John Masefield

STANDARD BOOK NUMBER:
8369-6108-0

LIBRARY OF CONGRESS CATALOG CARD NUMBER:
70-80376

To C.

INTRODUCTORY

IT is curious that a sea-going people such as the English should have written so little poetry, of a high quality, about the sea and its sailors until comparatively recent times. It might be said that until the end of the eighteenth century our poets hardly saw the beauty of the sea, though they felt its terror. We have poems, such as Donne's "Storm" and "Calm," expressing its horrors and its desolation; and later we have poems, like Falconer's "Shipwreck," expressing its force and fury. These, in their way, are excellent, but they are not exhaustive. They recognize and make significant the grimmest aspects, and only those, of the sea, and of the life of its followers. In this they are not singular. In their loathing of the waters and of sea-life they resemble most early English sea poetry. Nearly all the English poets, from Chaucer to Keats, have a dislike for, or a dread of, the sea, and a hatred of sea-life and no high opinion of sailors. "Chaucer," says someone, "dismisses the sea with a shudder."

He accepts the Shipman as a roadmate, and describes him with delicate art, but he describes him as a ruffian who would rather break cargo than be sober, and to whom the ginger that is hot in the mouth is the one thing worth praying for of all the things in the world. Gower, his follower, seldom leaves dry land ; though for a page or so he sings gracefully about the Sirens. To the metrical romanticists the sea is a wilderness haunted by magical ships plying from wonderful countries. To the Elizabethans (as Shakespeare, Markham, Webster, and Heywood) it is a place of tempest, or the scene of battle, or the haunt of pirates. To the Jacobeans (as Browne, Fletcher, Dekker, and Daborne) it is magical or tempestuous, or the haunt of pirates. To Donne, as I have said, it was desolate and horrible. To Sackville, the courtier, it was little save a place of exile, where one could have wine and hard knocks and a little quiet dice, but no ladies. To Falconer it was dangerous and deadly.

None of these poets took delight in the contemplation of the sea. Shakespeare, indeed, invites to merriment upon the sands. Fletcher dreams about beautiful islands, peopled by goddesses or princesses. Heywood tells us of sea captains drinking wine at a tavern. The others " dismiss the sea with a shudder." Nashe alone seems to have a word of praise for her. To Nashe she is the original home of " Solyman Herring," " our dappert *Piemont Huldrick Herring*," " the puissant red herring, the golden *Hesperides* red herring, the *Meonian* red herring, the red herring of Red Herrings Hall." To Nashe she is the " glassy fieldes of Thetis," the " boiling desert," full of " careeringest billowes," over which go the smacks of Yarmouth " and never bruise one bubble." From Nashe alone does the sea get sympathetic treatment ; and the sympathy of Nashe is not worth a very great deal. It was not until the nineteenth century that she came to her

INTRODUCTORY

own. Then Keats, Shelley, Byron, Wordsworth, and a school of landscape painters taught us to regard her, as we regard her now, not as a hedge but as an outlet, not as an enemy but as a manifestation.

Our sea heroes have received, on the whole, as scanty recognition as their element. Until the beginning of the nineteenth century the poets who honoured our sailors were generally ballad-singers, greater in their zeal than in their poetry. There are a few poems " by eminent hands " to eminent sailors, such as Peele's address to Drake and Hawkins, the noble passage in Browne's Pastorals, Drayton's poem to the Virginian Voyage, and Marvell's poem to Blake ; but these are exceptions. As a rule our great poets have left our great seamen unsung. We have no great epic poem on the deeds of our sailors. The ballad-singers have done their best for us, and " the best in this kind " are excellent ballads, such as " Andrew Barton," and " The Winning of Cales," and the ballad of Vernon taking Porto Bello. Our true sea epics are written in prose rather than in verse. They are to be found in the three folios of Hakluyt, in the four quartos of Purchas, in Mandeville, in " Sir Francis Drake Reviv'd," in Sir Walter Raleigh's story of the *Revenge*, in the books of Exquemeling, Shelvocke, Dampier, Walter, Cook, and Burney. Of these epics, some three or four, not more, appear to have taken firm hold upon the national imagination.

Though the sea and the sea heroes have remained for the most part unsung, the fault is rather racial than personal. Until the nineteenth century the English had little sense of the majesty and grandeur of certain aspects of nature ; and though they could fear and turn to use, they could not glory in the splendour and beauty of breaking water. As a nation they have regarded their great men in something the same way. They have broken their hearts or obeyed them or accepted them blindly, but they have never gloried in them, so that we need not look, in books of early English poetry, for any rapture of perception of the sea's beauty, nor rapture of praise of a hero's noble effort. Our poetical strength is not in rapture nor in panegyric, but in narrative and in characterization, more especially the characterization of homely types. We have had few great poems of the sea, and no great epic of the sea heroes, but we have had unmatchable sea characters in our poetry and in our prose fiction.

The sailor has been expressed for us with perfect art and perfect truth, though he himself may complain of the treatment he has received. The poets have not loved him. They have not been attracted by him. They have dismissed him, not with a shudder, but with a volley of his own oaths or with a scrap of his own song, as a sort of monster, a sort of sea-bear, a sort of a bawling rough Commodore Trunnion. So far as I know there are not half a dozen attractive naval characters, created and celebrated in poetry or in prose fiction, prior to the early nineteenth century. If a poet or a novelist desired a common seaman or a sea captain in his art, he followed the type of Chaucer's shipman or of Shakespeare's boatswain for the one, and that of Congreve's " young Ben " or Smollett's Commodore, or Edmund

INTRODUCTORY

Thompson's Captain Mizen for the other. Heywood's sea captains, at the inn, are perhaps the best we have prior to Miss Austen and Captain Marryat, though our fiction makers have always done well with pirates, as with Captain Ward and Captain Roberts.

We cannot wonder that the poets have said so little that is beautiful about the sailor. There is little to say about him; and that little, to a perceptive person, is very readily apparent. The poetic, or sea-bear sailor, who bawls and drinks and raps you out oaths and bangs upon tables with his cudgel, is always to be found. One can find him on blue water ships at the present time; and where he exists he is the best man in the vessel. He is not fitted to command, but he is excellent before the mast. He has hardly changed since Chaucer's time. One could find a dozen like Chaucer's shipmen in any dock in Liverpool or New York or Sydney or San Francisco. He no longer wears " faldyng," or rough Irish frieze, but he is never without a knife (as he will tell you himself in a coarse proverb), and he is tanned by the wind and the sun, and he is a " good felawe," a good comrade, a stand-by in any sudden trouble. It is significant that Chaucer notes the goodness of his felaweship directly he has drawn his portrait. He describes him riding " as he couthe " (as well, that is, as a sailor generally rides—something like a sack), and he tells us of his clothes, and knife, and tan. Directly the man has been defined for us, Chaucer points out his chief characteristic—

> And certainly he was a good felawe,

that being the one supremely attractive thing in

all sailors. For the rest, he is a mere ruffian with a knavish trick of broaching the wine casks in the hold " while that the chapman sleep." " Of nyce conscience," or tenderness, or ordinary human mercy, he is careless. If he fights, and wins, he sews his prisoners in a topsail and dumps them overboard—

By water he sent hem hoom to every land ;

he " makes water-spaniels of them," as the Elizabethan lord hinted to his successful pirate. But with all his brutality and cunning he is a craftsman and a knowledgeable fellow. He " knows his terms of hunting and the sea card." He can reckon the tides, he knows the currents, he is a good pilot of the Channel and its ports of call, while he can stow a ship's hold like an artist. With all this, he is weather-beaten and toughened by the sea. He is hardy and " wise to undertake " ; not reckless, but valiant and trusty. On the whole, he is the most perfect sailor in creative writing, though, when we get him a little older and a little gentler, in Marryat's Swinburne, we like him rather better.

Shakespeare's sailor, Sebastian's " bawling, blasphemous, incharitable dog," is much such another. His lack of charity places him alongside the shipman, as it would place him alongside many sailors of the present day. He is without any " bowels of mercies," but he is diligent in his office, and a faithful servant, as long as there are planks beneath him. He has a fine contempt for shore-folk. To shore-folk he gives a rough tongue : " Keep your cabins," " Out of our way,

INTRODUCTORY

I say," "What do you here?" etc.; but his men are "my hearts" and "good hearts," good fellows whom he cheers and heartens. There are one or two sailors in Webster's comedies, and the best of these is something more human than either Shakespeare's sea-bear or than Smollett's sea-bulldog; but in forming the present volume I have tried to avoid quotations from plays. Such quotations can seldom be detached effectually from their context, unless they are purely descriptive. I must pass to the consideration of those sea ballads which, after all, make up the bulk of the sea poetry we possess.

The ballads are mostly ancient. One or two were written as late as 1820; and one, a very merry ballad on "Jack Robinson," may be as late as 1830. But most of them, certainly all of those with any serious pretensions to beauty, date from the sixteenth, seventeenth, and eighteenth centuries. They may be classed, as I have ventured to class them, in several broad divisions. They may be ballads which illustrate naval history; or ballads of sea life, its dangers, wonders, and delights; or ballads of tragical disaster, or of poetical justice, such as "Brown Robyn's Confession" or "Captain Glen." Many of them, and some of these are among the best, are love ballads, either from the sailor to his lady or vice versa. As a rule the lady's verses are to be preferred to the sailor's.

The earliest ballads which illustrate our sea history are the battle songs of Laurence Minot, who sings of the Fight at Sluys, and of the destruction of some Spanish pirates. After Minot there is a gap of rather more than two centuries.

The sea battles of the reign of Elizabeth inspire the next poems. There are many Elizabethan sea poems—too many, in fact, to be mentioned here. I will merely indicate Gervase Markham's poem on the last fight of the *Revenge*, the curious poem on Drake's "Indies Voyage," by Thomas Greepe, who made one in that adventure, and the excellent ballad of "The Winning of Cales." This last-mentioned ballad is one of the most vigorous in the language. I know of no poem, with the exceptions of Drayton's "Agincourt," and that older parent poem of the same name, which moves to quite such a triumphant music. It is a stirring piece of writing, and it is so full of "local colour," of little particular details of the actual events of the sack, that one feels that the writer was one of the pikemen, or "one of the lusty bragging bowmen," or "a fire blood, a vantbrace" with the soldiers and sailors engaged. The note

> In some places we did find, pyes baking left behind,
> Meat at fire roasting, and folkes run away

is admirable. A pie, or a roast joint, would be good purchase indeed to any poor sailor, particularly to those who had been living on the poor john and beer of the Elizabethan lazareets. The remark about the materials of the bonfire, a little lower down, is also realistic. I fancy that the man who wrote the lines

> With their fat wainscots, their presses and bedsteads,
> Their joint-stools and tables a fire we made

had lent a hand in the piling up of the gear before

INTRODUCTORY

the torch was set to it. The destruction of the Spanish Armada inspired two or three ballads, but only one of them (that included in this volume) has any literary merit. The defeat of the Armada seems to have been less fruitful to the poets than the defeat of various pirates. Among the best of the sea-battle ballads are those describing the overcoming of Sir Andrew Barton, a Scottish knight who scoured the Channel and intercepted English merchant-ships during the reign of Henry VIII. Sir Andrew was not, in the strict sense, a pirate, as his quarrel was with the Portuguese, but he stopped so many English traders in his search for Portuguese goods that it became necessary "to reason with him." He has inspired many ballads, but this old sixteenth-century ballad is by far the most stirring of them. Sometimes, as in the versions of the ballad which are still familiar to English country folk, he figures as Henry, or Sir Henry, Martyn, one of three Scottish brothers who cast dice, or "kevels," to decide which of them should turn pirate to support the others. The ancient ballad gives a very curious picture of a sea fight. The actual fighting was perhaps a little more determined, and at closer range; but still, in reading the ballad, one creates a fine image of the battle, the ships lying near together, in a good deal of smoke from fire pots and the like, while the archers, in the little gilded tops, keep shooting at the officers. Apart from its historical and pictorial worth, the ballad is manly and grand. There is nobility in the rover's cry—

> "Fight on, my men," Sir Andrew sayes,
> " A little I'me hurt, but yett not slaine ;
> *I'le but lye downe and bleede a while,*
> And then I'le rise and fight agayne."

Sir Andrew is never less than a hero. He has style ; he is no " gentleman of fortune " like Bonnet or Roberts. He dies like a king, and his dead face wears such a nobleness that his very enemies lament him.

More popular than Sir Andrew was a later pirate, whose name for many years was terrible to the English. He inspired a poetical play, two chap-books, a number of ballads, and one knows not how many Royal Proclamations. This was John Ward, a Kentish fisherman, who, after a short service aboard the *Lion's Whelp* man-of-war, turned pirate, with a crew of drunken mates, and at last turned Turk and settled down at Tunis. He became head of a sort of colony of pirates, with whom he roved the Mediterranean, to the destruction of trade. He pillaged many English and Venetian ships, and amassed great wealth. In the height of his prosperity he took for partner one Dansker, or Dansekar, a Dutchman, with whom he afterwards quarrelled. Dansekar eventually obtained a pardon from Henri IV of France, and passed his old age in the service of the Duke of Guise. Ward retired in time " to make his peace with God." When his nerve began to fail he built himself a marble palace among the Tunis orange gardens, where he lived royally, " more like a prince than a pirate," till he died of old age. William Lithgow supped with him there, and seems to have enjoyed his supper.

The ballads about Ward are not historical

INTRODUCTORY

They describe a wonderful battle between a king's ship, the *Rainbow*, and Ward's cruiser. They give the fortunes of the fight to Ward, but the glory to the *Rainbow*, or to a " damsel," a " gallant damsel," a " damsel of fame " who handled the king's ship when her captain was hurt. There was a ship called the *Rainbow* then in the Navy, but she never fought with Ward, nor did any royal ship, so far as we can learn, unless it were the *Lion's Whelp* (Ward's old ship), which King James sent to the Mediterranean to suppress piracy. It is probable that the ballads contain some germ of truth. Perhaps some merchantman named the *Rainbow* escaped from a running fight with Ward, and perhaps her captain, or some man aboard her, made the ballad in the glory of his heart. And perhaps some lover, with an heroical lady, imagined the circumstances of the " damsel of fame."

Sir Francis Drake's achievements on the Spanish Main near Venta Cruz in 1572 were celebrated, some seventy years later, in an opera by Sir William Davenant. He was not neglected by his contemporaries, as has been stated too frequently, for in addition to Peele's send-off he is hymned by Charles FitzGeffery and by his follower Thomas Greepe. Robert Blake, the Admiral of the *Parliament*, was honoured during his life, by Andrew Marvell, in a fine poem. The seventeenth century is rich in sea poems ; and with these two " copies of verses " we may bracket Heywood's poem on " The Sovereign of the Seas," Browne's splendid fragment on the decay of sea adventure, and a number of rousing ballads. After the Restoration we have Sackville's " To all you

Ladies," and a few love ballads of the " Come all ye " kind, and a drinking song which means business.

The eighteenth century gives us several interesting poems. We have one very fine ballad on the death of Admiral Benbow, and a bragging strophe in honour of Admiral Vernon. " The Taking of Porto Bello " (for the sixth or seventh time in our national history) caused the nation to lose its wits. The ballad in this collection preserves one little mite of the general enthusiasm. Those who collect old china will know how frequently the mugs and bowls and plates of 1740 and thereabouts are decorated with Vernon's face, or with pictures of his ships. The triumphant, not to say braggart, note of the ballad (which is a good ballad) may be compared with another note, another tune in the same orchestra, in the ballad of " Hosier's Ghost."

The eighteenth century was a piratical century, as well as a century of great naval achievement and discomfiture. We have a fragment on Captain Kidd, or Kyd, a pirate who made a great stir, not so much by his piracies as by the respectability of the society in which he moved, and the greatness of the names with which his was coupled at the time of his trial. The fragment may still be heard at sea. It is sung to the very excellent tune of Samuel Hall :

> My name is Captain Kidd,
>   Captain Kidd.
> My name is Captain Kidd,
>   Captain Kidd.
> My name is Captain Kidd
>   And wickedly I did ;
> God's laws I did forbid,
>   As I sailed.

> My topsails they did shake
>   As I sailed.
> My topsails they did shake
>   As I sailed.
> My topsails they did shake,
>   And the merchants they did quake,
> For many did I take
>   As I sailed.

The ruffian " Blackbeard " is also celebrated in a ballad ; but Roberts, a more distinguished pirate, remains unsung, though he has been movingly chronicled. The buccaneers of an earlier generation receive sentimental poetical tributes to this day. During their lives they received little honour, and deserved rather less than they received.

The great French wars of the late eighteenth and early nineteenth centuries inspired a mass of verse, mostly execrable, from which one may gather a few good ballads. Captain Marryat's hearty " Port Admiral " and " The Captain stood on the Carronade " are the best of them ; and the mawkish nonsense of the Dibdins and their kind, the worst. Prince Hoare's " Arethusa " is an admirable ballad, not perfect in its form by any means, but full of spirit :

> On deck five hundred men did dance,
> The stoutest they could find in France.
> We with two hundred did advance
> On board of the *Arethusa*.

There is also a rousing though vainglorious ballad on some of the British naval victories under Jervis, Duncan, and Nelson. It goes to the tune of " The Roast Beef of Old England." To one with a voice like a gale of wind it may be confidently recommended. Nelson receives a number of memorial verses, some of them of great dignity; but his victories roused little music save that of drums for many years after his final triumph. One of the very best of the sea ballads of this period is that called "Spanish Ladies," a poem in which some unknown sailor describes his voyage home, and the picking up of the various headlands, the Dodman, Ram Head, the Start, etc., as the ship comes leisurely up Channel towards the Downs. Rather later we have the excellent ditty of "Jack Robinson," by Thomas Hudson, a poem in which the ancient man-of-war's man, with his grog and his pigtail, takes his final leave of us.

Of the ballads which illustrate life at sea, none are quite so good as the earliest. The poem of the pilgrims, sailing from "Sandwych or Winchelsee," to some French port, from which they could tramp to Compostella, is as vivid and as vigorous as a poem could well be. One can hardly read it without imaging the ship, some tub of a dromond, as she goes butting through the Channel, with her foresail dark with sprays as high as the yard, and her deck like Rachel mourning for her children, and her cabins like woe unutterable. It makes one a little squeamish even to read it. There are the groans and the misery and the loud talking at the bows, and the wire-hum of the wind in the rigging, and the "O tally on," "O-y-ho," of the sailors crying out; and groans and more groans, and misery, and then the mockery of the call to dinner. But the poem does not bring one very far. It is good of its kind, but there are better kinds. There are the magical and terrible ballads, such as "The Selchie," "The Demon Lover," "Brown Robyn's Confession," and others, which show us other

INTRODUCTORY xxi

aspects of the sea. These ballads are among the finest in the language. No one could have written a poem like "The Selchie" (with its suggestion of uncanny prescience in the human, inhuman creature) who had not brooded long by the seas, and gone a-gazing into the water after immortal and terrible things, such as people the green pools. "Brown Robyn's Confession" is one of many such. The tale of Jonah is one of the eternal tales. It appears in the folk-lore of most lands, and I can well believe that, if a ship were to meet with head-winds for several months, in the present year, her sailors would speculate unpleasantly, among themselves, as to the cause of it. A good instance of the Jonah ballad is "Captain Glen." This ballad is an example of the terrible fo'c'sle ballad, which the old sailors sometimes sing when they are cheerful. It is not good poetry, but I know no poem which has so deep an effect, when sung as the sailors sing it, in a steady, clear, slightly changing tone, which brings out, as the chorus in a tragedy, with ever-increasing presage, the line

As we went to New Barbary.

The dangers and miseries of life at sea have been sung by many sailors, and I have given ballads enough, I hope, to back my statement. Of the joys of life at sea it does not become a sailor to sing. Such joys as the sea gives are rather those of hope and unrest. The joy that one finds here and there in sea ballads is joy that the voyage is over, or will soon be over, with honour, profit, or safety to the sailor; or joy that the woman he loves is still alive. It is in his love ballads that the sailor shows himself most joyous. The virtue he praises most in women is constancy, for that is the virtue he is likeliest to appreciate. Women are invariably constant to him, perhaps because they have so much temptation to be otherwise. The love tragedies, such as they are which darken this section of my anthology are tragedies due, as all such tragedies are due, not to the women but to the men, in their weakness or their strength.

I have said that one of the joys the sea gives is the joy of unrest. This joy has been expressed in poetry during the last three generations, so perfectly that I have no need to indicate particular names. The glory and the beauty of the water have been hymned in glorious and lovely verse. I wish to express my gratitude to those living poets who have allowed me to quote their poems in that section of this anthology which treats of the beauty and wonder of the sea. I am confident that when the poetry of our time is reckoned up it will be said that one of its chief triumphs is that it has proclaimed the majesty and glory of the dominion of water. It is unnecessary for me to speak of poems like " The Forsaken Merman " ; but before closing this essay I should like to point out the extreme beauty of some of the modern sea poems in this volume. Our early poets have told us of the sea's terrors, and our early ballad singers have told us of our sea victories. It has been the task of modern poets—Mr. Binyon, Mr. Bridges, Mr. Kipling, Mr. Newbolt, and Mr. D. C. Scott—to tell us of the magical attraction of the sea, and to set before us, in ringing and strenuous verses, the nobility of those who have made the seas our heritage.

JOHN MASEFIELD

OMISSIONS

I REGRET extremely that I have been unable to include any poem by Mr. Swinburne. The reasons which forbid that inclusion also force me to omit the two splendid poems, "The Revenge, a Ballad of the Fleet," and the "Voyage of Maeldune," by Alfred Lord Tennyson. Another lamentable, but unfortunately necessary, omission is that of any poem by Mr. A. F. Brady, an Australian poet, whose "Ways of Many Waters" contain the best poems yet written about the merchant sailor and the man-of-war's man.

If in the preparation of this book I have omitted any noble poem, through my own negligence or ignorance, I am sorry; but

Fortune it will take its place, let a man do all he can.

NOTE

I WISH to thank the following poets and publishers for their kindness in granting me permission to avail myself of copyright material :—

Mr. and Mrs. Charles Ashbee, for their rendering of " Ich stand auf hohen Berge " (" Song Book of the Guild of Handicraft," Essex House Press) ; Mr. Laurence Binyon, for " John Winter " (" London Visions," Elkin Mathews) ; Mr. Robert Bridges, for " A Passer-By " (" Shorter Poems," Daniel, Oxford) ; the Rev. Father John Gray, for " Wings in the Dark " and " The Flying Fish " (" Silverpoints," John Lane ; and No. 4 of " The Dial ") ; Messrs. Macmillan, for the late Charles Kingsley's ballad " The Last Buccaneer " ; Mr. R. E. M'Gowan, for " A Young Man's Fancy " ; Mr. T. Sturge Moore, for " The Rower's Chant " (" The Vinedresser," Unicorn Press) ; Messrs. G. P. Putnam's Sons, for the three poems of Walt Whitman ; Mr. Henry Newbolt, for " Messmates " and " Drake's Drum " (" The Island Race " and " Admirals All," Elkin Mathews). Mr. Duncan Campbell Scott, for " The Piper of Arll," " At Les Eboulements " (" Labour and the Angel," Boston, Copeland & Day) ; and for " Off Riviere du Loup " (" The Magic House," Methuen & Co.) ; Messrs. Smith Elder, for the use of the lyric from " Paracelsus " in the collected edition of Robert

Browning's Works); Mr. A. T. Quiller-Couch, for "Victoria" and "Dolor Oogo" ("Poems and Ballads," Methuen); and Messrs. Chatto and Windus, for "Christmas at Sea" (from "Ballads"), by the late R. L. Stevenson.

I also wish to thank the editor and proprietors of the "Manchester Guardian" for allowing me to reprint an article on "Chanties" from their issue of August 16, 1905; and Mr. Rudyard Kipling and Messrs. Appleton & Sons, for the use of the poem "The Last Chanty" ("Seven Seas," Methuen & Co., London, and D. Appleton & Sons, New York).

TABLE OF CONTENTS

	PAGE
INTRODUCTION	
Old Sailors	1

MISCELLANEOUS POEMS

WALT WHITMAN	
Song for All Seas, All Ships	3
JOHN KEATS	
Sonnet	4
ROBERT BRIDGES	
A Passer By	5
JOHN GRAY	
Wings in the Dark	6
DUNCAN CAMPBELL SCOTT	
At Les Éboulements	7
THOMAS L. BEDDOES	
To Sea	7
T. STURGE MOORE	
Rower's Chant	8
LAURENCE BINYON	
John Winter	9
DUNCAN CAMPBELL SCOTT	
Off Rivière du Loup	12
ROBERT BROWNING	
Song from "Paracelsus"	13
ANONYMOUS	
Outwards	15
ALFRED LORD TENNYSON	
The Lotus Eaters	15
GERMAN FOLK-SONG, ADAPTED BY CHARLES AND JANET ASHBEE	
"Ich stand auf hohen Berge"	17
WALT WHITMAN	
After the Sea-Ship	19
JOHN GRAY	
The Flying Fish	19
HENRY NEWBOLT	
Messmates	26

A SAILOR'S GARLAND

	PAGE
WILLIAM SHAKESPEARE	
From "King Richard III"	27
WALT WHITMAN	
The World below the Brine	28
WILLIAM SHAKESPEARE	
Song from "The Tempest"	29
DUNCAN CAMPBELL SCOTT	
The Piper of Arll	29
LORD BYRON	
From "Childe Harold's Pilgrimage"	35
H. W. LONGFELLOW	
Lost Youth	37
RUDYARD KIPLING	
The Last Chanty	38

POEMS ILLUSTRATING OUR SEA HISTORY

LAURENCE MINOT	
The Sea-Fight at Sluys, June 24, 1340	42
Winchelsea Fight, or the Humbling of the Spaniards	46
ANONYMOUS	
Sir Andrew Barton	47
CHARLES FITZ-GEFFERY	
The English Captains	58
SIR WILLIAM DAVENANT	
Sir Francis Drake Reviv'd	64
CHARLES FITZ-GEFFERY	
On Sir Francis Drake	67
ANONYMOUS	
Sir Richard Grenville's Farewell	69
THOMAS GREEPE	
The Taking of Cartagena	70
WILLIAM WARNER	
From Albion's England	74
The Defeat of the Spanish Armada	77
GEORGE PEELE	
A Farewell to the most famous Generals, Sir John Norris and Sir Francis Drake, Knights	79
ANONYMOUS	
The Sailor's Onely Delight	82
ANONYMOUS	
The Winning of Cales	86
GERVASE MARKHAM	
End of the Last Fight of the *Revenge*	89
HENRY NEWBOLT	
Drake's Drum	96

TABLE OF CONTENTS xxix

PAGE

CHARLES FITZ-GEFFERY
    The Last Voyage of Sir Francis Drake and
        Sir John Hawkins - - - 97
WILLIAM WARNER
    From Albion's England - - - 102
MICHAEL DRAYTON
    To the Virginian Voyage - - - 102
ANONYMOUS
    The Honour of Bristol - - - 105
WILLIAM BROWNE
    From Britannia's Pastorals - - 109
THOMAS HEYWOOD
    An Epigram upon His Majesty's Great
        Ship (the *Sovereign of the Seas*) lying
        in the Dock at Woolwich - - 110
ANONYMOUS
    The Famous Fight at Malago - - 113
ANDREW MARVELL
    On the Victory obtained by Admiral
        Blake over the Spaniards in the Bay
        of Santa Cruz - - - 116
GEORGE HARRISON
    The Epitaph Acrostick on Robert Blake - 121
ANONYMOUS
    The Royal Victory - - - 122
ANONYMOUS
    The Second of November - - 125
ANONYMOUS
    Admiral Benbow - - - - 127
ANONYMOUS
    The Death of Admiral Benbow - - 128
ANONYMOUS
    Admiral Hosier's Ghost - - - 130
ANONYMOUS
    Brave News from Admiral Vernon - 133
ANONYMOUS
    Bold Sawyer - - - - 136
DAVID GARRICK
    Heart of Oak - - - - 138
WILLIAM COWPER
    On the Loss of the *Royal George* - - 139
ANONYMOUS
    Admiral Rodney's Triumph on the 12th
        of April - - - - 141
ANONYMOUS
    A New Song on Parker the Delegate
        Head of the Mutiny at Sheerness - 142
PRINCE HOARE
    The *Arethusa* - - - - 144

xxx A SAILOR'S GARLAND

	PAGE
ANONYMOUS	
A New Song on Lord Nelson's Victory at Copenhagen	145
ANONYMOUS	
The Brave Tars of Old England	147
ANONYMOUS	
Trafalgar	151
ANONYMOUS	
The Battle of Trafalgar	153
A. T. QUILLER-COUCH	
Victoria, June 22, 1893	155

POEMS OF SAILORS AND OF LIFE AT SEA

GEOFFREY CHAUCER	
The Shipman	158
ANONYMOUS	
The Sailing of the Pilgrims from Sandwich towards St. James of Compostella	159
ANONYMOUS	
Sir Patrick Spens	161
WILLIAM SHAKESPEARE	
From "The Tempest"	165
ANONYMOUS	
The Saylor's Song	168
ANONYMOUS	
A Ballad of Sea Fardingers, describing Evil Fortune	168
ANONYMOUS	
Sir Walter Raleigh Sailing in the Lowlands	170
ANONYMOUS	
The *Goulden Vanitee*	172
ANONYMOUS	
The *Golden Vanity* (a modern version)	175
JOHN DONNE	
The Storm	176
WILLIAM FALCONER	
From "The Shipwreck"	178
JOHN DONNE	
The Calm	183
MARTYN PARKER	
Neptune's Raging Fury	185
ANONYMOUS	
The Distressed Sailor's Garland	189
CAPTAIN JACK MITFORD, R.N.	
A Gale of Wind (from "Adventures of Johnny Newcome")	195
ANONYMOUS	
The *Benjamin's* Lamentations	199

TABLE OF CONTENTS xxxi

	PAGE
ANONYMOUS	
The Leadsman's Song	202
R. L. STEVENSON	
Christmas at Sea	203
ANONYMOUS	
The Whale	206
ANONYMOUS	
Spanish Ladies	208
ANONYMOUS	
The Greenwich Pensioner	209
ANONYMOUS	
Comfortable Song on the Poor Sailors	210
ANONYMOUS	
Sailors' Delight	211
FREDERICK MARRYAT	
Port Admiral	211
The Captain stood on the Carronade	214
ANONYMOUS	
The Press-Gang	216
ANONYMOUS	
Captain Bover	217
ANONYMOUS	
The *Flash* Frigate	217
LORD BYRON	
The Man-o'-War ("Childe Harold's Pilgrimage")	219
T. HUDSON	
Jack Robinson	220
CAPTAIN JACK MITFORD, R.N.	
The Fight (from "Adventures of Johnny Newcome")	221

THE STORY OF JONAH. POEMS OF MERMAIDS AND OF THE SEA SPIRITS

The Story of Jonah	228
Captain Glen	230
Brown Robyn's Confession	233
William Grismond's Downfall	234
S. T. COLERIDGE	
The Ancient Mariner	237
MATTHEW ARNOLD	
The Forsaken Merman	258
A. T. QUILLER-COUCH	
Dolor Oogo	263
ANONYMOUS	
The Merman Rosmer	265
Ho! for Lubberland	269

xxxii A SAILOR'S GARLAND

	PAGE
GEORGE CHAPMAN	
Ulysses and the Sirens	271
JOHN GOWER	
The Story of Ulysses	273
ANONYMOUS	
The Silkie of Sule Skerrie	274
The Daemon Lover	275
The Mermaid	277

POEMS OF LOVE AND THE AFFECTIONS

The Lass of Lochroyan	278
The Seaman's Happy Return	285
Constance and Anthony	289
THOMAS NASHE AND CHRISTOPHER MARLOWE	
From "The Tragedie of Dido"	295
WILLIAM SHAKESPEARE	
Stephano's Song	296
ANONYMOUS	
The Lowlands of Holland	296
The Maydens of London	297
The Gallant Seaman's Resolution	299
The Seaman's Reply	302
The Gallant Seaman's Return	303
The Gallant Seaman's Song	304
A Sailor	305
CHARLES SACKVILLE	
To all you Ladies	306
ANONYMOUS	
The Seaman's Compass	309
R. E. McGOWAN	
A Young Man's Fancy	314
ANONYMOUS	
The Fair Maid's Choice	315
The Sailor Laddie	317
CAPTAIN THOMSON	
Song to Mary	320
ANONYMOUS	
The North Country Collier	320
The Bold Privateer	321
CHARLES DIBDIN	
Tom Bowling	322

POEMS OF PIRATES AND SMUGGLERS

ANONYMOUS	
John Dory	324
Henry Martyn	325

TABLE OF CONTENTS xxxiii

PAGE

ANONYMOUS
- Dansekar the Dutchman - 326
- Captain Ward and the *Rainbow* - 329
- As we were a-Sailing - 332
- The Salcombe Seaman's Flaunt - 333
- Teach the Rover - 335

CHARLES KINGSLEY
- The Last Buccaneer - 338

LORD MACAULAY
- The Last Buccaneer - 340

ANONYMOUS
- The Smuggler - 341

CHANTIES

EDITOR'S NOTE
- Lowlands - 348
- Storm Along - 349
- Whiskey! Johnny - 349
- John François - 351
- Blow the Man Down - 352
- Roll the Cotton Down - 354
- Reuben Ranzo - 355
- Roll and Go - 356
- Roll him Over - 357
- Hanging Johnny - 358
- Sally Brown - 359
- Poor Old Joe - 359
- Tommy's Gone - 360
- A long Time Ago - 361
- Blow, Bullies, Blow - 362
- The Rio Grande - 363
- Sebastopol - 364
- The Banks of the Sacramento - 365
- The Maid of Amsterdam - 366
- Hand over Hand - 367
- Haul away, O - 368
- Haul the Bowline - 368
- Runaway Chorus - 370
- Paddy Doyle - 371
- Leave her, Johnny - 371

INDEX OF AUTHORS

Arnold, Matthew, 258.
Ashbee, Charles and Janet, 17.

Beddoes, T. L., 7.
Binyon, Laurence, 9.
Bridges, Robert, 5.
Browne, William, 109.
Browning, Robert, 13.
Byron, Lord, 35, 219.

Chapman, George, 271.
Chaucer, Geoffrey, 158.
Coleridge, S. T., 237.
Cowper, William, 139.

Davenant, Sir William, 64.
Dibdin, Charles, 322.
Donne, John, 176, 183.
Drayton, Michael, 102.

Falconer, William, 178.
Fitz-Geffery Charles, 58, 67, 97.

Garrick, David, 138.
Gower, John, 273.
Gray, John, 6, 19.
Greepe, Thomas, 70.

Harrison, George, 121.
Heywood, T., 110.
Hoare, Prince, 144.
Hudson, T., 220.

Keats, John, 4.

Kingsley, Charles, 338.
Kipling, Rudyard, 38.

Longfellow, H. W., 37.

Macaulay, Lord, 340.
McGowan, R. E., 314.
Markham, Gervase, 89.
Marlowe, Christopher, 295.
Marryat, Frederick, 211, 214.
Marvell, Andrew, 116.
Minot, Laurence, 42, 46.
Mitford, Jack, 195, 221.
Moore, T. Sturge, 8.

Nashe, T., 295.
Newbolt, Henry, 26, 96.

Parker, Martyn, 185.
Peele, George, 79.

Quiller-Couch, A. T., 155, 263.

Sackville, Charles, 306.
Scott, Duncan C., 7, 12, 29.
Shakespeare, William, 27, 29, 165, 296.
Stevenson, R. L., 203.

Tennyson, Lord, 15.
Thomson, Captain, 320.

Warner, William, 74, 102.
Whitman, Walt, 3, 19, 28.

A SAILOR'S GARLAND

Old Sailors

Of old Sailors, the song you would hear,
And we old Fiddlers have forgot who they were,
But all we remember, shall come to your ear,
    That were old Sailors of the Queen's
    And the Queen's old Sailors.

With Sir Francis Drake, that was the next man
To the old brave Portugall (who first it began)
To sail through the Straits of Magellan
    Like an old Sailor of the Queen's
    And the Queen's old Sailor.

That put the proud Spanish Armada to wrack,
And travelled all o'er the old World, and came back
In his old ship, laden with gold and old sack
    Like an old Sailor of the Queen's
    And the Queen's old Sailor.

With a silver jugful of jewels and the Spanish King's bed,
And banners flying in his rigging all white and red,
And a drum to beat a bravery when he lay dead,
    Like an old Sailor of the Queen's
    And the Queen's old Sailor.

With a courtly Candish, that seconded him
And taught his old sails the same passage to swim,
And dighted them, therefore, with cloth of gold trim
    Like an old Sailor of the Queen's
    And the Queen's old Sailor.

With an old brave Raleigh, who twice and agen
Sailed over most part of the salt seas, and then
Wrote a brave old history with his old pen
      Like an old Sailor of the Queen's
      And the Queen's old Sailor.

With an old George Anson, who beat round the Horn
With his ships falling to pieces and his sails all torn,
And made Spanish dollars as common as seed corn
      Like an old Sailor of the Queen's
      And the Queen's old Sailor.

With many an old sailor, on many an old ship,
Who hoisted out many a barrel on to many an old slip,
And went below to his hammock or to a can of flip
      Like an old Sailor of the Queen's
      And the Queen's old Sailor.

With many an old brave captain we shall never know,
Who walked the decks under the colours when the winds did blow,
And made the planks red with his blood before they carried him below
      Like an old Sailor of the Queen's
      And the Queen's old Sailor.

And in Davy Jones's Taverns may they sit at ease,
With their old tarpaulin aprons over their old knees,
Singing their old sea ballads and yarning of the seas
      Like good old Sailors of the Queen's
      And the Queen's old Sailors.

(Adapted)

MISCELLANEOUS POEMS

Song for All Seas, All Ships

I

To-day a rude brief recitative,
Of ships sailing the seas, each with its special flag
    or ship-signal,
Of unnamed heroes in the ships—of waves spread-
    ing and spreading far as the eye can reach,
Of dashing spray, and the winds piping and
    blowing,
And out of these a chant for the sailors of all
    nations,
Fitful, like a surge.

Of sea-captains young or old, and the mates, and
    of all intrepid sailors,
Of the few, very choice, taciturn, whom fate can
    never surprise nor death dismay,
Pick'd sparingly without noise by thee old ocean,
    chosen by thee,
Thou sea that pickest and cullest the race in time,
    and unitest nations,
Suckled by thee, old husky nurse, embodying thee,
Indomitable, untamed as thee.

(Ever the heroes on water or on land, by ones or
    twos appearing,
Ever the stock preserv'd and never lost, though
    rare enough for seed preserv'd.)

II

Flaunt out O sea your separate flags of nations!
Flaunt out visible as ever the various ship-signals!
But do you reserve especially for yourself and for
    the soul of man one flag above all the rest,
A spiritual woven signal for all nations, emblem
    of man elate above death,
Token of all brave captains and all intrepid sailors
    and mates,
And all that went down doing their duty,
Reminiscent of them, twined from all intrepid
    captains young or old,
A pennant universal, subtly waving all time, o'er
    all brave sailors,
All seas, all ships.

WALT WHITMAN

Sonnet on the Sea

It keeps eternal whisperings around
  Desolate shores, and with its mighty swell
  Gluts twice ten thousand caverns, till the spell
Of Hecate leaves them their old shadowy sound.
Often 'tis in such gentle temper found,
  That scarcely will the very smallest shell
  Be mov'd for days from whence it sometime fell,
When last the winds of heaven were unbound,
Oh ye! who have your eyeballs vex'd and tir'd,
  Feast them upon the wideness of the Sea;
  Oh ye! whose ears are dinn'd with uproar rude,
Or fed too much with cloying melody,—
  Sit ye near some old cavern's mouth, and brood
Until ye start, as if the sea-nymphs quir'd!

JOHN KEATS

A Passer By

Whither, O splendid ship, thy white sails crowding,
Leaning across the bosom of the urgent West,
That fearest nor sea rising, nor sky clouding,
Whither away, fair rover, and what thy quest?
Ah, soon, when Winter has all our vales opprest,
When skies are cold and misty, and hail is hurling,
Wilt thou glide on the blue Pacific, or rest
In a summer haven asleep, thy white sails furling?

I there before thee, in the country that well thou knowest,
Already arrived am inhaling the odorous air:
I watch thee enter unerringly where thou goest,
And anchor queen of the strange shipping there,
Thy sails for awnings spread, thy masts bare:
Nor is aught from the foaming reef to the snow-capped, grandest
Peak, that is over the feathery palms more fair
Than thou, so upright, so stately, and still thou standest.

And yet, O splendid ship, unhailed and nameless,
I know not if, aiming a fancy, I rightly divine
That thou hast a purpose joyful, a courage blameless,
Thy port assured in a happier land than mine.
But for all I have given thee, beauty enough is thine,
As thou, aslant with trim tackle and shrouding,
From the proud nostril curve of a prow's line
In the offing scatterest foam, thy white sails crowding.

ROBERT BRIDGES

Wings in the Dark

FORTH into the warm darkness faring wide—
More silent momently the silent quay—
Towards where the ranks of boats rock to the tide,
Muffling their plaintive gurgling jealously.

With gentle nodding of her gracious snout,
One greets her master till he steps aboard:
She flaps her wings impatient to get out;
She runs to plunder, straining every cord.

Full-winged and stealthy like a bird of prey
All tense the muscles of her seemly flanks;
She the coy creature that the idle day
Sees idly riding in the idle ranks.

Backward and forth, over the chosen ground,
Like a young horse, she drags the heavy trawl
Content; or speeds her rapturous course unbound,
And passing fishers through the darkness call,

Deep greeting, in the jargon of the sea.
Haul upon haul, flounders and soles and dabs,
And phosphorescent animalculæ,
Sand, sea drift, weeds, thousands of worthless crabs.

Darkling upon the mud the fishes grope,
Cautious to stir, staring with jewel eyes;
Dogs of the sea, the savage congers mope,
Winding their sulky march meander-wise.

Suddenly all is light and life and flight,
Upon the sandy bottom, agate strewn.
The fishers mumble, waiting till the night
Urge on the clouds, and cover up the moon.

JOHN GRAY

At Les Éboulements

A GLAMOUR on the phantom shore
  Of golden pallid green,
Gray purple in the flats before,
  The river streams between.

From hazy hamlets one by one,
  Beyond the island-bars,
The casements in the setting sun
  Flash back in violet stars.

A brig is straining out for sea,
  To Norway or to France she goes,
And all her happy flags are free,
  Her sails are flushed with rose.
                    DUNCAN CAMPBELL SCOTT

To Sea

To sea, to sea! The calm is o'er;
The wanton water leaps in sport,
And rattles down the pebbly shore;
The dolphin wheels, the sea-cows snort,
And unseen mermaids pearly song
Comes bubbling up the weeds among.
  Fling broad the sail, dip deep the oar:
  To sea, to sea! The calm is o'er.

To sea, to sea! Our white-wing'd bark
Shall billowing cleave its wat'ry way,
And with its shadow, fleet and dark,
Break the caved Triton's azure day,

Like mountain eagle soaring light
O'er antelopes on Alpine height.
  The anchor heaves, the ship swings free,
  Our sails swell full: to sea, to sea!
                        T. L. BEDDOES

Rower's Chant

Row till the land dip 'neath
  The sea from view.
Row till a land peep up,
  A home for you.

Row till the masts sing songs
  Welcome and sweet.
Row till the waves outstripped,
  Give up dead beat.

Row till the sea-nymphs rise
  To ask you why
Rowing you tarry not
  To hear them sigh.

Row till the stars grow bright
  Like certain eyes.
Row till the noon be high
  As hopes you prize.

Row till you harbour in
  All longing's port.
Row till you find all things
  For which you sought.
                        T. STURGE MOORE

John Winter

WHAT ails John Winter, that so oft
   Silent he sits apart?
The neighbours cast their looks on him;
   But deep he hides his heart.

In Deptford streets the houses small
   Huddle forlorn together.
Whether the wind blow or be still,
   'Tis soiled and sorry weather.

But over these dim roofs arise
   Tall masts of ocean ships.
Whenever John Winter looked on them,
   The salt blew on his lips.

He cannot pace the street about,
   But they stand before his eyes!
The more he shuns them, the more proud
   And beautiful they rise.

He turns his head, but in his ear
   The steady Trade-Winds run,
And in his eye the endless waves
   Ride on into the sun.

His little child at evening said,
   " Now tell us, dad, a tale
Of naked men that shoot with bows,
   Tell of the spouting whale!"

He told old tales, his eyes were bright,
   His wife looked up to see,
And smiled on him: but in the midst
   He ended suddenly.

He bade his boys good-night, and kissed
  And held them to his breast.
They wondered and were still, to feel
  Their lips so fondly pressed.

He sat absorbed in silent gloom.
  His wife lifted her head
From sewing, and stole up to him,
  "What ails you, John?" she said.

He spoke no word. A silent tear
  Fell softly down her cheek.
She knelt beside him, and his hand
  Was on her forehead meek.

But even as his tender touch
  Her dumb distress consoled,
The mighty waves danced in his eyes
  And through the silence rolled.

There fell a soft November night,
  Restless with gusts that shook
The chimneys, and beat wildly down
  The flames in the chimney nook.

John Winter lay beside his wife,
  'Twas past the mid of night.
Softly he rose, and in dead hush
  Stood stealthily upright.

Softly he came where slept his boys,
  And kissed them in their bed;
One stretched his arms out in his sleep:
  At that he turned his head.

JOHN WINTER

And now he bent above his wife,
  She slept a sleep serene,
Her patient soul was in the peace
  Of breathing slumber seen.

At last, he kissed one aching kiss,
  Then shrank again in dread,
And from his own home guiltily
  And like a thief he fled.

But now with darkness and the wind
  He breaths a breath more free,
And walks with calmer steps, like one
  Who goes with destiny.

And see, before him the great masts
  Tower with all their spars
Black on the dimness, soaring bold
  Among the mazy stars.

In stormy rushings through the air
  Wild scents the darkness filled,
And with a fierce forgetfulness
  His drinking nostril thrilled.

He hasted with quick feet, he hugged
  The wildness to his breast,
As one who goes the only way
  To set his heart at rest.

When morning glimmered, a great ship
  Dropt gliding down the shore.
John Winter coiled the anchor ropes
  Among his mates once more.

LAURENCE BINYON

Off Rivière du Loup

O SHIP incoming from the sea
With all your cloudy tower of sail,
Dashing the water to the lee,
And leaning grandly to the gale.

The sunset pageant in the west
Has filled your canvas curves with rose,
And jewelled every toppling crest
That crashes into silver snows!

You know the joy of coming home,
After long leagues to France or Spain
You feel the clear Canadian foam
And the gulf water heave again.

Between these sombre purple hills
That cool the sunset's molten bars,
You will go on as the wind wills,
Beneath the river's roof of stars.

You will toss onward towards the lights
That spangle over the lonely pier,
By hamlets glimmering on the heights,
By level islands black and clear.

You will go on beyond the tide,
Through brimming plains of olive sedge,
Through paler shadows light and wide,
The rapids piled along the ledge.

At evening off some reedy bay
You will swing slowly on your chain,
And catch the scent of dewy hay,
Soft blowing from the pleasant plain.

DUNCAN CAMPBELL SCOTT

Song from "Paracelsus"

Over the sea our galleys went,
With cleaving prows in order brave,
To a speeding wind and a bounding wave—
  A gallant armament:
Each bark built out of a forest-tree
  Left leafy and rough as first it grew,
And nailed all over the gaping sides,
Within and without, with black bull-hides,
Seethed in fat and suppled in flame,
To bear the playful billows' game:
So each good ship was rude to see,
Rude and bare to the outward view,
  But each upbore a stately tent;
Where cedar pales in scented row
Kept out the flakes of the dancing brine:
And an awning drooped the mast below,
In fold on fold of the purple fine,
That neither noontide nor starshine
Nor moonlight cold which maketh mad
  Might pierce the regal tenement.
When the sun dawned, oh, gay and glad
We set the sail and plied the oar:
But when the night-wind blew like breath,
For joy of one day's voyage more,
We sang together on the wide sea,
Like men at peace on a peaceful shore;
Each sail was loosed to the wind so free,
Each helm made sure by the twilight star,
And in a sleep as calm as death,
We, the voyagers from afar,
  Lay stretched along, each weary crew
In a circle round its wondrous tent,
Whence gleamed soft light and curled rich scent,

And with light and perfume music too ;
So the stars wheeled round, and the darkness past,
And at morn we started beside the mast,
And still each ship was sailing fast !

Now, one morn, land appeared—a speck
Dim trembling betwixt sea and sky ;
" Avoid it," cried our pilot, " check
　The shout, restrain the eager eye ! "
But the heaving sea was black behind
For many a night and many a day,
And land, though but a rock, drew nigh ;
So we brake the cedar-pales away,
Let the purple awning flap in the wind,
　And a statue bright was in every deck !
We shouted, every man of us,
And steered right into the harbour thus,
With pomp and pæan glorious.

A hundred shapes of lucid stone !
　All day we built its shrine for each,
A shrine of rock for every one—
Nor paused till in the westering sun
　We sat together on the beach
To sing, because our task was done.
When lo ! what shouts and merry songs !
What laughter all the distance stirs !
A loaded raft with happy throngs
Of gentle islanders !

" Our isles are just at hand," they cried ;
　" Like cloudlets faint in even sleeping,
Our temple-gates are opened wide,
　Our olive-groves thick shade are keeping
For these majestic forms "—they cried.

THE LOTUS-EATERS

Oh, then we awoke with sudden start
From our deep dream, and knew, too late,
How bare the rock, how desolate,
Which had received our precious freight;
   Yet we called out—" Depart!
Our gifts, once given, must here abide.
   Our work is done; we have no heart
To mar our work," we cried.

ROBERT BROWNING

Outwards

OVER the dim blue rim of the sea
   Comes the pale gold disc of the moon;
The topsails slat as we pass the quay,
   And the yard goes up with a tune.

We are outward bound for the west to-night,
   And the yard goes up with a cheer;
And the bells will ring in the town to-night,
   And the men in the inns will hear.

And the carts will creak in the lanes to-night,
   And the girls will dance to the band;
But we shall be out with the sails to fist,
   And the topsail-sheets to hand.

The Lotus-Eaters

" COURAGE!" he said, and pointed toward the land,
" This mounting wave will roll us shoreward soon."
In the afternoon they came unto a land

In which it seemed always afternoon.
All round the coast the languid air did swoon,
Breathing like one that hath a weary dream.
Full-faced above the valley stood the moon ;
And like a downward smoke, the slender stream
Along the cliff to fall and pause and fall did seem.

A land of streams ! some, like a downward smoke,
Slow-dropping veils of thinnest lawn, did go ;
And some thro' wavering lights and shadows broke,
Rolling a slumbrous sheet of foam below.
They saw the gleaming river seaward flow
From the inner land : far off, three mountain-tops,
Three silent pinnacles of aged snow,
Stood sunset-flush'd : and, dew'd with showery drops,
Up-clomb the shadowy pine above the woven copse.

The charmed sunset linger'd low adown
In the red West : thro' mountain clefts the dale
Was seen far inland, and the yellow down
Border'd with palm, and many a winding vale
And meadow, set with slender galingale ;
A land where all things always seem'd the same !
And round about the keel with faces pale,
Dark faces pale against that rosy flame,
The mild-eyed melancholy Lotus-eaters came.

Branches they bore of that enchanted stem,
Laden with flower and fruit, whereof they gave
To each, but whoso did receive of them,
And taste, to him the gushing of the wave

Far, far away did seem to mourn and rave
On alien shores; and if his fellow spake,
His voice was thin, as voices from the grave;
And deep-asleep he seem'd, yet all awake,
And music in his ears his beating heart did make.

They sat them down upon the yellow sand,
Between the sun and moon upon the shore;
And sweet it was to dream of Fatherland,
Of child, and wife, and slave; but evermore
Most weary seem'd the sea, weary the oar,
Weary the wandering fields of barren foam.
Then some one said, "We will return no more";
And all at once they sang, "Our island home
Is far beyond the wave; we will no longer roam."

ALFRED LORD TENNYSON

"Ich Stand Auf Hohen Berge"

Air—GERMAN FOLK SONG

I STOOD on a mighty mountain
  Looking over the sea;
And there I spied a ship at anchor,
There I spied a ship riding at anchor,
  And she beckoned to me.

Then she signalled with white flags,
  With flags green and blue,
And the captain sent me out a little boat,
Sent me out a little leaping jolly boat,
  With the pick of his ship's crew.

We tossed in the yellow sunset,
  We climbed the ship's side;
And the captain paced about the quarter-deck,
Yes, the captain paced the windy quarter-deck
  As he watched for the tide.

She'd a cargo of crimson roses
  And anemones blue;
And a dozen ton of shining beryl stones,
Yes, a dozen ton of sea-green beryl stones
  For to make her ride true.

" Say, captain, where's she bound for
  With her cargo of flowers ? "
" Oh, we're sailing out into the West, my lad,
Sailing out into the wondrous West, my lad,
  For a thousand good hours.

" We are bound for the Isle of Fancy,
  Through moonlight, through foam;
And who knows if we shall land our beryl stones
Land our hundred bags of shining beryl stones,
  Or our brave ship bring home."

" If her masts now should be broken,
  Her compass be lost;
If the captain should misread his reckoning,
Through the western stars misread his reckoning
  Ere the green sea be crossed ? "

" Nay, tear up the gallant anchor,
  Let all her sails run;
And we'll cheer the merry lads of Devonshire,
(Yes, we're all of us stout lads of Devonshire !)
  And away towards the Sun ! "

                    CHARLES AND JANET ASHBEE

After the Sea-Ship

AFTER the sea-ship, after the whistling winds,
After the white-grey sails taut to their spars and ropes,
Below, a myriad myriad waves hastening, lifting up their necks,
Tending in ceaseless flow toward the track of the ship,
Waves of the ocean bubbling and gurgling, blithely prying,
Waves, undulating waves, liquid, uneven, emulous waves,
Toward that whirling current, laughing and buoyant, with curves,
Where the great vessel sailing and tacking displaced the surface,
Larger and smaller waves in the spread of the ocean yearnfully flowing,
The wake of the sea-ship after she passes, flashing and frolicsome under the sun,
A motley procession with many a fleck of foam and many fragments,
Following the stately and rapid ship, in the wake following.

WALT WHITMAN

The Flying Fish

I

MYSELF am Hang, the buccaneer,
Whom children love and brave men fear
Master of courage, come what come,
Master of craft and called Sea-scum.

Student of wisdom and waterways,
Course of moons and the birth of days :
To him in whose heart all things be,
I bring my story from the sea.

The same am I as that sleek Hang,
Whose pattens along the stone quay clang
In sailing time : whose pile is high
In the mart when the merchants come to buy ;

Am he who cumbers his lowly hulk
With refuse bundles of feeble bulk ;
Turns sailor's eyes to the weather skies ;
Bows low to the master of merchandise ;

Who hoists his sail with the broken slats :
Whose lean crew is scarcely food for his rats ;
Am he who creeps from tower top ken
And utmost vision of all men.

Ah then ! am he who changes line,
And no man knoweth that course of mine ;
Am he, sir Sage, who sails to the sea
Where an island and other wonders be.

After six days we sight the coast ;
And my palace top ; (should the sailor boast)
Sail rattles down ; and then we ride,
Mean junk and proud, by my palace side.

For there lives a junk in that ancient sea,
Where the gardens of Hang, and his palace be ;
O my fair junk ! which once aboard
The pirate knows no living lord.

THE FLYING FISH

Its walls are painted water-green
Like the green sea's self, both shade and sheen,
Lest any mark it. (The pirate's trade
Is to hover swiftly and make afraid.)

Its sails are fashioned of lithe bamboo,
All painted blue as the sky is blue,
So it be not seen till the prey be nigh.
(Hang loves not that the same should fly.)

In midst of the first a painted sun
Gleams gold like the celestial yon.
In midst of the second a tender moon,
That a lover might kiss his flute and swoon,

Or maid touch lute at sight of the third,
Pictured with all the crystal herd.
So the silly ships are mazed at sight
Of night by day and day by night;

For wind and water a goodlier junk
Than all that have ever sailed or sunk.
Which junk was theirs: none fiercer than
My fathers since the fall of man.

So cotton rags lays Hang aside;
Lays bare the sailor's gristly hide;
He wraps his body in vests of silk,
Ilk is as beautiful as ilk.

Then Hang puts on his ancient mail,
Silver and black, and scale on scale,
Like dragons, which his grandsire bore
Before him, and his grandsire before.

He binds his legs with buskins grim,
Tawny and gold for the pride of him.
His feet are bare, like his who quelled
The dragon; his feet are feet of eld.

His head is brave with a lac-wrought casque,
The donning which is a heavy task;
Its lappets are spiked like a dolphin's fin;
'Tis strapped with straps of tiger skin.

The passions of his fathers whelm
The heart of Hang when he wears their helm.
Then Hang grows wrinkled betwixt his eyes,
He frowns like a devil, devilwise.

His eyeballs start, his mark is red
Like to the last judge of the dead;
His nostrils gape; his mouth is the mouth
Of the fish that swims in the torrid south.

His beard the pirate Hang lets flow.
He lays his hand on his father's bow:
Wherewith a cunning man of strength
Might shoot a shaft the vessel's length.

I have another of crimson lac,
Of a great man's height, so the silk be slack.
The bolt departs with a brazen clang,
'Tis drawn with the foot, and the foot of Hang.

Such house and harness become me when
I wait upon laden merchantmen;
'Twixt tears and the sea, 'twixt brine and brine,
They shudder at sight of me and mine.

THE FLYING FISH

Of the birds that fly in the farthest sea,
Six are more strange than others be;
Under its tumble, among the fish,
Six are a marvel passing wish.

First is a hawk, exceeding great;
He dwelleth alone, he hath no mate;
His neck is bound with a yellow ring;
On his breast is the crest of an ancient king.

The second bird is exceeding pale,
From little head to scanty tail;
She is striped with black on either wing,
Which is rose-lined like a costly thing.

Though small the bulk of the brilliant third,
Of all blue birds 'tis the bluest bird,
They fly in bands; and seen by day,
By the side of them the sky is grey.

I mind the fifth, I forget the fourth,
Save that it comes from east and north;
The fifth is an orange white-billed duck;
He diveth for fish like the god of Luck;

He hath never a foot on which to stand,
For water yields and he loves not land.
This is the end of many words,
Save one, concerning marvellous birds.

The great-faced dolphin is first of fish,
He is devil-eyed and devilish.
Of all the fishes is he most brave;
He walks the sea like an angry wave.

The second, the fishes call their lord.
Himself a bow, his face is a sword;
His sword is armed with a hundred teeth;
Fifty above and fifty beneath.

The third hath a scarlet suit of mail,
The fourth is nought but a feeble tail.
The fifth is a whip with a hundred strands;
And every arm hath a hundred hands.

The last strange fish is the last strange bird.
Of him no sage hath even heard;
He roams the sea in a gleaming horde,
In fear of the dolphin and him of the sword.

He leaps from the sea with a silken swish.
He beats the air does the flying fish.
His eyes are round with excess of fright,
Bright as the drops of his pinions' flight.

In sea and sky he hath no peace,
For the five strange fish are his enemies.
And the five strange fowls keep watch for him
They know him well by his crystal gleam.

Oftwhiles, sir Sage, on my junk's white deck,
Have I seen this fish-bird come to wreck;
Oftwhiles (fair deck) 'twixt bow and poop,
Have I seen that piteous sky fish stoop.

Scaled bird, how his snout and gills dilate,
All quivering and roseate!
He pants in crystal and mother-of-pearl,
While his body shrinks and his pinions furl.

THE FLYING FISH

His beauty passes like bubbles blown;
The white bright bird is a fish of stone.
The bird so fair, for its putrid sake,
Is flung to the dogs in the junks' white wake.

II

Have thought, son Pirate, some such must be
As the beast thou namest in yonder sea.
Else, bring me a symbol from nature's gear
Of aspiration born of fear.

Hast been, my son, to the doctor's booth
Some day when Hang had a qualm to soothe?
Hast noted the visible various sign
Of each flask's virtue, son of mine?

Rude picture of insect seldom found,
Of plant that thrives in marshy ground,
Goblin of east wind, fog or draught,
Sign of the phial's potent craft?

'Tis even thus where the drug is sense,
Where wisdom is more than frankincense,
Wit's grain than a pound of pounded bones;
Where knowledge is redder than ruby stones.

Hast thou marked how poppies are sign of sin?
How bravery's mantle is tiger skin?
How earth is dark and dumb with care?
How song is the speech of all the air?

(Thou hast? Thou'rt wise in thy sailor kind.
Not every fruit is known by its rind.)

I've a truth distilled and strained and casked ;
Thou hast brought the symbol it sorely asked.

A tree is the sign most whole and sure
Of aspiration plain and pure.
Of the variation one must wend
In search of the sign to the world's wide end.

Thy fish is the fairest of all that be
In the throbbing heart of yonder sea.
He says in his iridescent heart ;
I am gorgeous-eyed and a fish apart.

My back has the secret of every shell,
The Hang of fishes knows me well ;
Scales of my breast are softer still,
The ugly fishes devise my ill.

He prays the maker of water-things
Not for a sword, but cricket's wings ;
Not to be one of the sons of air ;
To be rid of the water is all his prayer.

All his hope is a fear-whipped whim,
All directions are one to him.
There are seekers of wisdom no less absurd,
Son Hang, than thy fish that would be a bird.
JOHN GRAY

Messmates

He gave us all a good-bye cheerily
  At the first dawn of day ;
We dropped him down the side full drearily
  When the light died away.

It's a dead dark watch that he's a-keeping there,
And a long, long night that lags a-creeping there,
Where the Trades and the tides roll over him
  And the great ships go by.

He's there alone with green seas rocking him
  For a thousand miles round;
He's there alone with dumb things mocking him,
  And we're homeward bound.
It's a long, lone watch that he's a-keeping there,
And a dead cold night that lags a-creeping there,
While the months and the years roll over him
  And the great ships go by.

I wonder if the tramps come near enough—
  As they thrash to and fro,
And the battleship's bells ring clear enough
  To be heard down below;
If through all the lone watch that he's a-keeping
    there,
And the long, cold night that lags a-creeping
    there
The voices of the sailor-men shall comfort him
  When the great ships go by.

HENRY NEWBOLT

From "King Richard III"

I saw a thousand fearful wrecks;
A thousand men that fishes gnaw'd upon;
Wedges of gold, great anchors, heaps of pearl,
Inestimable stones, unvalued jewels,
All scatter'd in the bottom of the sea.
Some lay in dead men's skulls; and, in those holes

Where eyes did once inhabit, these were crept
(As 'twere in scorn of eyes) reflecting gems,
That woo'd the slimy bottom of the deep,
And mock'd the dead bones that were scatter'd by.
WILLIAM SHAKESPEARE

The World Below the Brine

THE world below the brine,
Forest at the bottom of the sea, the branches and leaves,
Sea-lettuce, vast lichens, strange flowers and seeds, the thick tangles, openings and pink turf,
Different colours, pale grey and green, purple, white and gold, the play of light through the water,
Dumb swimmers there among the rocks, coral, gluten, grass, rushes, and the aliment of the swimmers,
Sluggish existences grazing there suspended, or slowly crawling close to the bottom,
The sperm-whale at the surface blowing air and spray, or disporting with his flukes,
The leaden-eyed shark, the walrus, the turtle, the hairy sea-leopard, and the sting-ray,
Passions there, wars, pursuits, tribes, sight in those ocean-depths, breathing that thick-breathing air, as so many do,
The change thence to the sight here, and to the subtle air breathed by beings like us who walk this sphere,
The change onward from ours to that of beings who walk other spheres.
WALT WHITMAN

Song from "The Tempest"

FULL fathom five thy father lies;
Of his bones are coral made;
These are pearls that were his eyes:
Nothing of him that does fade,
But doth suffer a sea-change
Into something rich and strange.
Sea-nymphs hourly ring his knell;
    Ding-dong.
Hark! now I hear them—ding-dong, bell.
WILLIAM SHAKESPEARE

The Piper of Arll

THERE was in Arll a little cove
Where the salt wind came cool and free:
A foamy beach that one would love,
If he were longing for the sea.

A brook hung sparkling on the hill,
The hill swept far to ring the bay;
The bay was faithful, wild or still,
To the heart of the ocean far away.

There were three pines above the comb.
That, when the sun flared and went down,
Grew like three warriors reiving home
The plunder of a burning town.

A piper lived within the grove,
Tending the pasture of his sheep;
His heart was swayed with faithful love,
From the springs of God's ocean clear and deep.

And there a ship one evening stood,
Where ship had never stood before;
A pennon bickered red as blood,
An angel glimmered at the prore.

About the coming on of dew,
The sails burned rosy, and the spars,
Were gold, and all the tackle grew
Alive with ruby-hearted stars.

The piper heard an outland tongue,
With music in the cadenced fall;
And when the fairy lights were hung,
The sailors gathered one and all.

And leaning on the gunwales dark,
Crusted with shells and dashed with foam,
With all the dreaming hills to hark,
They sang their longing songs of home.

When the sweet airs had fled away,
The piper, with a gentle breath,
Moulded a tranquil melody
Of lonely love and longed for death.

When the fair sound began to lull,
From out the fire flies and the dew,
A silence held the shadowy hull,
Until the eerie song was through.

Then from the dark and dreary deck,
An alien song began to thrill;
It mingled with the drumming beck,
And stirred the braird upon the hill.

THE PIPER OF ARLL

Beneath the stars each sent to each
A message tender, till at last
The piper slept upon the beach,
The sailors slumbered round the mast.

Still as a dream till nearly dawn,
The ship was bosomed on the tide;
The streamlet murmuring on and on,
Bore the sweet water to her side.

Then shaking out her lawny sails,
Forth on the misty sea she crept;
She left the dawning of the dales,
Yet in his cloak the piper slept.

And when he woke he saw the ship,
Limned black against the crimson sun;
Then from the disc he saw her slip,
A wraith of shadow—she was gone.

He threw his mantle on the beach,
He went apart like one distraught,
His lips were moved—his desperate speech
Stormed his inviolable thought.

He broke his human-throated reed,
And threw it in the idle rill;
But when its passion had its meed,
He found it in the eddy still.

He mended well the patient flue,
Again he tried its various stops;
The closures answered tight and true,
And starting out in piercing drops,

A melody began to drip
That mingled with a ghostly thrill
The vision-spirit of the ship,
The secret of his broken will.

Beneath the pines he piped and swayed,
Master of passion and of power;
He was his soul and what he played,
Immortal for a happy hour.

He, singing into nature's heart,
Guiding his will by the world's will,
With deep, unconscious, childlike art
Had hung his soul out and was still.

And then at evening came the bark
That stirred his dreaming heart's desire;
It burned slow lights along the dark
That died in glooms of crimson fire.

The sailors launched a sombre boat,
And bent with music at the oars;
The rhythm throbbing every throat,
And lapsing round the liquid shores,

Was that true tune the piper sent,
Unto the wave-worn mariners,
When with the beck and ripple blent
He heard that outland song of theirs.

Silent they rowed him, dip and drip,
The oars beat out an exequy,
They laid him down within the ship,
They loosed a rocket to the sky.

THE PIPER OF ARLL

It broke in many a crimson sphere
That grew to gold and floated far,
And left the sudden shore-line clear,
With one slow-changing, drifting star.

Then out they shook the magic sails,
That charmed the wind in other seas,
From where the west line pearls and pales,
They waited for a ruffling breeze.

But in the world there was no stir,
The cordage slacked with never a creak,
They heard the flame begin to purr
Within the lantern at the peak.

They could not cry, they could not move,
They felt the lure from the charmed sea;
They could not think of home or love
Or any pleasant land to be.

They felt the vessel dip and trim,
And settle down from list to list;
They saw the sea-plain heave and swim
As gently as a rising mist.

And down so slowly, down and down,
Rivet by rivet, plank by plank;
A little flood of ocean flown
Across the deck, she sank and sank.

From knee to breast the water wore,
It crept and crept ere they were ware.
Gone was the angel at the prore,
They felt the water float their hair.

They saw the salt plain spark and shine,
They threw their faces to the sky;
Beneath a deepening film of brine
They saw the star-flash blur and die.

She sank and sank by yard and mast,
Sank down the shimmering gradual dark;
A little drooping pennon last
Showed like the black fin of a shark.

And down she sank, till, keeled in sand,
She rested safely balanced true,
With all her upward gazing band,
The piper and the dreaming crew.

And there unmarked of any chart,
In unrecorded deeps they lie.
Empearled within the purple heart
Of the great sea for aye and aye.

Their eyes are ruby in the green
Long shaft of sun that spreads and rays,
And upward with a wizard sheen
A fan of sea-light leaps and plays.

Tendrils of or and azure creep
And globes of amber light are rolled,
And in the gloaming of the deep
Their eyes are starry pits of gold.

And sometimes in the liquid night
The hull is changed, a solid gem,
That glows with a soft stony light,
The lost prince of a diadem.

And at the keel a vine is quick,
That spreads its bines and works and weaves
O'er all the timbers, veining thick
A plenitude of silver leaves.

                    DUNCAN CAMPBELL SCOTT

The Sea

THERE is a pleasure in the pathless woods,
There is a rapture on the lonely shore,
There is society where none intrudes,
By the deep Sea, and music in its roar:
I love not man the less, but Nature more,
From these our interviews, in which I steal
From all I may be, or have been before,
To mingle with the universe, and feel
What I can ne'er express, yet cannot all conceal.

Roll on, thou deep and dark blue Ocean—roll!
Ten thousand fleets sweep over thee in vain;
Man marks the earth with ruin—his control
Stops with the shore;—upon the watery plain
The wrecks are all thy deed, nor doth remain
A shadow of man's ravage, save his own,
When for a moment, like a drop of rain,
He sinks into thy depths with bubbling groan,
Without a grave, unknell'd, uncoffin'd and unknown.

His steps are not upon thy paths—thy fields
Are not a spoil for him—thou dost arise
And shake him from thee; the vile strength he wields
For earth's destruction thou dost all despise,

Spurning him from thy bosom to the skies,
And send'st him, shivering in thy playful spray,
And howling, to his Gods, where haply lies
His petty hope in some near port or bay,
And dashest him again to earth—there let him lay.

The armaments which thunderstrike the walls
Of rock-built cities, bidding nations quake,
And monarchs tremble in their capitals,
The oak leviathans, whose huge ribs make
Their clay creator the vain title take
Of lord of thee, and arbiter of war;
These are thy toys, and, as the snowy flake,
They melt into thy yeast of waves, which mar
Alike the Armada's pride, or spoils of Trafalgar.

Thy shores are empires, changed in all save thee—
Assyria, Greece, Rome, Carthage, what are they?
Thy waters wasted them while they were free,
And many a tyrant since: their shores obey
The stranger, slave or savage; their decay
Has dried up realms to deserts:—not so thou,
Unchangeable save to thy wild waves' play—
Time writes no wrinkle on thine azure brow—
Such as creation's dawn beheld, thou rollest now.

Thou glorious mirror, where the Almighty's form
Glasses itself in tempests: in all time,
Calm or convulsed—in breeze, or gale, or storm,
Icing the pole, or in the torrid clime
Dark-heaving;—boundless, endless, and sublime—

The image of Eternity—the throne
Of the Invisible ; even from out thy slime
The monster's of the deep are made ; each zone
Obeys thee ; thou goest forth, dread, fathomless,
    alone.

And I have loved thee, Ocean ! and my joy
Of youthful sports was on thy breast to be
Borne, like thy bubbles, onward : from a boy
I wanton'd with thy breakers—they to me
Were a delight ; and if the freshening sea
Made them a terror—'twas a pleasing fear,
For I was as it were a child of thee,
And trusted to thy billows far and near,
And laid my hand upon thy mane—as I do here.
                             LORD BYRON
            (" Childe Harold's Pilgrimage ")

Lost Youth

OFTEN I think of the beautiful town
  That is seated by the sea ;
Often in thought go up and down
The pleasant streets of that dear old town,
  And my youth comes back to me,
    And a verse of a Lapland song
    Is haunting my memory still :
  " A boy's will is the wind's will
And the thoughts of youth are long, long
    thoughts."

I can see the shadowy lines of its trees,
  And catch in sudden gleams,
The sheen of the far-surrounding seas,

And islands that were the Hesperides
   Of all my boyish dreams.
      And the burden of that old song,
         It murmurs and whispers still:
   " A boy's will is the wind's will,
And the thoughts of youth are long, long thoughts."

I remember the black wharves and the slips
   And the sea-tides tossing free ;
And the Spanish sailors with bearded lips
And the beauty and mystery of the ships
   And the magic of the sea.
      And the voice of that wayward song
         Is singing and saying still :
   " A boy's will is the wind's will,
And the thoughts of youth are long, long thoughts."

H. W. LONGFELLOW

The Last Chanty

"AND THERE WAS NO MORE SEA"

THUS said the Lord in the vault above the Cherubim,
Calling to the Angels and the Souls in their degree
      " Lo ! Earth has passed away
         On the smoke of Judgment Day,
That Our word may be established shall We gather up the sea ? "

Loud sang the souls of the jolly, jolly mariners :
" Plague upon the hurricane that made us furl and flee !

THE LAST CHANTY

But the war is done between us
In the deep the Lord hath seen us—
Our bones we'll leave the barracout and God may sink the sea!"

Then said the soul of Judas that betrayed Him:
"Lord hast Thou forgotten Thy covenant with me?
How once a year I go
To cool me on the floe?
And Ye take my day of mercy if Ye take away the sea!"

Then said the soul of the Angel of the Off-shore Wind:
(He that bits the thunder when the bull-mouthed breakers flee)
"I have watch and ward to keep
O'er Thy wonders on the deep,
And Ye take mine honour from me if Ye take away the sea."

Loud sang the souls of the jolly, jolly mariners:
"Nay, but we were angry, and a hasty folk were we!
If we worked the ship together
Till she foundered in foul weather,
Are we babes that we should clamour for a vengeance on the sea?"

Then said the souls of the slaves that men threw overboard:
"Kennelled in the picaroon a weary band were we;
But Thy arm was strong to save,
And it touched us on the wave,
And we drowsed the long tides idle till Thy Trumpets tore the sea."

Then cried the soul of the stout Apostle Paul
   to God:
"Once we frapped a ship, and she laboured
   woundily.
      There were fourteen score of these,
      And they blessed Thee on their knees,
When they learned Thy Grace and glory under
   Malta by the sea."

Loud sang the souls of the jolly, jolly mariners:
Plucking at their harps, and they plucked un-
   handily:
      "Our thumbs are rough and tarred,
      And the tune is something hard—
May we lift a Deapsea Chanty such as seamen use
   at sea?"

Then said the souls of the gentlemen adventurers,
Fettered wrist to bar all for red iniquity:
      "Ho, we revel in our chains
      O'er the sorrow that was Spain's
Heave or sink it, leave or drink it, we were masters
   of the sea!"

Up spake the soul of a grey Gothavn 'speck-
   shioner—
(He that led the flinching in the fleets of fair
   Dundee)
      "Oh the ice-blink white and near,
      And the bowhead breaching clear!
Will Ye whelm them all for wantonness that
   wallow in the sea?"

Loud sang the souls of the jolly, jolly mariners,
Crying: "Under Heaven, here is neither lead nor lee

THE LAST CHANTY

> Must we sing for evermore
> On the windless, glassy floor?
Take back your golden fiddles and we'll beat to open sea."
> Then stooped the Lord, and He called the good sea up to Him,
And 'stablished His borders unto all Eternity,
> That such as have no pleasure
> For to praise the Lord by measure,
They may enter into galleons and serve Him on the sea.

Sun, wind, and cloud shall fail not from the face of it,
Stinging, ringing spindrift, nor the fulmar flying free;
> *And the ships shall go abroad*
> *To the Glory of the Lord*
Who heard the silly sailor-folk and gave them back their sea.

RUDYARD KIPLING (" The Seven Seas ")

POEMS ILLUSTRATING OUR SEA HISTORY

The Sea-Fight at Sluys

JUNE 24, 1340

LISTEN, and the battle I shall begin,
Of Englishmen and Normans in the Swyn.

Minot with mouth had meant to make
True saws and sad for some men's sake.
The words of Sir Edward makes me to wake,
Would he salve us soon my sorrow should slake,
 Were my sorrow slaked soon would I sing,
 When God will Sir Edward shall us boot bring.

Sir Philip the Valois cast was in care;
And said Sir Hugh Kyret to Flanders should fare,
And have Normans enough to leave on his lare,
All Flanders to burn and make it all bare;
 But unkind coward, woe was him there,
 When he sailed in the Swyn it sowed him sair;
 Sore it them smarted that fared out of France;
 Englishmen learnèd them there a new dance.

The burgess(es) of Bruges were not to blame;
I pray, Jesu, save them from sin and from shame,
For they were soon at the Sluys all by a name,
 Where many of the Normans took mickle grame.

THE SEA-FIGHT AT SLUYS

When Bruges and Ypres hereof heard tell,
They sent Edward to wit that was in Orwell;
Then had he no liking longer to dwell,
He hasted him to the Swyn with sergeants snell,[1]
To meet with the Normans that false were and fell,
That had meant, if they might, all Flanders to quell.

King Edward unto sail full soon was dight,
With earls and barons and many a keen knight
They came before Blankbergh on St. John's night;
That was to the Normans a full sorry sight.
Yet trumped they and danced with torches full bright,
In the wild waning were their hearts light.

Upon the morn after, if I sooth say,
A merry man, Sir Robert, out of Morlay,
At half ebb in the Swyn sought he the way;
There taught men the Normans at buckler to play;
Helped them no prayer that they might pray;
The wretches are wonnen, their weapon is away.

The Earl of Northampton helped at that need,
And the wise men of words and worthy in weed,
Sir Walter the Maunay, God give him meed,
Was bold of body in battle to bede.[2]

The Duke of Lancaster was dight for to drive
With many a moody man that thought for to thrive,
Well and stalwartly stint he that strife[3]

[1] *Snell*, active, fiery.   [2] *Battle to bede*, to offer battle.
[3] *Stint he that strife*, did he end that battle.

That few of the Normans left they alive.
Few left they alive but did them to leap,
Men may find by the flood a hundred on heap.

Sir William of Clinton was easy to know,
Many stout bachelors brought he in a row.
It seemed with their shooting that it did snow,
The most of the Normans brought they full low;
Their boast was abated and their mickle pride,
For they might not flee, but there do they bide.

The good Earl of Gloucester, God make him glad,
Brought many bold men with bows full brade;
To bicker with the Normans boldly they bade,
And in midst of the flood did them to wade.
To wade were those wretches cast in the brim,
The caitiffs come out of France to learn them to swim.

I praise John Badding as one of the best;
Fair came he sailing out of the south-west,
To the proof of those Normans was he full prest,
Till he had fought his fill he had never rest.

John of Aile of the Sluys with a squadron full sheen
Was coming into Cagent,[1] cantly[2] and keen;
But soon was his trumping turned to teen;
Of him had Sir Edward his will I ween.

The shipmen of England sailed full swith,[3]
That none of the Normans from them might skrith.[4]

[1] *Cagent*, a village of Zeeland.
[2] *Cantly*, briskly, smartly.
[3] *Swith*, gaily, swiftly.
[4] *Skrith*, escape, or crawl away.

THE SEA FIGHT AT SLUYS

Whoso knew well his craft there might it kith [1]
Of all the good that they got gave they no tithe.

Two hundred and more ships on the sands
Had our Englishmen won with their hands;
The cogs [2] of England were brought out of bands,
And also the *Christopher* [3] that in the stream stands;
In that stound they stood, with streamers full still,
Till they wist full well Sir Edward's ill.

Sir Edward, our king worthy in wall, [4]
Fought well on that flood, fair mot him fall; [5]
As it is custom of king to comfort them all,
So thanked he goodly the great and the small.
He thanked them goodly, God give him meed,
Thus came our king in the Swyn till that good deed.

This was the battle that fell in the Swyn,
Where many Normans made mickle din;
Well were they armed up to the chin,
But God and Sir Edward gar'd their boast blin; [6]
Thus blinned their boast, as we well ken,
God assoil their souls, say all, Amen.

LAURENCE MINOT

[1] *Kith*, make a show of, exhibit.
[2] *Cogs*, or cocks, ships of burthen.
[3] *Christopher*, a flagship captured by the English.
[4] *Worthy in wall*, apparently a good fellow, a stout fighter, one worth wailing or bewailing when killed.
[5] *Fair mot him fall*, good luck to him.
[6] *Blin*, come to an end, cease.

Winchelsea Fight, or the Humbling of the Spaniards

> How King Edward and his menie,
> Met with the Spaniards in the sea.

I would not spare for to speak, wist I to speed,
Of wight men with weapons, and worthy in weed,
That now are driven to dale,[1] and dead all their deed,
They sail in the sea—ground fishes to feed;
Fell fishes they feed for all their great fare,[2]
It was in the waning that they came there.

They sailed forth in the Swyn in a summer's tide,
With trumps and tabors and mickle other pride;
The word of those war-men walked full wide,
The goods that they robbed in hold gan they it hide;
In hold have they hidden great wealths as I ween
Of gold and of silver, of scarlet and green.

When they sailed westward those wight men in war,
Their hurdis,[2] their anchors, hanged they on here:[4]
Wight men of the west nighèd them near,
And gar'd them stumble in the snare, might they no ferr.[5]

[1] *Driven to dale*, driven to the grave.
[2] *Their great fare*, their boasts and brags.
[3] *Hurdis*, a war girdle, or pavesse, of coloured canvas, which protected the sailors of a warship as they rowed or hauled.
[4] *On here*, aloft
[5] *No ferr*, so that they might go no farther.

Far might they not flit, but there must they fine,[1]
And that that before they reived then must they tine.[2]

Boy with thy black beard [3] I rede that thou blin,
And soon set thee to shrive with sorrow of thy sin;
If thou wert in England nought shouldst thou win,
Come thou more on that coast, thy bale shall begin.
There kindles thy care, keen men shall thee keep,
And do thee die on a day and dump in the deep.

Ye brought out of Bretayne[4] your custom with care,
Ye met with the merchants and made them full bare;
It is good reason and tight that ye evil misfare
When ye would, in England, learn of a new lare.
New lore shall ye learn, Sir Edward to lout:[5]
For when ye stood in your strength you were all too stout.

LAURENCE MINOT

Sir Andrew Barton

THE FIRST PART

" WHEN Flora with her fragrant flowers
Bedeckt the earth so trim and gaye,

[1] *Fine*, come to an end.   [2] *Tine*, lose.
[3] *Boy with thy black beard*, " a most notorious pirate," named Barbenoire, who may have been in the Spanish ships destroyed by " Sir Edward " in the battle here celebrated.
[4] *Out of Bretayne*, the Spanish pirates had raided the Brittany coasts.
[5] *To lout*, to salute.

And Neptune with his daintye showers
   Came to present the monthe of Maye ";
King Henrye rode to take the ayre,
   Over the river of Thames past hee ;
When eighty merchants of London came,
   And downe they knelt upon their knee.

" O yee are welcome, rich merchants ;
   Good saylors, welcome unto mee."
They swore by the rood, they were saylors good,
   But rich merchànts they cold not bee :

" To France nor Flanders dare we pass :
   Nor Bordeaux voyage dare we fare ;
And all for a rover that lyes on the seas,
   Who robbs us of our merchant ware."

King Henrye frownd and turned him rounde,
   And swore by the Lord, that was mickle of
      might,
" I thought he had not beene in the world,
   Durst have wrought England such unright."
The merchants sighed, and said, " Alas ! "
   And thus they did their answer frame,
" He is a proud Scott, that robbs on the seas,
   And Sir Andrewe Barton is his name."

The king lookt over his left shouldèr,
   And an angrye look then looked hee :
" Have I never a lorde in all my realme,
   Will feitch yond traytor unto mee ? "
" Yea, that dare I," lord Howard sayes ;
   " Yea, that dare I with heart and hand ;
If it please your grace to give me leave,
   Myselfe wil be the only man."

SIR ANDREW BARTON

"Thou art but yong," the kyng replyed:
  "Yond Scott hath numbred manye a yeare."
"Trust me, my liege, Ile make him quail,
  Or before my prince I will never appeare."
"Then bowemen and gunners thou shalt have,
  And chuse them over my realme so free;
Besides good mariners, and shipp-boyes,
  To guide the great shipp on the sea."

The first man, that lord Howard chose,
  Was the ablest gunner in all the realm,
Thoughe he was threescore yeeres and ten;
  Good Peter Simon was his name.
"Peter," sais hee, "I must to the sea,
  To bring home a traytor live or dead:
Before all others I have chosen thee,
  Of a hundred gunners to be the head."

"If you, my lord, have chosen mee
  Of a hundred gunners to be the head,
Then hang me up on your maine-mast tree,
  If I miss my marke one shilling bread."[1]
My lord then chose a boweman rare,
  Whose active hands had gained fame.
In Yorkshire was this gentleman borne,
  And William Horseley was his name.

"Horseley," sayd he, "I must with speede
  Go seeke a traytor on the sea,
And now of a hundred bowemen brave
  To be the head I have chosen thee."
"If you," quoth hee, "have chosen mee
  Of a hundred bowemen to be the head,
On your main-mast Ile hanged bee,
  If I miss twelvescore one penny bread."

[1] An old English word for *breadth*.

With pikes and gunners, and bowemen bold,
  This noble Howard is gone to the sea;
With a valyant heart and a pleasant cheare,
  Out at Thames mouth sayled he.
And days he *scant* had sayled three,
  Upon the " voyage " he tooke in hand,
But there he mett with a noble shipp,
  And stoutely made itt stay and stand.

" Thou must tell me," lord Howard said,
  " Now who thou art, and what's thy name;
And shewe me where thy dwelling is:
  And whither bound, and whence thou came.
" My name is Henry Hunt," quoth hee
  With a heavye heart, and a carefull mind;
" I and my shipp doe both belong
  To the Newcastle, that stands upon Tyne."

" Hast thou not heard, nowe, Henrye Hunt,
  As thou hast sayled by daye and by night,
Of a Scottish rover on the seas;
  Men call him sir Andrew Barton, knight ? "
Then ever he sighed, and sayd " Alas ! "
  With a grieved mind, and well away !
" But over-well I knowe that wight,
  I was his prisoner yesterday.

" As I was sayling uppon the sea,
  A Burdeaux voyage for to fare;
To his *hach-borde* he clasped me,
  And robd me of all my merchant ware:
And mickle debts, God wot, I owe,
  And every man will have his owne;
And I am nowe to London bounde,
  Of our gracious king to beg a boone."

SIR ANDREW BARTON

" That shall not need," lord Howard sais ;
  " Lett me but once that robber see,
For every penny tane thee froe
  It shall be doubled shillings three."
" Nowe God forefend," the merchant said,
  " That you shold seek so far amisse !
God keepe you out of that traitor's hands !
  Full litle ye wott what a man hee is.

" Hee is brasse within, and steele without,
  With beames on his topcastle stronge ;
And eighteen pieces of ordinance
  He carries on each side along :
And he hath a pinnace deerlye dight,
  St. Andrew's cross that is his guide ;
His pinnace beareth ninescore men,
  And fifteen cannons on each side.

" Were ye twentye shippes, and he but one ;
  I sweare by kirke, and bower, and hall ;
He wold overcome them everye one,
  If once his beames they do downe fall." [1]
" This is cold comfort," sais my lord,
  " To wellcome a stranger thus to the sea :
Yet Ile bring him and his shipp to shore,
  Or to Scottland hee shall carrye mee."

[1] It should seem from hence that before our marine artillery was brought to its present perfection, some naval commanders had recourse to instruments or machines, similar in use, though perhaps unlike in construction, to the heavy dolphins made of lead or iron used by the ancient Greeks, which they suspended from beams or yards fastened to the mast, and which they precipitately let fall on the enemy's ships, in order to sink them by beating holes through the bottoms of their undecked Triremes, or otherwise damaging them. These are mentioned by Thucydides, lib. vii. p. 256, ed. 1564, folio, and are more fully explained in " Schefferi de Militia," lib. ii. cap. 5, p. 136, ed. 1653, 4to.—*Bishop Percy's Note.*

"Then a noble gunner you must have,
  And he must aim well with his ee,
And sinke his pinnace into the sea,
  Or else hee never orecome will bee:
And if you chance his shipp to borde,
  This counsel I must give withall,
Let no man to his topcastle goe
  To strive to let his beams downe fall.

"And seven pieces of ordinance,
  I pray your honour lend to mee,
On each side of my shipp along,
  And I will lead you on the sea.
A glasse Ile sett, that may be seene,
  Whether you sayle by day or night;
And to-morrowe, I sweare, by nine of the clocke
  You shall meet with Sir Andrewe Barton knight."

THE SECOND PART

THE merchant sett my lorde a glasse
  Soe well apparent in his sight,
And on the morrowe, by nine of the clocke,
  He shewed him Sir Andrew Barton knight.
His hachebord it was "gilt" with gold,
  Soe deerlye *dight* it dazzled the ee:
"Nowe by my faith," lord Howarde sais,
  "This is a gallant sight to see.

"Take in your *ancyents*, standards eke,
  So close that no man may them see;
And put me forth a white willowe wand,
  As merchants use to sayle the sea."
But they stirred neither top, nor mast;[1]
  Stoutly they passed Sir Andrew by.

[1] i.e. did not salute.

SIR ANDREW BARTON

"What English churles are yonder," he sayd,
  "That can soe little curtesye?

"Now by the roode, three yeares and more
  I have beene admirall over the sea;
And never an English nor Portingall
  Without my leave can pass this way."
Then called he forth his stout pinnace;
  "Fetch backe yond pedlars nowe to mee:
I sweare by the masse, yon English churles
  Shall all hang att my maine-mast tree."

With that the pinnace itt shott off,
  Full well lord Howard might it ken;
For itt stroke down my lord's fore mast,
  And killed fourteen of his men.
"Come hither, Simon," sayes my lord,
  "Looke that thy word be true, thou said;
For at my maine-mast thou shalt hang,
  If thou misse thy marke one shilling bread."

Simon was old, but his heart itt was bold.
  His ordinance he laid right lowe;
He put in chain full nine yardes long,[1]
  With other great shott lesse, and moe,
And he lette goe his great gunnes shott:
  Soe well he settled itt with his ee,
The first sight that Sir Andrew sawe,
  He saw his pinnace sunke in the sea.

And when he saw his pinnace sunke,
  Lord, how his heart with rage did swell!
"Nowe cutt my ropes, itt is time to be gon;
  Ile fetch yond pedlars backe mysell."

[1] i.e. discharged chain shot.

When my Lord sawe Sir Andrewe loose,
  Within his heart hee was full *faine*:
"Nowe spread your ancyents, strike up drummes,
  Sound all your trumpetts out amaine."

"Fight on, my men," Sir Andrewe sais,
  "Weale howsoever this *geere will sway*;
Itt is my lord admirall of England,
  Is come to seek mee on the sea."
Simon had a sonne, who shott right well,
  That did Sir Andrewe mickle scare;
In att his decke he gave a shott,
  Killed threescore of his men of warre.

Then Henrye Hunt with rigour hott
  Came bravely on the other side,
Soone he drove downe his fore-mast tree
  And killed fourscore men beside.
"Nowe, out alas!" Sir Andrewe cryed,
  "What may a man now thinke, or say?
Yonder merchant theefe, that pierceth mee,
  He was my prisoner yesterday.

"Come hither to me, thou Gordon good,
  That aye wast readye att my call;
I will give thee three hundred markes,
  If thou wilt let my beames downe fall."
Lord Howard hee then call'd in haste,
  "Horseley, see thou be true in stead;
For thou shalt at the maine-mast hang,
  If thou misse twelvescore one penny bread."

Then Gordon swarved the maine-mast tree,
  He swarved it with might and maine;

SIR ANDREW BARTON

But Horsley with a bearing [1] arrowe,
　Stroke the Gordon through the braine;
And he fell unto the haches again,
　And sore his deadlye wounde did bleed:
Then word went through Sir Andrew's men,
　How that the Gordon hee was dead.

"Come hither to mee, James Hambilton,
　Thou art my only sister's sonne,
If thou wilt let my beames down fall,
　Six hundred nobles thou hast wonne."
With that he swarved the maine-mast tree,
　He swarved it with nimble art;
But Horseley with a broad arrowe
　Pierced the Hambilton through the heart:

And downe he fell upon the deck,
　That with his blood did streame amaine:
Then every Scott cryed, "Well-away!
　Alas a comelye youth is slaine!"
All woe begone was Sir Andrew then,
　With grief and rage his heart did swell:
"Go fetch me forth my armour of proofe,
　For I will to the topcastle mysell."

"Goe fetch me forth my armour of proofe;
　That gilded is with gold soe cleare:
God be with my brother John of Barton!
　Against the Portingalls hee it ware;
And when he had on his armour of proofe,
　He was a gallant sight to see:
Ah! nere didst thou meet with living wight,
　My deere brothèr, could cope with thee."

[1] *sc.* that carries well, etc.

" Come hither, Horseley," sayes my lord,
  "And looke your shaft that itt goe right,
Shoot a good shoote in time of need,
  And for it thou shalt be made a knight."
" Ile shoot my best," quoth Horseley then,
  "Your honour shall see, with might and maine ;
But if I were hanged at your maine-mast,
  I have now left but arrowes twaine."

Sir Andrew he did swarve the tree,
  With right good will he swarved then :
Upon his breast did Horseley hitt,
  But the arrow bounded back agen.
Then Horseley spyed a privye place
  With a perfect eye in a secrette part ;
Under the spole of his right arme
  He smote Sir Andrew to the heart.

" Fight on, my men," Sir Andrew sayes,
  "A little Ime hurt, but yett not slaine ;
Ile but lye downe and bleede a while,
  And then Ile rise and fight againe.
Fight on, my men," Sir Andrew sayes,
  "And never flinche before the foe ;
And stand fast by St. Andrewes crosse
  Untill you heare my whistle blowe."

They never heard his whistle blow,—
  Which made their hearts waxe sore adread :
Then Horseley say'd, "Aboard, my lord,
  For well I wott Sir Andrew's dead."
They boarded then his noble shipp,
  They boarded it with might and maine
Eighteen score Scots alive they found,
  The rest were either maimed or slaine.

SIR ANDREW BARTON

Lord Howard tooke a sword in hand,
  And off he smote Sir Andrewes head,
"I must have left England many a daye
  If thou wert alive as thou art dead."
He caused his body to be cast
  Over the hatchbord into the sea,
And about his middle three hundred crownes:
  "Wherever thou land this will bury thee."

Thus from the warres Lord Howard came,
  And backe he sayled ore the maine,
With mickle joy and triumphing
  Into Thames mouth he came againe.
Lord Howard then a letter wrote,
  And sealed it with seale and ring;
"Such a noble prize have I brought to your grace,
  As never did subject to a king:

"Sir Andrewes shipp I bring with mee;
  A braver shipp was never none:
Nowe hath your grace two shipps of warr,
  Before in England was but one."
King Henryes grace with royall cheere
  Welcomed the noble Howard home,
"And where," said he, "is this rover stout,
  That I myselfe may give the doome?"

"The rover, he is safe, my liege,
  Full many a fadom in the sea;
If he were alive as he is dead,
  I must have left England many a day:
And your grace may thank four men i' the ship
  For the victory wee have wonne,
These are William Horseley, Henry Hunt,
  And Peter Simon, and his sonne."

To Henry Hunt, the king then sayd,
  " In lieu of what was from thee tane,
A noble a day now thou shalt have,
  Sir Andrewes jewels and his chayne.
And Horseley, thou shalt be a knight,
  And lands and livings shalt have store;
Howard shall be erle Surrye hight,
  As Howards erst have been before.

" Nowe, Peter Simon, thou art old,
  I will maintaine thee and thy sonne:
And the men shall have five hundred markes
  For the good service they have done."
Then in came the queene with ladyes fair
  To see Sir Andrewe Barton knight:
They weened that hee were brought on shore,
  And thought to have seen a gallant sight.

But when they see his deadlye face,
  And eyes soe hollow in his head,
" I wold give," quoth the king, " a thousand markes,
  This man were alive as hee is dead:
Yett for the manfull part hee playd,
  Which fought soe well with heart and hand,
His men shall have twelvepence a day,
  Till they come to my brother king's high land."

The English Captains

COURAGEOUS CABOT, brave Venetian born,
Fostered with honour-breathing English air,
Victorious Henry's name the more t' adorn,
And to Emblazon Troynovant the fair,

THE ENGLISH CAPTAINS

Unto the far-most climates made repair:
And by the Southern and Septentrion
Measured the fame of famous Albion.

Lightless and nameless Prima-vista lay,
Till from his eyes it borrowed name and light;
Flora did never Florida array,
Roses not lilies shewed their shining sprite,
Till it was ros'd and lilied with his sight:
Thrice happy sight that verdant spring composes,
By strewing lands with lilies and with roses.

By Labrador's high promontory Cape,
Beyond the isles of Cuba, CABOT sailed,
Discovering Baccalaos uncouth shape:
The mighty Silver-River not concealed,
His tributary sands to him revealed,
Nor 'dainèd it to be a tributor
Unto the Ocean's mighty emperor.

Honour of England, brave Sebastian,
Mirror of Britain's magnanimity,
Although by birth a right Venetian,
Yet for thy valour, art, and constancy,
Due unto England from thy infancy:
Venice, thou claimst his berth, England his art,
Now judge thyself which hath the better part.

WYNDHAM, although thy rash temerity,
Hast'ning for endless gain, gain hast'ned end;
And through improvident celerity,
Too soon accelerated death did send:
Yet since so far thy valour did extend,
And death for rashness made full satisfaction,
Why should not fame advance thy valorous action?

With like misfortune (though unlike advise)
Did fame-ennobled WILLOUGHBY intend
A famous action's hapless enterprize ;
Arzina saw his lamentable end,
Which her eternal winter's frost did send :
Though freezing cold benumbed his vital flame,
Heat shall not hurt, nor cold consume his Fame.

Fortune not always good, nor alway ill,
Willing to show her mercy with her power,
Feasted on other's falls (as seemed) her fill,
Smiled with a mild aspect on CHANCELLOUR,
Making herself his daily oratour :
Hereby, quoth she, the world shall know my powers
How Fortune sometimes laughs as well as lowers.

Forthwith for him a bark herself she framed,
Enchanting it with an almighty charm ;
Which she the blissful *Bonaventure* named,
Which wind, nor wave, nor heat, nor cold could harm.
While her omnipotence the same did arm,
Guiding it safely to Moscovia,
Safely reducing it from Russia.

Bold with success, and proud on Fortune's favour
Again his lofty sails he doth advance,
Allured by silver's soul-attractive savour :
But fortune (like the moon in change and chance,
That never twice doth shew like countenance)
At Pettisligo drenched him in the seas :
Thus most she hurts, when most she seems to please.

THE ENGLISH CAPTAINS

Ask the Wingandicoa savages,
They can relate of GRENVILLE and his deeds;
The Isles of Flores, and Azores, these
Extol his valour and victorious meeds;
While Spain's griped heart fresh streams of anguish bleeds:
His worth with all the world his praise made even,
But he scorned earth, and therefore went to Heaven.

What Time-out-sliding thought so far could fly,
As did heroic CAVENDISH drive his sails?
The great Magores' Kingdom did he see,
Where freezing Boreas rings his northern peals,
'Gainst whose benumbing blast no heat avails:
His prowess hath been known to Malacca
And to her neighbour-bordering Bengala.

Knighted by honour in desert's fair field,
Death-scorning GILBERT, chronicled by fame,
To England's Monarchess did force to yield
The savage land (that Newfound now we name)
Making wild people mild, submisse and tame.
O, were men's lives unto their praise's tied!
Then, noble Gilbert, hadst thou never died.

If searching labyrinths inextricable,
By hard adventures and ambiguous ways,
To purchase glory and renown be able,
And meritorious of eternal praise:
Then FROBISHER out-lives the Sybil's days:
What death took from his life, this gives his name:
Death hath no dart to slay deserved fame

Rich China, and fair Met' Incognita,
Admired his valour and extolled his fame,
Cathaia, and the great America,
The dangerous Straits that do yet bear his name,
Are monumental annals of the same;
Annals, wherein posterity shall read,
How Fame the living salves, revives the dead.

Now drop, my pen, in ink of dreary tears,
A name of late of laughter and of joy;
But now (O death, the agent of our fears)
A name of dolour and of dire annoy,
The sad memorial of the Fates destroy:
HAWKINS (O, now my heart, cleave thou asunder)
In naming him (meseems) I name a wonder.

Nestor in wisdom, art, and policy,
Nestor in knowledge, skill, and prudency,
Nestor in counsel and in gravity,
Nestor in wit, foresight, and modesty,
Nestor in might and magnanimity:
O would he had (as he had Nestor's hairs)
Enjoyèd Nestor's age, and Nestor's years.

A mortal man more than a man of late,
If mortal man more than a man may be,
Since his life's calendar is out of date,
And death's new-year exacts his 'customed fee,
No more a man, not mortal now is he:
No more a man because of breath bereaven,
Mortal no more, because a Saint in Heaven.

CLIFFORD, a name that still was ominous,
Prefiguring an high-resolvèd mind,
Victorious, venturous, vertuous, valorous,

Eternal adjuncts to that noble kind,
By nature's secret influence assigned;
Who can deny that names are ominous?
For Clifford's name hath still been valorous.

Nectar-tongued SYDNEY, England's Mars and Muse,
Heroic DEVEREUX had never sent
Their royal blood to earth's unworthy use;
Nor FROBISHER his breath at Brest had spent,
We should not WINGFIELD'S loss so much lament;
Such worthies might have saved their vital breath,
By one accursed vassal's worthy death.

Then might victorious CLIFFORD yet survive,
And with renown-invested BASKERVILLE
Re-greet fair Albion's shining shore alive;
No Spaniard had triumphed in his ill,
Nor boasted he so brave a knight did kill:
If, but by one, whose worth his worth could stain,
He had not been slain, he had not been slain.

Sleep you securely, O thrice blessed bones,
The sacred relics of so fair a Saint,
In your rich tomb enchased with precious stones,
Till honour shall your destiny prevent,
And Fame revive the breath that Fates have spent;
And if no Homer will display your name,
Accept a Cherilus to do the same.

Live, O live ever, ever-living Sprites,
Wherever live the sprites of virtuous livers,
Heavens have your souls, the Earth your fame inherits:
But when Earth's massy apple turns to shivers,
And fire conjoins that nature now dissevers,

That hold's your souls shall then your fames
    contain;
For Earth shall end, your praise shall still remain.

What though you left your bodies far from home,
And some on seas, and some died on the sand,
Losing the honour of your father's tomb,
Which may seek, few have, none understand?
Heaven is as near from sea, as from the land:
What though your country-tomb you could not
    have?
You sought your country's good, not country's
    grave.

More than most blest (if more than most may be)
Spirits of more than most renownèd wights:
But if of more than most be no degree,
As much as most you are, victorious Knights.
Earth's admirations, and the Heaven's delights;
And as, in worth, you were Superlatives,
So shall you be, in Fame, Infinitives.

                    CHARLES FITZ-GEFFERY.

Sir Francis Drake Reviv'd

The Steersman: Aloof, and aloof, and steady I steer!
    'Tis a boat to our wish,
    And she slides like a fish,
When cheerily stemmed, and when you row clear.
    She now has her trim!
    Away let her swim.
Mackrels are swift in the shine of the moon:
And herrings in gales when they wind us,
But, timing our oars, so smoothly we run,
That we leave them in shoals behind us.

The Mariners : Then cry, One and all!
                Amain! For Whitehall!
The Diegoes we'll board to rummage their hold;
And drawing our steel, they must draw out
    their gold.

The Steersman : Our master and 's mate, with
                bacon and pease,
    In cabins keep aboard;
    Each as warm as a lord.
    No queen, lying in, lies more at her ease.
    Whilst we lie in wait
    For reals of eight,
And for some gold quoits which fortune must
    send :
But, alas, how their ears will tingle,
When finding, though still little Hectors we
    spend,
Yet still all our pockets shall jingle.

The Mariners : Then cry, One and all!
                Amain! For Whitehall!
The Diegoes we'll board to rummage their hold;
And drawing our steel, they must draw out
    their gold.

The Steersman : But oh, how the Purser shortly
                will wonder,
    When he sums in his book
    All the wealth we have took,
    And finds that we'll give him none of
        the plunder;
    He means to abate
    The tithe for the state;
Then for our owners some part he'll discount :
But his fingers are pitched together;

Where so much will stick, that little will mount,
When he reckons the shares of either.
The Mariners: Then cry, One and all!
              Amain! For Whitehall!
The Diegoes we'll board to rummage their hold;
And drawing our steel, they must draw out
    their gold.

The Steersman: At sight of our gold, the boat-
              swain will bristle,
    But not finding his part,
    He will break his proud heart,
    And hang himself straight in the chain
        of his whistle.
    Abaft and afore,
    Make way to the shore.
Softly as fishes which slip through the stream,
That we may catch their sentries napping.
Poor little Diegoes, they now little dream
Of us the brave warriors of Wapping.
The Mariners: Then cry, One and all!
              Amain! For Whitehall!
The Diegoes we'll board to rummage their hold;
And drawing our steel, they must draw out
    their gold.

(From the opera, " The History of Sir Francis Drake,"
by Sir William Davenant, 1659. The opera is founded
on the prose narrative, "Sir Francis Drake Revived."
" One and All," " Amain," and " For Whitehall," were
familiar war-cries of the mid-seventeenth century.
" Amain " was the sailor's summons to an enemy to
surrender his ship. The word " board " is used here
as Sir Toby Belch uses it in " Twelfth Night." The
attack planned was a land attack, and the only " board-
ing " done was the stopping of a train of mules carrying
silver and gold.)

On Sir Francis Drake

You, whose exploits the world itself admired,
Admire the strange exploits of peerless Drake;
And you whom neither lands nor seas have tired,
Have tired your tongues when they rehearsal make
What hard adventures he did undertake;
Then if that such Atlantes are too weak,
What marvell if this weight our shoulders break?

O you once matchless monarchs of the seas,
But now advanced to an higher place,
Invested Vice-roys and high Satrapes,
In that fair palace near the milken race;
O think not that his praise doth yours deface:
If he be justly praised, you justly graced,
Your graces by his praise are not defaced.

What though his worth above yours is extolled?
Yet thereby is not yours extenuated:
What though your neighbour's jewels dearer sold,
Than for the price whereat your gem is rated?
What thereby is your diamond abated?
Wherefore to give both him and you your due
I say he was the best, the next were you.

. . . . . .

So in the May-tide of his summer age,
Valour enmoved the mind of vent'rous Drake,
To lay his life with winds and waves in gage,
And bold and hard adventures t' undertake,
Leaving his country for his country's sake:
Loathing the life that cowardice doth stain,
Preferring death, if death might honour gain.

At *Cuba* silver, at *Coquimbo* gold,
At *China* cloth and precious silks he found.
Pearl at the Pearlèd Isles he did behold;
Rich cochineels hoarded did abound,
Embosom'd in Tichamachalco's ground:
Thus his industrious labour still did raise
The public profit and his private praise.

   .   .   .   .   .   .

He that hath been where none but he hath been
Leaving the world behind him as he went;
He that hath seen that none but he hath seen,
Searching if any other world unkent,
Lay yet within the Ocean's bosom pent:
Even he was Drake: O could I say he is,
No music would revive the soul like this.

He that did pass the Straits of Magellan,
And saw the famous island Mogadore:
He that unto the Isle of Mayo came,
Where winter yieldeth grapes in plenteous store:
He that the Isle of Fogo passed before,
A second Etna, where continual smoke
Of brimstone-burning vaults the air doth choke.

He that at Brava saw perpetual Spring
Gracing the trees with never-fading green,
Like laurel branches ever flourishing:
He that at Taurapaza's port had been:
He that the rich Molucca's Isles had seen:
He that a new found Albion descried,
And safely home again his bark did guide.

   .   .   .   .   .   .

CHARLES FITZ-GEFFERY

Sir Richard Grenville's Farewell, on His Sailing for Foreign Parts in the Year 1585

A Ballad in Praise of Seafaring Men

Who seeks the way to win renown,
Or flies with wings of high desire,
Who seeks to wear the laurel crown,
Or hath the mind that would aspire,
Let him his native soil eschew,
Let him go range, and seek a new.

Each haughty heart is well content,
With every chance that shall betide;
No hag can hinder his intent;
He steadfast stands, though fortune slide.
The sun, quoth he, doth shine as well
Abroad, as erst where I did dwell.

In change of streams each fish can live,
Each fowl content with every air,
Each haughty heart remaineth still,
And not be drowned in deep despair:
Wherefore I judge all lands alike,
To haughty hearts who fortune seek.

To pass the seas some think a toil,
Some think it strange abroad to roam;
Some think it a grief to leave their soil,
Their parents, kinfolk, and their home.
Think so who list, I like it not;
I must abroad to try my lot.

Who list at home at cart to drudge,
And cark and care for worldly trash,
With buckled shoes let him go trudge,
Instead of lance or whip to slash;
A mind that base his kind will show
Is carrion meet to feed a crow.

If Jason of that mind had been,
The Grecians when they came to Troy,
Had never so the Trojans foiled
Nor put them all to such annoy:
Wherefore who lust may live at home,
To purchase fame I will go roam.
(Sloame MS. 2497, fol. 47)

The Taking of Cartagena

(FROM THE TRUE AND PERFECTE NEWES OF THE WORTHY ENTERPRISES OF SIR FRANCIS DRAKE, 1586)

THE Mariners the while provide
For victuals and fresh water sweet:
With other commodities beside,
Which was conveyed aboard the fleet.
Commandment then was given straightway:
"All men aboard without delay."

Then presently they sailèd thence,
To one rich island they were bent:
But wind and storm turned their pretence,
And other course they then invent.
With Cartagena they set at last,
Where all their fleet their anchors cast

THE TAKING OF CARTAGENA

This town was strong, well fenced about,
Four hundred soldiers under pay:
Four hundred Indians in a scout,
Besides their townsmen in array.
For they had news that Drake would come:
And they thought sure to be his doom.

Their fort well manned and fortified,
Five sconces wherein good ordnance was:
Three galleys then were amplified,
With fifteen pieces of good brass.
Full little then they feared the Drake:
For they thought sure to make him quake.

One mischief more they did devise,
Whereby they thought to spoil our men:
Many poisoned pricks in sundry wise,
Amidst their way they fastened then.
To prick their shins they did purpôse:
But the Lord God did that disclose.

Nine hundred men were set on land,
And marching forth then all by night:
Until they came unto the strand,
Where pricks with poisoned heads were dight.
The water low, as God's will was:
'Twixt strand and seas they safely pass.

Then in the morn before daylight,
They came full in their enemy's face:
Then all at once with force and might,
They ran upon them in a race.
For all their force and thundering shot:
One of their sconces soon they got.

As God shut up the Lion's jaws,
From 'noying His Prophet Daniell:
And eke preserved from tyrant's paws,
The three children of Israel.
And saved them in the oven so hot:
So He conveyed away their shot.

Our captains then, most valiantly,
To courage their soldiers for to fight:
Did jeopard themselves then foremostly,
Which made their enemies dread their might,
Bold soldiers put foes to shame:
To win their country honour and fame.

From sconce to sconce they then retire,
Their lofty hearts right soon were quailed:
They left their holds and fled for fear,
Then with their heels they best prevail.
And as they fled strange news they tell:
"These be no men but fiends of Hell."

Their ordnance and artillery,
Which in their holds did then remain,
Our men achieve with victory,
The town, like case, they won certain.
Their ensigns then they did display
Upon their walls; none durst say nay.

The soldiers then seek for their prey,
Some for their bellies likewise did care:
Though breakfast sharp, now, care away,
Their dinner's sweet and wholesome fare.
Bread and victuals they found good store
With wine and sugar as erst before. [1]

[1] At San Domingo.

THE TAKING OF CARTAGENA

They make a sconce amidst the street,
And placed great ordnance in the same
To charge the watch when 't came to night,
To daunt their foes, their rage to tame.
Being shot off, their thundering sound
So shook their Church, the roof fell down.

This town also they kept a space,
And eke the Friary there beside;
These townsmen then with humble grace,
Besought the general at that tide.
To release their town he would vouchsave
And they would give what he would have.

All things provided orderly,
And brought unto the water's side,
Munitions and artillery,
Was all embarkèd at that tide,
The mariners, without delay,
These things aboard with speed convey.

. . . . . .

Then when aboard their ships they come,
They were received joyfully,
A peal of guns, with thundering soune,
For one hour's space even pierced the sky.
Their drums struck up, their trumpets sound
Their victories which did abound.

Their yards across hoist at the top,
Their anchors weighed then presently:
Their sails displayed, their good ships lop,
The mariners stand their tacklings by.
Each helm belayed with good respect,
As skilful masters did direct.
                    " *Quoth* THOMAS GREEPE "

From Albion's England

THE Spaniard's long time care and cost, invincible surnam'd,
Was now afloat, whilst Parma too from Flanders hither aim'd,
Like fleet, of eight score ships, and odd, the ocean never bore,
So huge, so strong, and so complete, in every strength and store:
Carracks, galleons, argosies, and galliasses, such
That seem'd so many castles, and their tops the clouds to touch.
These on the Lizards shew themselves, and threaten England's fall;
But there with fifty ships of ours that fleet was fought withal.
Howbeit of a greater sort our navy did consist,
But part kept diet in the port, that might of health have miss'd,
Had Spain's Armada of our wants in Plymouth's haven wist.
The rest had eye on Parma, that from Flanders armour threats:
Meanwhile Lord Charles our Admiral, and Drake did worthy feats:
Whose fearless fifty mole-hills bow'd their tripled mountain's base,
And even at first (so pleas'd it God) pursued as if in chase.
By this (for over-idle seem'd to English hearts the shore)
Our gallants did embark each where and made our forces more.

But in such warlike order then their ships at anchor lay,
That we, unless we them disperse, on bootless labour stay.
Nor lacked policy that to that purpose made us way.
Ours fired divers ships, that down the current sent, so scared,
That cables cut, and anchors lost, the Spaniards badly fared.
Dispersed thus, we spare not shot, and part of them we sink,
And part we board, the rest did fly, not fast enough they think.
Well guided little axes so force tallest oaks to fall,
So numbrous herds of stately harts, fly beagles few and small,
Nine days together chas'd we them, not actious, save in flight:
About eight thousand perished by famine, sea, and fight.
For treasure, ships, and carriages, lost honour, pris'ners ta'en,
The Spaniards hardly 'scaping hence, 'scapt not rebukes in Spain.
Well might thus much (as much it did) cheer England, but much more
Concurrency from one to all to stop that common sore.
Even Catholics (that erred name doth please the Papists) were
As forward in this quarrel as the foremost arms to bear;
Recusants and suspects of note: of others was no care,

And had not our God-guided fight on seas prevailed, yet
The Spaniards, land whereso they could, had with our armies met,
Our common courage wish'd no less, so lightly fear'd we foes
Such hope in God, such hate of them, such hearts to barter blows.
Here flam'd the Cyclop's forges, Mars his armoury was here,
Himself he sheds in us, and with our cause ourselves we cheer.
But (which had scarrified our wounds, if wounded, with the balm
Of her sweet presence, so applaus'd as in sea storms a calm)
Her royal self, Elizabeth our sovereign gracious Queen,
In magnanimous majesty amidst her troops was seen,
Which made us weep for joy, nor was her kindness less to us.
Think nothing letting then that might the common cause discuss,
Where prince and people have in love a sympathy as thus.
Howbeit force, nor policy, but God's sole providence,
Did clear fore-boasted conquest and benighted thraldom hence.
He in Sennacherib his nose did put his hook, and brought
Him back again the way he came without performing aught;
He fought for us, alonely we did shout and trumpets sound,

When as the walls of Jericho fell flat unto the ground.
Yea lest (for erst did never hear like strong supplies befall,
Like loyal hearts in everyone, like warlike minds in all,
Less spare of purses, more foresight, and valiant guides to act,
As shew'd our hardy little fleet that battle never slack'd)
Lest these, I say, might have been said the cause that we subdued,
Even God to glorify Himself, our gained cause pursued,
Without our loss of man, or mast, or foe once touching shore,
Save such as wreck'd were prisoners, or but landing, liv'd not more.
And in the public prayers we did His defence implore,
So being victors, publicly, we yielded thanks therefor.
Her Highness' self (good cause she had) in view of every eye,
On humbled knees did give Him thanks that gave her victory.
   Remaineth, what she won, what Spain and Rome did lose in fame :
   Remaineth, Popes use potentates but to retrieve their game.

WILLIAM WARNER

The Defeat of the Spanish Armada

SOME years of late, in eighty-eight
   As I do well remember,

It was, some say, the tenth of May,
  And, some say, in September,
  And, some say, in September.

The Spanish train launch'd forth amain,
  With many a fine bravado,
Their (as they thought, but it proved not)
  Invincible Armado,
  Invincible Armado.

There was a little man, that dwelt in Spain,
  Who shot well in a gun-a,
Don Pedro hight, as black a wight
  As the Knight of the Sun-a,
  As the Knight of the Sun-a.

King Philip made him Admiral,
  And bid him not to stay-a,
But to destroy both man and boy,
  And so to come away-a,
  And so to come away-a.

Their navy was well victualled
  With biscuit, pease, and bacon;
They brought two ships, well fraught with whips,
  But I think they were mistaken,
  But I think they were mistaken.

Their men were young, munition strong,
  And, to do us more harm-a,
They thought it meet to join the fleet,
  All with the Prince of Parma,
  All with the Prince of Parma.

They coasted round about our land,
  And so came in by Dover;

But we had men set on them then
  And threw the rascals over,
  And threw the rascals over.

The Queen was then at Tilbury,
  What more could we desire-a?
And Sir Francis Drake, for her sweet sake,
  Did set them all on fire-a,
  Did set them all on fire-a.

Then, straight, they fled, by sea and land,
  That one man killed threescore-a;
And had not they all ran away,
  In truth he had killed more-a,
  In truth he had killed more-a.

Then let them neither brag nor boast,
  But if they come agen-a,
Let them take heed, they do not speed
  As they did, you know when-a.
  As they did, you know when-a.

A Farewell to the most Famous Generals, Sir John Norris and Sir Francis Drake, Knights

HAVE done with care, my hearts, aboard amain,
With stretching sails to plough the swelling waves;
Bid England's shore and Albion's chalky cliffs
Farewell; bid stately Troynovant adieu,
Where pleasant Thames, from Isis' silver head,
Begins her quiet glide, and runs along

To that brave bridge, the bar that thwarts her
    course,
Near neighbour to that ancient Stony Tower,
The glorious hold that Julius Cæsar built.
Change love for arms; gird-to your arms, my
    boys!
Your rests and muskets take, take helm and targe,
And let God Mars his consort make you mirth,—
The roaring cannon, and the brazen trump,
The angry sounding drum, the whistling fife,
The shrieks of men, the princely courser's neigh.
Now vail your bonnets to your friends at home.
Bid all the lovely British dames adieu,
That under many a standard well-advanced,
Have his the sweet alarms and braves of love;
Bid theatres and proud tragedians,
Bid Mahmet, Scipio, mighty Tamburlaine,
King Charlemagne, Tom Stukely and the rest,
Adieu. To arms, to arms, to glorious arms
With noble Norris, and victorious Drake,
Under the sanguine cross, brave England's badge,
To propagate religious piety,
And hew a passage with your conquering swords
By land and sea, wherever Phœbus' eye,
Th' eternal lamp of Heaven, lends us light;
By golden Tagus, or the western Inde,
Or through the spacious bay of Portugal,
The wealthy ocean-main, the Tyrrhene sea,
From great Alcides' pillars branching forth
Even to the gulf that leads to lofty Rome;
There to deface the pride of Antichrist,
And pull his paper walls and popery down,—
A famous enterprise for England's strength,
To steel your swords on Avarice' triple crown,
And cleanse Augeas' stalls in Italy.

A FAREWELL

To arms, my fellow-soldiers. Sea and land
Lie open to the voyage you intend ;
And sea or land, bold Britons, far and near,
Whatever course your matchless virtue shapes,
Whether to Europe's bounds, or Asian plains,
To Afric's shore, or rich America,
Down to the shades of deep Avernus' crags,
Sail on, pursue your honours to your graves :
Heaven is a sacred covering for your heads,
And every climate virtue's tabernacle,
To arms, to arms, to honourable arms !
Hoist sail, weigh anchors up, plough up the seas
With flying keels, plough up the land with swords :
In God's name venture on ; and let me say
To you, my mates, as Cæsar said to his,
Striving with Neptune's hills : " You bear,"
    quoth he,
" Cæsar, and Cæsar's fortune in your ships."
You follow them whose swords successful are :
You follow Drake, by sea the scourge of Spain,
The dreadful dragon, terror to your foes,
Victorious in his return from Inde,
In all his high attempts unvanquished ;
You follow noble Norris, whose renown
Won in the fertile fields of Belgia,
Spreads by the gates of Europe to the courts
Of Christian kings and heathen potentates.
You fight for Christ, and England's peerless
    Queen,
Elizabeth, the wonder of the world,
Over whose throne the enemies of God
Have thundered erst their vain successless braves.
O, ten-times-treble happy men, that fight
Under the cross of Christ and England's queen,
And follow such as Drake and Norris are !

All honours do this cause accompany ;
All glory on these endless honours waits ;
These honours and this glory shall He send,
Whose honour and whose glory you defend.
>> GEORGE PEELE (1589)

The Sailor's Onely Delight[1]

Shewing the brave fight between the *George-Aloe*, the *Sweepstake*, and certain Frenchmen at sea.

THE *George-Aloe*, and the *Sweepstake*, too,
With hey, with hoe, for and a nony no.
O, they were Merchant-men, and bound for Safee
And alongst the Coast of Barbary.

The *George-Aloe* to anchor came
With hey, etc.
And the jolly *Sweepstake* kept on her way
And alongst, etc.

They had not sayled leagues two or three,
With hey, etc.
But they met with a French Man-of-War upon the Sea,
And alongst, etc.

All haile, all haile, you lusty Gallants,
With hey, etc.
Of whence is your fair Ship, and whither are you bound ?
And alongst, etc.

[1] This poem is quoted in the play of the "Two Noble Kinsmen," by Shakespeare and Fletcher. Act III, Scene v.

THE SAILOR'S ONELY DELIGHT

We are Englishmen, and bound for Safee,
   With hey, etc.
Of whence is your fair Ship, and whither are you bound?
   And alongst, etc.

Amaine, Amaine,[1] you gallant Englishman,
   With hey, etc.
Come you French Swads,[2] and strike down your sayle,
   And alongst, etc.

They laid us aboard on the Starboard side,
   With hey, etc.
And they overthrew us into the Sea so wide,
   And alongst, etc.

When tidings to the *George-Aloe* came,
   With hey, etc.
That the jolly *Sweepstake* by a Frenchman was ta'en,
   And alongst, etc.

To top, To top,[3] thou little Ship-boy,
   With hey, etc.
And see if this French Man-of-War thou canst descry,
   And alongst, etc.

A Sayle, a Sayle, under our lee,
   With hey, etc.

[1] *Amain*, surrender.
[2] *Swads* (query *Swabs*?), swabbers, the ship's scavengers, the pumpers, and sea-menials.
[3] *Top*, the platform on the masts above the lower yards of ships.

Yea, and another under her obey,
    And alongst, etc.

Weigh anchor, weigh anchor, O jolly Boat-swain,
    With hey, etc.
We will take this Frenchman, if we can,
    And alongst, etc.

We had not sayled leagues two or three,
    With hey, etc.
But we met the French Man-of-War upon the Sea,
    And alongst, etc.

All haile, All haile, you lusty Gallants,
    With hey, etc.
Of whence is your faire Ship, and whither are you bound?
    And alongst, etc.

O, wee are Merchant-men and bound for Safee,
    With hey, etc.
Ay, wee are French-men, and war upon the sea,
    And alongst, etc.

Amaine, Amaine, you English Dogges,
    With hey, etc.
Come aboard, you French rogues, and strike down your sailes.
    And alongst, etc.

The first good shot that the *George-Aloe* shot,
    With hey, etc.
He made the Frenchman's heart sore afraid,
    And alongst, etc.

THE SAILOR'S ONELY DELIGHT

The second shot the *George-Aloe* did afford,
  With hey, etc.
He struck their Main-mast over the board,
  And alongst, etc.

Have mercy, have mercy, you brave English Men,
  With hey, etc.
O, what have you done with our Brethren on shore,
  As they sayled in Barbarie?

We laid them aboard the Starboard side,
  With hey, etc.
And we threw them into the Sea so wide,
  And alongst, etc.

Such mercy as you have shewed unto them,
  With hey, etc.
Then the like mercy shall you have again,
  And alongst, etc.

Wee laid them aboard the Larboard side,
  With hey, etc.
And wee threw them into the Sea so wide,
  And alongst, etc.

Lord, how it grieves our hearts full Sore,
  With hey, etc.
To see the drown'd Frenchmen swim along the shore,
  And alongst, etc.

Now gallant Seamen all, adieu,
  With hey, etc.
This is the last Newes I can write to you,
  To England's Coast from Barbarie.

The Winning of Cales

"The subject of this ballad is the taking of the city of *Cadiz* (called by our sailors corruptly *Cales*) on June 21, 1596, in a descent made on the coast of Spain, under the command of the Lord Howard, admiral, and the Earl of Essex, general."

LONG the proud Spaniards had vaunted to conquer us,
   Threatening our country with fyer and sword;
Often preparing their navy most sumptuous
   With as great plenty as Spain could afford.
      Dub a dub, dub a dub, thus strike their drums:
      Tantara, tantara, the Englishman comes.

To the seas presently went our lord admiral,
   With knights courageous and captains full good;
The brave Earl of Essex, a prosperous general,
   With him prepared to pass the salt flood.
      Dub a dub, etc.

At Plymouth speedilye, took they ship valiantlye,
   Braver ships never were seen under sayle,
With their fair colours spread, and streamers ore their head,
   Now bragging Spaniards, take heed of your tayle.
      Dub a dub, etc.

Unto Cales cunninglye, came we most speedilye,
   Where the kinges navy securelye did ryde;
Being upon their backs, piercing their butts of sacks,
   Ere any Spaniards our coming descryde.
      Dub a dub, etc.

THE WINNING OF CALES

Great was the crying, the running and ryding,
  Which at that season was made in that place ;
The beacons were fyred, as need then required ;
  To hyde their great treasure they had little space.
    Dub a dub, etc.

There you might see their ships, how they were fyred fast,
  And how their men drowned themselves in the sea ;
There might you hear them cry, wayle and weep piteously,
  When they saw no shift to scape thence away.
    Dub a dub, etc.

The great *St. Phillip*, the pryde of the Spaniards,
  Was burnt to the bottom, and sunk in the sea ;
But the *St. Andrew*, and eke the *St. Matthew*,
  Wee took in fight manfullye and brought away.
    Dub a dub, etc.

The Earl of Essex, most valiant and hardye,
  With horsemen and footmen marched up to the town ;
The Spanyards, which saw them, were greatly alarmed,
  Did fly for their savegard, and durst not come down.
    Dub a dub, etc.

"Now," quoth the noble Earl, "courage my soldiers all,
  Fight and be valiant, the spoil you shall have ;
And be well rewarded all from the great to the small ;

But looke that the women and children you save."
    Dub a dub, etc.

The Spaniards at that sight, thinking it vain to fight,
    Hung upp flags of truce and yielded the towne ;
Wee marched in presentlye, decking the walls on hye,
    With English colours which purchase renowne.
    Dub a dub, etc.

Entering the houses then, of the most richest men,
    For gold and treasure we searched eche day ;
In some places wè did find, pyes baking left behind,
    Meate at fire rosting, and folkes run away.
    Dub a dub, etc.

Full of rich merchandize, every top catched our eyes,
    Damasks and sattens and velvets full fayre ;
Which soldiers mèasur'd out by the length of their swords ;
    Of all commodities eche had a share.
    Dub a dub, etc.

Thus Cales was taken, and our brave general
    March'd to the market-place, where he did stand :
There many prisoners fell to our several shares,
    Many crav'd mercye, and mercye they fannd.
    Dub a dub, etc.

When our brave General saw they delayed all,
    And wold not ransome their towne as they said,

With their fair wanscots, their presses and bed-
    steads,
  Their joint-stools and tables a fire we made;
    And when the town burned all in flame,
    With tara, tantara, away we all came.

The End of the Last Fight of the *Revenge*

(SEPTEMBER 11–14, 1591)

BUT when the morning's dewy locks drunk up
A misty moisture from the Ocean's face,
Then might he see the source of sorrow's cup,
Plainly prefigured in that hateful place :
And all the miseries that mortals sup
From their great grandsire Adam's band, disgrace
For all that did encircle him, was his foe,
And that encircled, model of true woe.

His masts were broken, and his tackle torn,
His upper work hew'd down into the sea,
Naught of his ship above the surge was born,
But even levelled with the Ocean lay,
Only the ship's foundation (yet that worn)
Remained a trophy in that mighty fray ;
Nothing at all above the head remained,
Either for covert, or that force maintained.

Powder for shot was spent and wasted clean,
Scarce seen a corn to charge a piece withal,
All her pikes broken, half his best men slain,
The rest, sore wounded, on Death's agents call,
On the other side, her foe in ranks remain,
Displaying multitudes, and store of all

Whatever might avail for victory,
Had they not wanted heart's true valiancy.

When Grenville saw his desperate dreary case,
Merely despoiled of all successful thought,
He calls before him all within the place,
The Master, Master-Gunner, and them taught
Rules of true hardiment to purchase grace;
Shows them the end their travail's toil had bought,
How sweet it is, swift Fame to over-go,
How vile to dive in captive overthrow.

" Gallants," he saith, " since three o'clock last noon,
Untill this morning, fifteen hours by course,
We have maintained stout war, and still undone
Our foes assaults, and driven them to the worse,
Fifteen Armado's boardings have not won
Content or ease, but been repelled by force,
Eight hundred cannon shot against her side,
Have not our hearts in coward colours dyed.

. . . . . .

Since losing, we unlost keep strong our praise,
And make our glories gainers by our ends,
Let not the hope of hours (for tedious days
Unto our lives no longer circuit lends).
Confound our wondered actions and assays,
Whereon the sweet of mortal ears depends,
But as we live by wills victorious,
So let us die victors of them and us.

. . . . . .

And thus resolved, since other mean is reft,
Sweet Master-Gunner, split our keel in twain,
We cannot live, whom hope of life hath left,

Dying, our deaths more glorious lives retain.
Let not our ship, of shame and foil bereft,
Unto our foemen for a prize remain;
Sink her, and sinking, with the Greek we'll cry,
Best not to be, or being soon to die."

Scarce had his words ta'en wings from his dear
    tongue,
But the stout Master-Gunner, ever rich
In heavenly valour and repulsing wrong,
Proud that his hands by action might enrich
His name and nation with a worthy song,
Towered his heart higher than eagle's pitch,
And instantly endeavours to effect
Grenville's desire, by ending Death's defect.

But the other Master, and the other Mates,
Dissented from the honour of their minds,
And humbly prayed the Knight to rue their
    states,
Whom misery to no such mischief binds;
To him they allege great reasons, and dilates
Their foes amazements, whom their valour blinds,
And makes more eager t' entertaine a truce,
Than they to offer words for war's excuse.

They show him divers gallant men of might,
Where wounds, not mortal, gave hope of recure,
For their sakes sue they to divorce this night
Of desperate chance, called unto Death's black lure.
Their lengthened lives, their country's care might
    right,
And to their Prince they might good hopes assure.
Then quoth the Captain, "Dear Knight, do not
    spill

The lives of whom Gods and Fates seek not to kill.

And where thou sayst the Spaniards shall not brave
T' have ta'en one ship due to our virgin Queen,
O know, that they, nor all the world can save,
This wounded bark, whose like no age hath seen,
Six foot she leaks in hold, three shot beneath the wave,
All whose repair so insufficient been,
That when the sea shall angry work begin,
She cannot choose but sink and die therein.

Besides, the wounds and bruisings which she bears,
Are such, so many, so incurable,
As to remove her from this place of fears,
No force, no wit, no mean, nor man is able ;
Then since that peace prostrate to us repairs,
Unless our selves, our selves make miserable,
Herculean Knight, for pity, pity lend,
No fame consists in wilful desperate end."

. . . . .

O when Sir Richard saw them start aside,
More chained to life than to a glorious grave,
And those whom he so oft in dangers tried,
Now trembling seek their hateful lives to save,
Sorrow and rage, shame, and his honour's pride,
Choking his soul, madly compelled him rave,
Until his rage with vigour did confound
His heavy heart, and left him in a swound.

The Master-Gunner, likewise seeing Fate,
Bridle his fortune and his will to die,

With his sharp sword sought to set ope the gate,
By which his soul might from his body fly,
Had not his friends perforce preserved his state,
And locked him in his cabin, safe to lie,
Whilst others swarmed where hapless Grenville lay,
By cries recalling life, late run away.

In this too restless turmoil of unrest,
The poor *Revenge's* Master stole away,
And to the Spanish Admiral addrest
The doleful tidings of this mournful day,
(The Spanish Admiral who then oppresst,
Hovering with doubt, not daring t' end the fray,)
And pleads for truce, with soldier-like submission,
Annexing to his words a straight condition.

Alonzo, willing to give end to arms,
For well he knew Grenville would never yield,
Able his power stood like unnumbered swarms,
Yet daring not on stricter terms to build,
He offers all what may allay their harms
Safety of lives, nor any thrall to wield,
Free from the galley, prisonment, or pain,
And safe return unto their soil again.

To this he yields, as well for his own sake,
Whom desperate hazard might endamage sore,
As for desire the famous Knight to take,
Whom in his heart he seemed to deplore,
And for his valour half a god did make,
Extolling him all other men before,
Admiring with an honourable heart,
His valour, wisdom, and his soldier's art.

. . . . .

Baçan made proud, unconquering t' over-come,
Swore the brave Knight nor ship he would not lose,
Should all the world in a petition come :
And therefore of his gallants, forty chose.
To board *Sir Richard*, charging them be dumb
From threatening words, from anger, and from blows,
But with all kindness, honour, and admire
To bring him thence, to further Fame's desire.

Sooner they boarded not the crazed bark,
But they beheld where speechless Grenville lay,
All smeared in blood, and clouded in the dark,
Contagious curtain of Death's tragic day ;
They wept for pity, and yet silent mark
Whether his lungs sent living breath away,
Which, when they saw in airy blasts to fly,
They strived who first should staunch his misery.

Anon came life, and lift his eyelids up,
Whilst they with tears denounce their General's will,
Whose honoured mind ought to retort the cup
Of Death's sad poison, well instruckt to kill :
Tells him what fame and grace his eyes might sup
From Baçan's kindness, and his surgeon's skill,
Both how he loved him, and admired his fame,
To which he sought to lend a living flame.

" Ay me," quoth Grenville, " simple men, I know
My body to your General is a prey,
Take it, and as you please my limbs bestow,
For I respect it not, 'tis earth and clay ;
But for my mind that mightier much much doth grow
To Heaven it shall, despite of Spanish sway."

He swounded and did never speak again,
This said, o'ercome with anguish and with pain.

They took him up, and to the General brought
His mangled carcass, but unmaimèd mind,
Three days he breathed, yet never spake he ought,
Albeit his foes were humble, sad, and kind;

Then forth came down the Lamb that all souls bought,
And his pure part, from worser parts refined,
Bearing his spirit up to the lofty skies,
Leaving his body, wonder to wonder's eyes.

You powers of Heaven, rain honour on his hearse,
And tune the Cherubins to sing his fame,
Let infants in the last age him rehearse,
And let no more honour be Honour's name:
Let him that will obtain immortal verse,
Conquer the style of Grenville to the same,
For till that fire shall all the world consume,
Shall never name, with Grenville's name presume.

Rest then, dear soul, in thine all-resting place,
And take my tears for trophies to thy tomb,
Let thy lost blood, thy unlost fame increase,
Make kingly ears thy praise's second womb:
That when all tongues to all reports surcease,
Yet shall thy deeds outlive the day of doom,
For even Angels in the Heavens shall sing,
Grenville unconquered died, still conquering.
            O utinam.
                    GERVASE MARKHAM

Drake's Drum

DRAKE he's in his hammock an' a thousand mile away,
   (Capten, art tha sleepin' there below ?)
Slung atween the round shot in Nombre Dios Bay
   An' dreamin' arl the time o' Plymouth Hoe.
Yarnder lumes the Island, yarnder lie the ships,
   Wi' sailor lads a-dancin' heel-an'-toe,
An' the shore-lights flashin', an' the night-tide dashin',
   He sees et arl so plainly as he saw et long ago.

Drake he was a Devon man, an' rüled the Devon seas,
   (Capten, art tha sleepin' there below ?),
Rovin' tho' his death fell, he went wi' heart at ease,
   An' dreamin' arl the time o' Plymouth Hoe.
"Take my drum to England, hang et by the shore,
   Strike et when your powder's runnin' low ;
If the Dons sight Devon, I'll quit the port o' Heaven,
   An' drum them up the Channel as we drummed them long ago."

Drake he's in his hammock till the great Armadas come,
   (Capten, art tha sleepin' there below ?),
Slung atween the round shot, listenin' for the drum,
   An' dreamin' arl the time o' Plymouth Hoe.
Call him on the deep sea, call him up the Sound,
   Call him when ye sail to meet the foe ;

Where the old trade's plyin' an' the old flag flyin',
  They shall find him ware an' wakin', as they
    found him long ago!

HENRY NEWBOLT

The Last Voyage of Sir Francis Drake, and Sir John Hawkins

WHENAS a Royal fleet, with joyful minds,
(O how mishap is nearest still to joy)
Daring their hopes and lives to sea and winds,
(Two trustless treasures full of annoy)
Did toward the Western Ind their course employ;
  Whose guide to Drake and Hawkins was
    assign'd,
  When they went forth, O who would stay
    behind?

Whether to win from Spain what was not Spain's,
Or to acquit us of sustained wrong,
Or intercept their Indian hoped gains,
Thereby to weaken them and make us strong;
Here to discuss to me doth not belong:
  Yet if grief may say truth by nature's laws,
  Ill was th' effect, how good so e'er the cause.

Now are they on the seas resolved to prove
The mercy of a mercy-wanting wave:
England behind them lies, there lies their love;
Before them and about them air they have,
And sometimes foggy mists their sight bereave;
  Beneath them, seas; above them skies they
    find;

>   Seas full of waves, skies threatening storms
>   and wind.

. . . . . .

Thus still ambiguous 'twixt fear and hope,
Fear in the storms and hope in calmer tide;
Passing Saint Michael's promontory top,
At length the bay of Portingale they spied,
Where not determining long time to abide,
>   Again they venture in their danger's source,
>   And to the Grand Canaries bend their course.

Now pass in silence, O my drooping pen,
So many famous towns and ports passed by,
Some took, some burnt, some unassaulted then,
As that Port Rico, place of misery,
Where (O!) great Hawkins and brave Clifford lie;
>   The taking of the city Hatch conceal,
>   Nor many other brave attempts reveal.

Only two base ignoble places tell,
Famous for nothing but for death and dread;
Where (O!) that, which my muse laments, befell,
The stages where our tragedy was played,
Th' one Scudo, th' other Portobella said:
>   Both to be razed out of memory
>   But for memorial of this tragedy.

O wherefore should so many famous places,
Worthy eternal memory of fame,
Be here concealed unworthy such disgraces,
And these two should be registered by name,
Though meritorious of eternal blame?
>   But some are sometime named to their
>   shames,
>   And therefore must I tell these places names.

DRAKE AND HAWKINS

Whether of both was in the greatest fault,
I know not, nor I care not much to know :
(Far deeper passions now my mind assault :)
Thus much I know (O that I knew not so !)
Both jointly joined to aggravate our woe ;
    Since he on whom his country's hope relied,
    At Scudo sickened, at Port Bella died.

  .   .   .   .   .

He that the bravest captain was accounted
Boldly to encounter with the proudest foe :
Now from his stately courser is dismounted,
And hath by death received an overthrow,
Unto the world's inconsolable woe ;
    The tournament turned to lamenting fears,
    And all the triumphs into ruthful tears.

  .   .   .   .   .

What say they ? Death doth grief and sorrow end ?
O how they are deceived in saying so !
Death only did this grief and sorrow send ;
Death was the only agent of our woe,
Death was our dreary and our dismal foe :
    For hath not death himself subdued Drake,
    The world beside could not him captive make.

This only comfort is unto us left,
(O simple comfort in so great distress !)
That no proud Spaniard hath his life bereft,
No man may boast he caused our wretchedness,
Nor triumph he subdued earth's worthiness :
    But only death our treasures hath bereven
    And that was due to earth he gave to heaven.

  .   .   .   .   .

As one that vows a solemn pilgrimage
To some canonised saint's religious shrine,

Doth leave his solitary hermitage,
And with a new incensed zeal divine,
Unto devotion doth his mind incline;
    Passing the way and day in meditation
    Beguiling both with holy contemplation.

At length with over-tired tedious race,
Always invoking Saints successive aid,
Arriveth at the sanctified place,
Where after all his orisons are said,
And due oblations to the saint are paid;
    Ravished in spirit with devoted zeal,
    Becomes a priest and will not home repeal.

So Drake the pilgrim of the world intending
A vowed voyage unto honour's shrine,
At length his pilgrimage in heaven had ending,
Where ravished with the joys more than divine,
That in the temple of the Gods do shine;
    There did a never dying life renew,
    Bidding base earth, and all the world, adieu.

. . . . .

We weep in vain because for him we weep.
Since he with saints in thought-surmounting joy,
At Jove's great festival doth revel keep
Where neither scarcity doth him annoy,
Nor loathed satiety his mind accloy:
    O since that he from us is gone to bliss,
    We do lament our own mishap, not his.

. . . . .

Spain, clap thy hands, while we our hands do wring,
And while we weep, laugh thou at our distress,
While we do sob and sigh, sit thou and sing,

Smile thou, while we lament with heaviness,
While we our grief, do thou thy joy express,
    Since he who made us triumph, and thee
        quake,
    Hath ceased to live; O most victorious
        Drake!

. . . . . .

Known to the heavens by honour long before,
Now by the presence of the immortal soul,
O new-made saint, (for now a man no more)
Admit my tender infant Muse to enroll
Thy name in honour's everlasting scroll:
  What though thy praises cannot live by me?
  Yet may I hope to live by praising thee.

. . . . .

Phœbus himself shall chronicle thy fame,
And of a radiant sunbeam make the pen;
The ink the milk whence Via Lactea came;
The empyrean heaven, the volume shall be then;
To register the miracle of men:
  The sun and moon the letters capital
  The stars the commas and the periods all.

Jove's silver foot-stool shall be library
That shall their acts and monuments contain;
Which that they may to after ages tarry
And as a true memorial still remain,
Eternity is the adamantine chain
  And that the heavens still on Drake's praise
    may look,
  The gods shall read and saints peruse the book.

Quis Martem tunica tectum adamantina
Digne scripserit?
                     CHARLES FITZ-GEFFERY

From Albion's England

OF world-admired *Drake* (for of his worth what
  argues more,
Than Fame envied? some, for was his so rich
  thought theirs to poor),
And his brave breeder *Hawkins* (yet be honoured
  every pen,
That, howsoever, honour them as high-resolvèd
  men)
In fiction, or in mystery, to read would less
  delight
Than would significantly some their glorious
  journeys write :
The pains of such invited pens such subject
  would requite.
Add *Gilbert*, *Frobisher*, of knights to make up five,
All in their better parts with God, with men their
  fames alive :
Add *Chilton*, *Oxnam*, *Fenton*, *Ward*, *Davis*,
  another *Drake*,
With divers here not catalogued, and for a chiefest
  take
All-actious *Candish*, and of these eternal pen-work
  make.

Omitted men, and named men, and lands (not
  here, indeed,
So written of as they deserve) at large in *Hakluyt*
  read.   WILLIAM WARNER

To the Virginian Voyage

You brave heroic minds,
Worthy your country's name,

That honour still pursue,
   Whilst loit'ring hinds
Lurk here at home, with shame.
   Go, and subdue.

Britons, you stay too long,
Quickly abroad bestow you,
And with a merry gale
   Swell your stretched sail,
   With vows as strong,
As the winds that blow you.

Your course securely steer,
West and by south forth keep,
Rocks, lee-shores, nor shoals,
   When Eolus scowls,
   You need not fear,
So absolute the deep.

And cheerfully at sea,
Success you still entice,
To get the pearl and gold,
   And ours to hold
   Virginia,
Earth's only Paradise.

Where Nature hath in store
Fowl, venison, and fish,
And the fruitful'st soil,
   Without your toil,
   Three harvests more
All greater than your wish.

And the ambitious vine
Crowns with his purple mass,

The cedar reaching high
  To kiss the sky;
  The cypress, pine,
And useful sassafras.

To whose, the golden age
Still Nature's laws doth give,
No other cares that tend,
  But them to defend,
  From winter's rage
That long there doth not live.

When as the luscious smell
Of that delicious land,
Above the seas that flows,
  The clear wind throws,
  Your hearts to swell
Approaching the dear strand.

In kenning of the shore
(Thanks to God first given)
O you, the happiest men,
  Be frolic then,
  Let cannons roar
Frighting the wide heaven.

And in regions far
Such heroes bring ye forth,
As those from whom we came,
  And plant our name
  Under that star
Not known unto our north.

And as there plenty grows
Of laurel everywhere,

Apollo's sacred tree,
  You it may see,
  A poet's brows
To crown, that may sing there.

Thy voyages attend,
Industrious Hakluyt,
Whose reading shall inflame
  Men to seek fame,
  And much commend
To after-times thy wit.
                    MICHAEL DRAYTON

The Honour of Bristol

ATTEND you and give ear awhile,
  And you shall understand,
Of a Battle fought upon the Sea,
  By a Ship of Command;
The fight it was so famous,
  That all Men's Hearts do fill,
And makes them cry, " *To Sea
With the Angel Gabriel.*"

The lusty ship of *Bristol*,
  Sail'd out adventurously,
Against the Foes of *England*,
  Their strength with them to try:
Well victual'd, rig'd, and mann'd,
  With good Provision still,
Which made them cry, " *To Sea
With the Angel Gabriel.*"

The Captain, famous *Netheway*,
  So he was call'd by name,

The Master's name *John Mines*,
    A man of noted Fame:
The Gunner *Thomas Watson*,
    A Man of perfect Skill.
With other valiant Hearts
    In the Angel Gabriel.

They, waiving up and down the Seas,
    Upon the Ocean Main,
"*It is not long ago,*" quoth they,
    "*Since* England *fought with* Spain,
Would we with them might meet
    Our minds for to fulfil,
We would play a noble Bout
    With our Angel Gabriel."

They had no sooner spoken,
    But straight appear'd in sight,
Three lusty Spanish vessels,
    Of warlike Force and Might;
With bloody Resolution,
    They fought out Blood to spill,
And vow'd to make a Prize
    Of our Angel Gabriel.

Then first came up their Admiral,
    Themselves for to advance,
In her she bore full forty-eight
    Pieces of Ordnance;
The next that then came near us,
    Was the Vice-Admiral,
Which shot most furiously,
    At the Angel Gabriel.

Our gallant Ship had in her
    Full forty fighting Men,

THE HONOUR OF BRISTOL

With twenty pieces of Ordnance,
   We play'd about them then ;
And with Powder, Shot, and Bullets,
   We did employ them still,
And thus began the Fight
   With our Angel Gabriel.

Our Captain to our Master said,
   "*Take courage, Master bold,*"
The Master to the Seamen said,
   "*Stand fast, my Hearts of Gold ;* "
The Gunner, unto all the rest,
   "*Brave hearts, be valiant still,*
Let us fight in the Defence
   Of our Angel Gabriel."

Then we gave them a Broadside,
   Which shot their Mast asunder,
And tore the Bow Spret of their Ship,
   Which made the Spaniards wonder ;
And caused them to cry,
   With voices loud and shrill,
" *Help, help, or else we sink*
   By the Angel Gabriel."

Yet desperately they boarded us,
   For all our valiant Shot,
Three score of their best fighting Men,
   Upon our Decks were got ;
And then, at their first entrance,
   Full thirty did we kill ;
And thus we cleared the decks
   Of the Angel Gabriel.

With that, their three ships boarded us,
   Again with might and main,

But still our noble Englishmen
   Cry'd out, " *A fig for Spain !* "
Though seven times they boarded us,
   At last we shew'd our skill,
And made them feel the Force
   Of our Angel Gabriel.

Seven hours this Fight continued,
   And many Men lay dead,
With purple Gore, and Spanish blood,
   The Sea was coloured red ;
Five hundred of their Men,
   We there, outright, did kill,
And many more were maim'd
   By the Angel Gabriel.

They, seeing of these bloody Spoils,
   The rest made haste away,
For why, they saw it was no boot,
   Any longer for to stay ;
Then they fled into *Cales,*
   And there they must lye still,
For they never more will dare to meet
   With our Angel Gabriel.

We had within our English Ship
   But only three Men slain,
And five men hurt, the which I hope
   Will soon be well again ;
At Bristol we were landed,
   And let us praise God still,
That thus hath blest our Men,
   And our Angel Gabriel.

Now let me not forget to speak
   Of the Gift giv'n by the Owner

Of the *Angel Gabriel*,
  That many years had known her;
Two hundred Pounds in Coin and Plate,
  He gave with free good will,
Unto them that bravely fought
  In the Angel Gabriel.

From Britannia's Pastorals

TIME never can produce men to o'ertake
The fames of Grenville, Davies, Gilbert, Drake,
Or worthy Hawkins, or of thousands more
That by their power made the Devonian shore
Mock the proud Tagus; for whose richest spoil
The boasting Spaniard left the Indian soil
Bankrupt of store, knowing it would quit cost
By winning this, though all the rest were lost.
As oft the sea-nymphs on her strand have set,
Learning of fishermen to knit a net,
Wherein to wind up their dishevelled hairs,
They have beheld the frolic mariners
For exercise (got early from their beds)
Pitch bars of silver, and cast golden sleds.

  .   .   .   .   .   .

Where Plym and Tamar with embraces meet,
Thetis weighs anchor now, and all her fleet;
Leaving that spacious Sound, within whose arms
I have those vessels seen, whose hot alarms
Have made Iberia tremble, and her towers
Prostrate themselves before our iron showers;
While their proud builders' hearts have been inclined
To shake, as our brave ensigns, with the wind.

  .   .   .   .   .   .

O by heroës were we led of yore,
And by our drums that thunder'd on each shore,
Struck with amazement countries far and near;
Whilst their inhabitants, like herds of deer
By kingly lions chased, fled from our arms.
If any did oppose instructed swarms
Of men immail'd, Fate drew them on to be
A greater fame to our got victory.
But now our leaders want; those vessels lie
Rotting, like houses through ill-husbandry;
And on their masts, where oft the ship-boy stood,
Or silver trumpets charmed the brackish flood,
Some wearied crow is set;
       and daily seen
Their sides, instead of pitch, caulked o'er with green.
 Ill-hap (alas) have you that once were known
By reaping what was by Iberia sown,
By bringing yellow sheaves from out their plain,
Making our barns the storehouse for their grain;
 When now as if we wanted land to till,
Wherewith we might our useless soldiers fill;
Upon their hatches where half-pikes were borne
In every chink rise stems of bearded corn:
Mocking our idle times that so have wrought us,
Or putting us in mind what once they brought us.
WILLIAM BROWNE

An Epigram upon His Majestie's Great Ship (the *Sovereign of the Seas*) Lying in the Docks at Woolwich

WHAT artist took in hand this ship to frame?
Or who can guess from whence these tall oaks came?

AN EPIGRAM

Unless from the full grown Dodonian grove,
A wilderness sole sacred unto Jove.

What eye such brave materials hath beheld ?
Or by what axes were these timbers felled ?
Sure Vulcan with his three Cyclopean swains,
Have forged new metals from their active brains,
Or else, that hatchet he hath grinded new,
With which he cleft Jove's skull, what time out-flew
The armed virago, Pallas, who inspires
With Art, with Science, and all high desires
She hath (no doubt) raptured our undertaker
This machine to devise first, and then make her.

How else could such a mighty mole be raised ?
To which Troy's horse (by Virgil so much praised,
Whose bulk a thousand armed men contained)
Was but a toy (compar'd) and that too feigned,
For she bears thrice his burden, hath room, where
Enceladus might rowe, and Triton steer :
But no such vessel could for them be made,
Had they intent by sea the gods to invade.
The Argo, stellified because 'twas rare,
With this ship's long-boat scarcely might compare.

Yet sixty Greek Heroës even in that
With oars in hand, upon their transtrae sat.
Her anchors, beyond weight, expanst and wide,
Able to wrestle against wind and tide :
Her big wrought cable like that massy chain
With which great Xerxes bounded in the main
'Tweene Sestos and Abydos, to make one
Europe and Asia, by that line alone.
Her five bright lanterns lustre round the seas,
Shining like five of the seven Hyades :
Whose clear eyes, should they, by oft weeping, fail
By these, our seamen might find Art to sail.
In one of which (which bears the greatest light)

Ten of the guard at once may stand upright :
What a conspicuous ray did it dart then ?
What more than a Titanian lustre, when
Our Phœbus, and bright Cynthia jointly sphered
In that one orb, together both appeared :
With whom seven other stars had then their station
All luminous, but lower, constellation
That lamp, the great Colosse held, who bestrid
The spacious Rhodian sea-arm, never did
Cast such a beam, yet ships of tallest size,
Past, with their masts erect, between his thighs.
Her main mast like a Pyramis appears,
Such as the Egyptian Kings were many years,
To their great charge, erecting, whilst their pleasure
To mount them high, did quite exhaust their treasure.
Whose brave top-top-top royal nothing bars,
By day, to brush the sun, by night the stars.
Her mainsail (if I do not much mistake
For Amphitrite might a kirtle make :
Or in the heat of summer be a fan
To cool the face of the great ocean.

She being angry, if she stretch her lungs,
Can rail upon her enemy, with more tongues
(Louder than Stentor's, as her spleen shall rise)
Than ever Juno's Argus saw with eyes.
I should but lose my self, and craze my brain,
Striving to give this glory of the main
A full description, though the Muses nine
Should quaff to me in rich Mendaeum wine.
Then O you marine gods, who with amaze,
On this stupendous work (emergent) gaze.
Take charge of her, as being a choice gem,
That much outvalue's Neptune's diadem.

THOMAS HEYWOOD (1629 ?)

The Famous Fight at Malago

Or the Englishmen's Victory over the Spaniards

Come all you brave sailors
  That sails on the main
I'll tell you of a fight
  That was lately in Spain;
And of five sail of frigates
  Bound to Malago,
For to fight the proud Spaniards,
  Our orders was so.

There was the *Henry* and *Ruby*
  And the *Antelope* also,
The *Greyhound* and the *Bryan*
  For fireships must go;
But so bravely we weighed,
  And played our parts
That we made the proud Spaniards
  To quake in their hearts.

Then we came to an anchor
  So nigh to the Mould,
" Methinks you proud English
  Do grow very bold ";
But we came to an anchor
  So near to the town,
That some of their churches
  We soon battered down.

They hung out their flag of truce,
  For to know our intent,
And they sent out their longboat
  To know what we meant;

But our Captain he answered
  Them bravely, it was so,
"For to burn all your shipping
  Before we do go."

"For to burn all our shipping
  You must us excuse,
'Tis not five sail of frigates
  Shall make us to muse";
But we burnt all their shipping
  And their gallies also,
And we left in the city
  Full many a widow.

"Come then," says our Captain,
  "Let's fire at the church,"
And down came their belfry,
  Which grièved them much;
And down came the steeple,
  Which standeth so high,
Which made the proud Spaniards
  To the nunnery fly

So great a confusion
  Was made in the town,
That their lofty buildings
  Came tumbling down;
Their wives and their children
  For help they did cry,
But none could relieve them
  Though danger was nigh.

The flames and the smoke,
  So increased their woe,
That they knew not whither
  To run nor to go;

Some to shun the fire
   Leapt into the flood,
And there they did perish
   In water and mud.

Our guns we kept firing,
   Still shooting amain,
Whilst many a proud Spaniard
   Was on the place slain;
The rest being amazèd
   For succour did cry,
But all was in vain,
   They had nowhere to fly.

At length, being forced,
   They thought it most fit,
Unto the brave English men
   For to submit;
And so a conclusion
   At last we did make,
Upon such conditions
   As was fit to take.

The Spanish Armado
   Did England no harm,
Twas but a bravado
   To give us alarm;
But with our five frigates
   We did them bumbaste,
And made them of Englishmen's
   Valour to taste.

When this noble victory
   We did obtain,
Then home we returned
   To England again;

When we were received
  With welcomes of joy,
Because with five frigates
  We did them destroy.

On the Victory Obtained by Admiral Blake

Over the Spaniards, in the Bay of Santa Cruz in the Island of Tenerife, 1657

Now does Spain's fleet her spacious wings unfold,
Leaves the new world, and hastens for the old ;
But though the wind was fair, they slowly swum,
Freighted with acted guilt, and guilt to come ;
For this rich load, of which so proud they are,
Was raised by tyranny, and raised for war.
Every capacious galleon's womb was filled
With what the womb of wealthy kingdoms yield ;
The new world's wounded entrails they had tore,
For wealth wherewith to wound the old once
    more ;
Wealth which all other's avarice might cloy,
But yet in them caused as much fear, as joy.
For now upon the main themselves they saw
That boundless empire, where you give the law ;
Of wind's and water's rage they fearful be,
But much more fearful are your flags to see.
Day, that to those who sail upon the deep,
More wished for and more welcome is than sleep,
They dreaded to behold, lest the sun's light,
With English streamers should salute their sight :
In thickest darkness they would choose to steer,
So that such darkness might suppress their fear :
At length it vanishes, and fortune smiles,
For they behold the sweet Canary isles,

VICTORY BY ADMIRAL BLAKE

One of which doubtless is by nature blessed
Above both worlds, since 'tis above the rest.
For lest some gloominess might stain her sky,
Trees there the duty of the clouds supply :
O noble trust which heaven on this isle pours,
Fertile to be, yet never need her showers !
A happy people, which at once do gain
The benefits, without the ills, of rain !
Both health and profit fate cannot deny,
Where still the earth is moist, the air still dry ;
The jarring elements no discord know,
Fuel and rain together kindly grow ;
And coolness there with heat does never fight,
This only rules by day, and that by night.
Your worth to all these isles a just right brings,
The best of lands should have the best of kings.
And these want nothing heaven can afford,
Unless it be, the having you their lord ;
But this great want will not a long one prove,
Your conquering sword will soon that want remove ;
For Spain had better, she'll ere long confess,
Have broken all her swords, than this one peace :
Casting that league off, which she held so long,
She cast off that which only made her strong.
Forces and art, she soon will feel, are vain,
Peace, against you, was the sole strength of Spain ;
By that alone those islands she secures,
Peace makes them hers, but war will make them yours.
There the rich grape the soil indulgent breeds,
Which of the gods the fancied drink exceeds.
They still do yield, such is their precious mould,
All that is good, and are not cursed with gold ;

With fatal gold, for still where that does grow,
Neither the soil, nor people, quiet know;
Which troubles men to raise it when 'tis ore,
And when 'tis raised does trouble them much more.
Ah, why was thither brought that cause of war,
Kind nature had from thence removed so far!
In vain does she those islands free from ill,
If fortune can make guilty what she will,
But whilst I draw that scene, where you, ere long,
Shall conquests act, you present are unsung.

For Santa Cruz the glad fleet takes her way;
And safely there casts anchor in the bay.
Never so many, with one joyful cry,
That place saluted, where they all must die.
Deluded men! Fate with you did but sport,
You 'scaped the sea, to perish in your port.
'Twas more for England's fame you should die there,
Where you had most of strength and least of fear.
The Peak's proud height the Spaniards all admire,
Yet in their breasts carry a pride much higher.
Only to this vast hill a power is given,
At once both to inhabit earth and heaven.
But this stupendous prospect did not near
Make them admire, so much as they did fear.

For here they met with news, which did produce
A grief, above the cure of grape's best juice.
They learned with terror, that nor summer's heat,
Nor winter's storms, had made your fleet retreat.
To fight against such foes was vain, they knew,
Which did the rage of elements subdue,
Who on the ocean, that does horror give
To all beside, triumphantly do live.

VICTORY BY ADMIRAL BLAKE

With haste they therefore all their galleons moor,
And flank with cannon from the neighbouring shore;
Forts, lines, and sconces, all the bay along,
They build, and act all that can make them strong.

Fond men! who knew not whilst such works they raise,
They only labour to exalt your praise.
Yet they by restless toil became at length,
So proud and confident of their made strength,
That they with joy their boasting general heard
Wish then for that assault he lately feared.
His wish he had, for now undaunted Blake,
With winged speed, for Santa Cruz does make.

For your renown, the conquering fleet does ride,
O'er seas as vast as is the Spaniard's pride.
Whose fleet and trenches viewed, you soon did say,
We to their strength are more obliged than they;
Wer't not for that, they from their fate would run,
And a third world seek out, our arms to shun.
Those forts, which there so high and strong appear,
Do not so much suppress, as show their fear.
Of speedy victory let no man doubt,
Our worst work passed, now we have found them out.
Behold their navy does at anchor lie,
And they are ours, for now they cannot fly.

This said, the whole fleet gave it their applause.
And all assume your courage, in your cause.
That bay they enter, which unto them owes

The noblest wreaths which victory bestows ;
Bold Stanier leads ; this fleet's designed by fate
To give him laurel, as the last did plate.

   The thundering cannon now begins the fight,
And, though it be at noon, creates a night ;
The air was soon, after the fight begun,
Far more inflamed by it, than by the sun.
Never so burning was that climate known ;
War turned the temperate, to the torrid zone.

   Fate these two fleets, between both worlds, had brought,
Who fight, as if for both those worlds they sought.
Thousands of ways, thousands of men there die,
Some ships are sunk, some blown up in the sky.
Nature ne'er made cedars so high aspire
As oaks did then, urged by the active fire
Which, by quick powder's force, so high was sent
That it returned to its own element.
Torn limbs some leagues into the island fly,
Whilst others lower, in the sea, do lie ;
Scarce souls from bodies severed are so far
By death, as bodies there were by the war.
The all-seeing sun ne'er gazed on such a sight,
Two dreadful navies there at anchor fight,
And neither have, or power, or will, to fly ;
There one must conquer, or there both must die.
Far different motives yet engaged them thus,
Necessity did them, but choice did us,
A choice which did the highest worth express,
And was attended by as high success ;
For your resistless genius there did reign,
By which we laurels reaped e'en on the main.
So prosperous stars, though absent to the sense,
Bless those they shine for by their influence.

Our cannon now tears every ship and sconce,
And o'er two elements triumphs at once.
Their galleons sunk, their wealth the sea does fill,
The only place where it can cause no ill.

Ah ! would those treasures which both Indias have
Were buried in as large, and deep a grave !
War's chief support with them would buried be,
And the land owe her peace unto the sea.
Ages to come your conquering arms will bless,
There they destroyed what had destroyed their peace ;
And in one war the present age may boast,
The certain seeds of many wars are lost.

All the foe's ships destroyed by sea or fire,
Victorious Blake does from the bay retire.
His siege of Spain he then pursues,
And there first brings of his success the news :
The saddest news that e'er to Spain was brought,
Their rich fleet sunk, and ours with laurel fraught,
Whilst fame in every place her trumpet blows,
And tells the world how much to you it owes.
                                    ANDREW MARVELL

The Epitaph Acrostick on Robert Blake

R est here in Peace the sacred Dust
O f valiant Blake, the good, the just,
B elov'd of all on every side,
E ngland's honour, once her pride,
R ome's terror, Dutch annoyer,
T ruth's defender, Spain's destroyer.

B ring no dry eyes unto this place :
L et not be seen in any case
A smiling or an unsad face.
K indle desires in every breast
E ternally with him to rest.

GEORGE HARRISON

On board the *Dunbar* in the Downs, Aug. 11, 1657.

The Royal Victory

OBTAINED (WITH THE PROVIDENCE OF ALMIGHTY GOD) AGAINST THE DUTCH FLEET, JUNE 2ND AND 3RD, 1665

LET *England*, and *Ireland*, and *Scotland* rejoice,
   And render thanksgiving with heart and with voice.
   That surly *Fanatick* that now will not sing,
   Is false to the Kingdom, and Foe to the King ;
        For he that will grutch,
        Our Fortune is sutch,
   Doth deal for the Devil, as well as the Dutch ;
For why should my nature or conscience repine,
At taking of his life, that fain would have mine.

So high a Victory we could not command,
Had it not been gain'd by an Almighty hand,
The great Lord of Battels did perfect this work,
For God and the King, and the good Duke of York ;
        Whose courage was such
        Against the *Low Dutch*,
   That vapour'd and swagger'd, like Lords in a hutch ;
But, let the bold Hollander burn, sink, or swim,
They have honour enough to be beaten by him.

THE ROYAL VICTORY

Fire, Aire, Earth, and Water, it seems were imployed,
To strive for the Conquest which we have injoy'd,
No honour, or profit, or safety can spring,
To those who do fight against God and the King;
        The Battel was hot,
        And bloudily fought,
  The Fire was like Rain, and like Hail was ye Shot,
For in this Ingagement ten thousand did bleed
Of *Flemmings*, who now are ye *Low Dutch* indeed.

In this cruel Conflict stout *Opdam* was slain,
By the great *Duke of York*, and lyes sunk in ye Main,
'Twas from ye Duke's Frigat that he had his doome,
And by the Duke's Valour he was overcome;
        It was his good Fate,
        To fall at that Rate,
  Who sink under Princes, are buried in State.
Since Valour and Courage in one grave must lye,
It is a great honour by great hands to dye.

That gallant bold fellow, ye Son of *Van Trump*,
Whose brains were beat out by the head of the *Rump*,
Ingaging with *Holmes*, a brave Captain of ours,
Retreated to *Neptune's* salt, waterie bowers:
        His Fate was grown grim,
        He no longer could swim,
  But he that caught Fishes, now Fishes catch him,
They eat up our Fish, without Reason or Lawes,
But now they are going to pay for the Sawce.

To mock at men's miserie is not my aime,
It never can add to an *Englishman's* fame,
But I may rejoyce that the Battel is woun,
Because in the Victory, God's will is done;
   Whose Justice appears
   In such great affairs,
 Who will for *Amboina* plague them and their Heirs,
For he that did comber his conscience with gilt,
In shedding of blood, his own shall be spilt.

In this cruel Contest (our fortune was such),
We tooke seventeen Men-of-War from the *Dutch*,
And likewise (as then the occasion requir'd
And as God would have it) fourteen more were fir'd:
   At *Amboina*, when
   They Tortur'd our Men,
 They look'd not to have the same paid them agen,
With Fire and with Water their Sinews they crack't,
In Fire and in Water they dy'd for the Fact.

According as our God of Battel commanded,
The best of their Vessels were Fir'd and Stranded,
All Ships, Men-of-War; for what Power hath Man
To fight with that Army, when God leads ye Van:
   They Steere and they Stem,
   But 'twas so extream,
 But men were neer dying, with killing of them;
They lost, when ye Muskets and Cannons so thunder'd,
Twice so many Thousand, as we have lost hundred.

'Twould make a brave Englishman's heart leap to see't.
But forty Ships made an escape of their Fleet,

Which our Men pursue with much courage and
  strength,
'Tis doubtless but we shall surprize them at length :
> If God be our guide,
> And stand by our side,
We shall be befriended with fair Wind and Tide,
If Providence prosper us with a good gale,
The *Dutch*, nor the Devil shall ever prevaile.

Prince *Rupert*, like lightning flew through their
  Fleet,
Like Flame mix'd with Powder, their Army did
  meet,
Ten thousand slain Bodies the Ocean ore spread,
That in few hours distance, were living and dead ;
> Their Admirals all,
> Save one there did fall,
And Death had command like a Chief General
Brave *Smith* in the *Mary* did shave out his way
As Reapers do Wheat, or as Mowers do Hay.

Stout *Lawson* and *Minn* there did play both their
  parts,
Who emptied their Guns in their Enemie's hearts,
The burly fat *Dutchman* being cut out in Slips,
The Vessels did look more like Shambles than Ships,
> God prosper the Fleete,
> And send they may meet
De Ruiter to make up the Conquest compleat,
God bless all the Princes, and every thing
That fights for ye Kingdom and prayes for ye King.

The Second of November

Iт was one November—the second day—
The admiral he bore away,

Intending for his native shore.
The wind at sou'-sou'-west did roar ;
There was likewise a terrible sky,
Which made the sea to run mountains high.

The tide of ebb it was not done,
But fiercely to the west did run ;
Which put us all in terrible fear,
Because there was not room for to veer.
The wind and weather increased sore,
And drove ten sail of us on shore.

Ashore went the *Northumberland*,
The *Harwich*, and the *Cumberland*,
The *Lion* and the *Warwick* too ;
But the *Elizabeth* had the most to rue—
She came stem on—her fore-foot broke,
And she sank the *Gloucester* at one stroke.

And now remains what is worse to tell,
The greatest ships had the greatest knell
The brave *C'ronation* and all her men
Was lost and drowned every one,
Except the mate and eighteen more
What in the long boat com'd ashore.

And thus they lost their precious lives ;
But the greatest loss was to their wives
Who, with their children left on shore,
Their husbands' watery death deplore,
And wept their loss with many tears—
(But grief endureth not for years).

Now you who've a mind to go to sea,
Pray take a useful hint from me,
And live at home, and be content
With what kind Providence has sent ;

For they were punish'd for their misdeeds,
In grumbling when they had no needs.

Now God preserve our noble Queen,
Likewise her Ministers serene;
And may they ever steer a course
To make things better 'stead of worse,
And England's flag triumphant fly,
The dread of every enemy.

Admiral Benbow

OH, we sail'd to Virginia, and thence to Fyal,
Where we water'd our Shipping, and so then weigh'd all;
Full in view on the sea, boys, seven sail we did espy,
So we hoisted our topsails, and sail'd speedily.

O we drew up our Squadron in a very nice line,
And we fought them courageously for four hours' time;
But the day being spent, and the night coming on,
We let them alone till the darkness was gone.

The very next morning the engagement prov'd hot,
And brave Admiral Benbow received a chain-shot;
O when he was wounded, to his merry men he did say,
"Take me up in your arms, boys, and carry me away."

O the guns they did rattle, and the bullets did fly,
While brave Admiral Benbow for help loud did cry,
"Carry me down to the Cockpit, there is ease for my smarts,
If my merry men should see me, 'twould sure break their hearts."

The very next morning, by the break of the day,
We hoisted our topsails, and so bore away;
We sailed for Port Royal where the people flocked much
To see brave Admiral Benbow carried to Kingston Church.

Come all you brave fellows wheresoever you have been,
Let us drink a good health to the King and the Queen;
And another good health to the girls that we know,
And a third in remembrance of brave Admiral Benbow.

The Death of Admiral Benbow

(To the tune of " Samuel Hall," or " As I Sailed ")

Come all you sailors bold,
　Lend an ear,
Come all you sailors bold,
　Lend an ear:
'Tis of our Admiral's fame,
Brave Benbow called by name,
How he fought on the main
　You shall hear.

Brave Benbow he set sail
　For to fight,
Brave Benbow he set sail
　For to fight:
Brave Benbow he set sail,
With a fine and pleasant gale,
But his captains they turned tail
　In a fight.

THE DEATH OF ADMIRAL BENBOW

Says Kirkby unto Wade,
  " I will run,"
Says Kirkby unto Wade,
  " I will run :
I value not disgrace,
Nor the losing of my place,
My foes I will not face
  With a gun."

'Twas the *Ruby* and *Noah's Ark*,
  Fought the French,
'Twas the *Ruby* and *Noah's Ark*,
  Fought the French :
And there was ten in all,
Poor souls they fought them all,
They recked them not at all
  Nor their noise.

It was our Admiral's lot,
  With a chain-shot,
It was our Admiral's lot,
  With a chain-shot :
Our Admiral lost his legs,
And to his men he begs
" Fight on, my boys," he says,
  " 'Tis my lot."

While the surgeon dressed his wounds,
  Thus he said,
While the surgeon dressed his wounds,
  Thus he said,
" Let my cradle now in haste
On the quarter-deck be placed,
That the Frenchmen I may face,
  Till I'm dead."

And there bold Benbow lay,
  Crying out,
And there bold Benbow lay,
  Crying out:
" O let us tack once more,
We'll drive them to the shore,
As our fathers did before
  Long ago."

Admiral Hosier's Ghost

"Was a party song written by the ingenious author of 'Leonidas,' on the taking of Porto Bello from the Spaniards by Admiral Vernon, 22nd November, 1739. The case of Hosier, which is here so pathetically represented, was briefly this: In April 1726, that commander was sent with a strong fleet into the Spanish West Indies, to block up the galleons in the ports of that country, or, should they presume to come out, to seize and carry them into England; he accordingly arrived at the Bastimentos, near Porto Bello, but being employed rather to overawe than to attack the Spaniards, with whom it was probably not our interest to go to war, he continued long inactive on that station, to his own great regret. He afterwards removed to Carthagena, and remained cruising in those seas, till far the greater part of his men perished deplorably by the diseases of that unhealthy climate. This brave man, seeing his best officers and men thus daily swept away, his ships exposed to inevitable destruction, and himself made the sport of the enemy, is said to have died of a broken heart. Such is the account of Smollett, compared with that of other less partial writers."—*Bishop Percy's Note.*

As near Porto Bello lying
  On the gently swelling flood,
At midnight with streamers flying
  Our triumphant navy rode:
There while Vernon sate all-glorious
  From the Spaniards' late defeat:
And his crews, with shouts victorious,
  Drank success to England's fleet:

ADMIRAL HOSIER'S GHOST

On a sudden shrilly sounding,
   Hideous yells and shrieks were heard;
Then each heart with fear confounding,
   A sad troop of ghosts appear'd.
All in dreary hammocks shrouded,
   Which for winding-sheets they wore,
And with looks by sorrow clouded
   Frowning on that hostile shore.

On them gleam'd the moon's wan lustre,
   When the shade of Hosier brave
His pale bands were seen to muster,
   Rising from their watery grave,
O'er the glimmering wave he hy'd him,
   Where the *Burford* [1] rear'd her sail,
With three thousand ghosts beside him,
   And in groans did Vernon hail.

Heed, oh heed our fatal story,
   I am Hosier's injur'd ghost,
You who now have purchas'd glory
   At this place where I was lost!
Tho' in Porto Bello's ruin
   You now triumph free from fears,
When you think on our undoing,
   You will mix your joy with tears.

See these mournful spectres sweeping
   Ghastly o'er this hated wave,
Whose wan cheeks are stain'd with weeping;
   These were English captains brave.
Mark those numbers pale and horrid,
   Those were once my sailors bold:
Lo, each hangs his drooping forehead,
   While his dismal tale is told.

[1] Admiral Vernon's ship.

I, by twenty sail attended,
　　Did this Spanish town affright ;
Nothing then its wealth defended
　　But my orders not to fight.
Oh ! that in this rolling ocean
　　I had cast them with disdain,
And obey'd my heart's warm motion
　　To have quelled the pride of Spain !

For resistance I could fear none,
　　But with twenty ships had done
What thou, brave and happy Vernon,
　　Hast achiev'd with six alone.
Then the Bastimentos never
　　Had our foul dishonour seen,
Nor the sea the sad receiver
　　Of this gallant train had been.

Thus like thee, proud Spain dismaying,
　　And her galleons leading home,
Though condemn'd for disobeying,
　　I had met a traitor's doom.
To have fallen, my country crying
　　He has play'd an English part,
Had been better far than dying
　　Of a griev'd and broken heart.

Unrepining at thy glory,
　　Thy successful arms we hail ;
But remember our sad story,
　　And let Hosier's wrongs prevail.
Sent in this foul clime to languish,
　　Think what thousands fell in vain,
Wasted with disease and anguish,
　　Not in glorious battle slain

Hence with all my train attending
  From their oozy tombs below,
Thro' the hoary foam ascending,
  Here I feed my constant woe :
Here the Bastimentos viewing,
  We recall our shameful doom,
And our plaintive cries renewing,
  Wander thro' the midnight gloom

O'er these waves for ever mourning
  Shall we roam depriv'd of rest,
If to Britain's shores returning
  You neglect my just request ;
After this proud foe subduing,
  When your patriot friends you see,
Think on vengeance for my ruin,
  And for England sham'd in me.

Brave News from Admiral Vernon

(1740)

Come, loyal Britons all, rejoice, with joyful acclamation,
And join with one united voice upon this just occasion,
To Admiral Vernon drink a health, likewise to each brave fellow
Who with that noble Admiral was, at the taking of Porto Bello.

From Jamaica he did sail, with Commodore Brown to attend him,
Against the Spaniards to prevail, for which we must commend him,

At Porto Bello he arrived, where each brave gallant
    fellow
With Admiral Vernon bravely fought at the taking
    of Porto Bello.

Two men-of-war of twenty guns, likewise five
    guarda costa,
They in the harbour quickly took, to surrender
    they were forced, sir,
And then the town he summoned straight, to
    surrender to his will, O,
Which they refusing, he did shake the town of
    Porto Bello.

He did bombard it above two days, and they again
    returned it,
The bombs and mortars they did play, he vowed
    that he would burn it,
Which, when they came to understand he was so
    brave a fellow,
They did surrender, out of hand, the town of
    Porto Bello.

Then with his men he went on shore, who straight
    began to plunder,
'Tis as they served our ships before, and therefore
    'tis no wonder;
With plenty of rum and good strong wine, our men
    did soon get mellow,
They swore that never a house should stand in
    the town of Porto Bello.

The governor to the Admiral sent, and to him
    made an offer,
And thirty thousand pieces of eight, the houses
    to save did proffer;

To which the Admiral did accept with a right and
    good free will, O,
And therefore let the houses stand, in the town
    of Porto Bello.

The Iron Castle he destroyed, and all the guns he
    seizèd,
The Spaniards ne'er were more annoyed, he did just
    what he pleasèd.
The *Southsea*, snow, he did release, and many an
    English fellow
From plundering these could not be kept, in the
    town of Porto Bello.

Besides, brave Vernon freely gave, amongst his
    men as follows,
Who bravely did themselves behave, full thirty
    thousand dollars ;
This must their courage animate, each Tar is a
    rich fellow,
And this is good encouragement, for the taking
    of Porto Bello.

While trumpets they did loudly sound, and colours
    were displaying,
The prizes he did bring away, while sailors were
    huzzaying ;
And then they to Jamaica came, a glorious tale
    to tell, O,
Of the noble actions they had done in the taking
    of Porto Bello.

To our good King, now loudly sing, may
    Providence attend him.
To Admiral Vernon, toss a glass, may Heaven aye
    defend him,

To Commodore Brown, toss another down, and to each gallant fellow
Who did so bravely play his part at the taking of Porto Bello

Bob Sawyer

1758

Come all ye jolly sailors, with courage stout and bold,
Come enter with bold Sawyer, he'll clothe you all in gold,
    Repair on board the old *Nassau*,
      We'll make the French to stand in awe,
        She's manned with British boys.

Commodore Keppel with his good design,
Commanded the squadron, five sail of the line,
    The *Prince Edward* of forty guns,
    The *Firedrake* and *Furnace* bombs,
    To take Goree, it must be done,
      By true British boys.

The 29th of October, from Spithead we set sail,
Kind Neptune convey'd us with a sweet and pleasant gale,
    So, steering on the Barbary shore,
    Distance about ten leagues or more,
    The wind, at West, aloud did roar.
      Stand by, ye British boys.

So, steering on the lee shore until the break of day,
We spy'd a lofty sail on the Barbary shore to lay
    In great distress she seem'd to be,
    Her guns all overboard threw she,
    Which prov'd the *Litchfield* for to be,
      With all her British boys.

The wind blowing hard we could give them no relief,
A stretching on the lee shore, we touch'd at Teneriff,
    So watering the ships at Santa Cruz,
    Taking good wine for our ship's use,
    We sold our cloaths good wine to booze,
        Like brave British boys.

Our ship being water'd, and plenty of good wine,
We hoisted up our topsails and crost the tropic line,
    The wind at West the leading gale,
    Our gallant ship did sweetly sail,
    Steady along, she ne'er will fail,
        With all her British boys.

Steady a port! don't bring her by the lee!
Yonder is the flag staff at Goree, I do see,
    We brought the city within our sight.
    Anchored in Goree Bay that night,
    Clear'd our ships ready to fight,
        Like brave British boys.

Early the next morning the *Prince Edward of* forty guns,
Was station'd off the Island, to cover our two bombs,
    The old *Nassau* she led the van,
    With all her jovial fighting men,
    The drums did beat; to quarters stand,
        Like brave British boys.

We sail'd up to their batteries as close as we could lay,
Our guns from the top and poop aloud did play,

Which made the French cry, " Morbleu !
Diable ! what shall we do ? "
Here comes bold Sawyer, and all his crew,
    They're all British boys.

Then followed the *Dunkirk* and *Torbay*,
The guns aloud did rattle, the shells aloud did play,
    Which made the French their batteries shun,
    And from their trenches for to run,
    The flag was struck, the fight was done,
        Oh, huzza, my British boys.

Boast not of Frenchmen, nor yet of Maclome,
Sawyer's as big a hero as ever you did hear,
    Whilst the shot around him did flee,
    In engaging twice the Isle of Goree,
    As valiant men as ever you see,
        They are all British boys.

Here's a health to King George, our sovereign majesty,
Likewise to Bold Sawyer, that fought the French so free,
    Our officers and all our crew,
    Are valiant men as e'er you knew,
    So here's a health to all true blue,
        My brave British boys.

Heart of Oak

COME, cheer up, my lads ! 'tis to glory we steer,
To add something more to this wonderful year :
To honour we call you, not press you like slaves ;
For who are so free as the sons of the waves ?

> Heart of oak are our ships,
> Heart of oak are our men,
>   We always are ready :
>   Steady, boys, steady !
> We'll fight and we'll conquer again and again.
>
> We ne'er see our foes but we wish them to stay,
> They never see us but they wish us away,
> If they run, why, we follow, or run them ashore ;
> For if they won't fight us we cannot do more.
>   Heart of oak, etc.
>
> They swear they'll invade us, these terrible foes !
> They frighten our women, our children and beaux ;
> But should their flat bottoms in darkness get o'er,
> Still Britons they'll find to receive them on shore.
>   Heart of oak, etc.
>
> Britannia triumphant, her ships sweep the sea ;
> Her standard is Justice—her watchword, " Be free."
> Then cheer up, my lads ! with one heart let us sing,
> " Our soldiers, our sailors, our statesmen, and king."
>   Heart of oak, etc.

DAVID GARRICK

On the Loss of the *Royal George*

> TOLL for the brave !
>   The brave that are no more !
> All sunk beneath the wave,
>   Fast by their native shore !
>
> Eight hundred of the brave,
>   Whose courage well was tried,

Had made the vessel heel,
  And laid her on her side.

A land-breeze shook the shrouds,
  And she was overset;
Down went the *Royal George*,
  With all her crew complete.

Toll for the brave!
  Brave Kempenfelt is gone;
His last sea-fight is fought,
  His work of glory done.

It was not in the battle;
  No tempest gave the shock;
She sprang no fatal leak;
  She ran upon no rock.

His sword was in its sheath,
  His fingers held the pen,
When Kempenfelt went down,
  With twice four hundred men.

Weigh the vessel up,
  Once dreaded by our foes!
And mingle with our cup,
  The tears that England owes.

Her timbers yet are sound,
  And she may float again,
Full charged with England's thunder,
  And plough the distant main.

But Kempenfelt is gone,
  His victories are o'er,
And he and his eight hundred
  Shall plough the wave no more.

WILLIAM COWPER

Admiral Rodney's Triumph on the 12th of April

TRUE Britons all of each degree,
    Rejoice around the nation,
Full bumpers drink and merry be,
    Upon this just occasion,
Let mirth on every brow appear,
Rodney victorious is, we hear,
For he has drubbed haughty Mounseer,
    Success to gallant Rodney.

This fierce engagement did begin,
    About six in the morning,
And held till seven in the evening,
    To yield both parties scorning,
But when brave Rodney he came nigh,
He made De Grasse *peccavi* cry,
And forced the proud Mounseers to fly,
    Success to gallant Rodney.

Though they had thirty-seven sail,
    They could not save their bacon,
Their numbers nothing did avail,
    Their Admiral was taken.
Though Rodney had but thirty-four,
He forced the Mounseers to give o'er,
    Success to gallant Rodney.

He took five French sail of the line,
    And one was sunk in battle,
The Mounseers did the fight decline,
    Awed by his thunder's rattle.
Our tars did ply their guns so fast
Their leaded pills they made them taste,
De Grasse was forced his ship at last,
    To yield to gallant Rodney.

Our gallant tars they played their part,
    And like true sons of thunder,
They made the haughty Mounseer smart
    And forced him to knock under.
They mauled their masts, and rigging, too,
Their small shot just like hailstones flew,
The Mounseers roared out Sacre Dieu,
    And flew from gallant Rodney.

Upon the 12th of April last
    (Which was Fool's Day by old style),
He made a fool of famed De Grasse,
    Which sure will make you all smile.
Brave Rodney showed them George shall rule,
Drink Rodney's health in bumpers full,
Who made De Grasse an April Fool,
    Success to gallant Rodney.

A New Song on Parker the Delegate

HEAD OF THE MUTINY AT SHEERNESS

(To the tune of 'The Vicar of Bray')

I WILL not sing in Parker's praise,
    Disgraceful is the story,
Nor yet to seamen tune my lays,
    Eclipsed is now their glory;
Fell Faction's head they proudly rear,
    'Gainst Country and 'gainst King, sir
And on their land they now do try
    Destruction for to bring, sir.
        Then Britons all, with one accord,
            Fight for your Constitution,
        And let surrounding foes behold
            We want no Revolution.

PARKER THE DELEGATE

Parker the means has brought about
  Our seamen to corrupt, sir,
And like a daring traitor bold,
  Our trade doth interrupt, sir;
The ships at Sheerness rear the flag,
  The emblem of defiance,
With sorrow strikes us to reflect
  On them we've no reliance.

An Admiral he calls himself,
  Takes a Commander's station,
On board the *Sandwich* doth insult
  And braves the English nation;
Gives law, dispenses life and death,
  Or punishment disgraceful,
And by his arbitrary deeds
  Hath made himself most hateful.

A terror to each merchant ship,
  Detains, and doth them plunder,
And if they offer to sail by
  His guns do at them thunder;
Whate'er he likes he from them takes,
  And should they dare refuse, sir,
The captain's ordered to be flogged,
  Thus doth he them ill use, sir.

Five hundred pounds is the reward,
  The traitor to bring in, sir,
Who thus the bloody flag hath reared
  'Gainst Country and 'gainst King, sir;
Let's hope the villain quickly will
  To punishment be brought, sir,
Who like a daring traitor bold
  His country's ruin sought, sir.

Then Britons all, with one accord,
    Fight for your Constitution,
And let surrounding foes behold
    We want no Revolution.

The *Arethusa*

COME, all ye jolly sailors bold,
Whose hearts are cast in honour's mould,
While English glory I unfold,
    Huzza for the *Arethusa* !
She is a frigate tight and brave,
As ever stemmed the dashing wave ;
    Her men are staunch
    To their fav'rite launch,
And when the foe shall meet our fire,
Sooner than strike, we'll all expire
    On board of the *Arethusa*.

'Twas with the Spring fleet she went out
The English Channel to cruise about,
When four French sail, in show so stout,
    Bore down on the *Arethusa*.
The famed *Belle Poule* ahead did lie,
The *Arethusa* scorned to fly,
    Not a sheet, nor a tack,
    Nor a brace did she slack ;
Though the Frenchman laughed and thought it stuff,
But they knew not the handful of men, how tough,
    On board of the *Arethusa*.

On deck five hundred men did dance,
The stoutest they could find in France ;

We with two hundred did advance
    On board of the *Arethusa*.
Our captain hailed the Frenchman, " Ho ! "
The Frenchman then cried out, " Hallo ! "
    " Bear down, d'ye see,
    To our Admiral's lee ! "
" No, no," says the Frenchman, " that can't be."
" Then I must lug you along with me,"
    Says the saucy *Arethusa*.

The fight was off the Frenchman's land,
We forced them back upon the strand,
For we fought till not a stick could stand
    Of the gallant *Arethusa*.
And now we've driven the foe ashore
Never to fight with Britons more,
    Let each fill his glass
    To his fav'rite lass ;
A health to the captain and officers true,
And all that belong to the jovial crew
    On board of the *Arethusa*.

PRINCE HOARE

A New Song on Lord Nelson's Victory at Copenhagen

DRAW near, ye gallant seamen, while I the truth unfold,
Of as gallant a naval victory as ever yet was told,
The second day of April last, upon the Baltic Main,
Parker, Nelson, and their brave tars, fresh laurels there did gain.
    With their thundering and roaring, rattling and roaring,
    Thundering and roaring bombs.

Gallant Nelson volunteer'd himself, with twelve
    sail formed a line,
And in the Road of Copenhagen he began his grand
    design;
His tars with usual courage, their valour did
    display,
And destroy'd the Danish navy upon that glorious
    day.
    With their, etc.

With strong floating batteries in van and rear we
    find,
The enemy in centre had six ships of the line;
At ten that glorious morning, the fight begun, 'tis
    true,
We Copenhagen set on fire, my boys, before the
    clock struck two.
    With their, etc.

When this armament we had destroy'd, we anchor'd
    near the town,
And with our bombs were fully bent to burn their
    city down;
Revenge for poor Matilda's wrongs, our seamen
    swore they'd have,
But they sent a flag of truce on board, their city
    for to save.
    With their, etc.

For the loss of his eye and arm, bold Nelson does
    declare,
The foes of his country, not an inch of them he'll
    spare;
The Danes he's made to rue the day that they ever
    Paul did join,

Eight ships he burnt, four he sunk, and took six
of the line.
With their, etc.

Now drink a health to gallant Nelson, the wonder
of the world,
Who, in defence of his country his thunder loud
has hurled ;
And to his bold and valiant tars, who plough the
raging sea,
And who never were afraid to face the daring
enemy.
With their, etc.

The Brave Tars of Old England

(To the tune of " The Old English Roast Beef ")

LONG time of the sea had old England been Queen,
When republican France thought to alter the scene,
So she worked day and night to make up a marine,
 To fight the brave tars of old England,
 And to fight with the bold British tars.

But the day they met Howe on the seas they may
rue,
For to show them the difference he very well knew,
Twixt tri-coloured cockades and true English blue,
 Huzza, for the tars of old England,
 And huzza for the bold British tars.

They were swept from the sea on the land high and
dry,
Till they ventured their luck in a fog once to try ;

But a storm sent them back pleased in harbour to
   lie,
  Secure from the tars of old England,
  Secure from the bold British tars.

Yet unwilling with Britain's domain to agree,
They made up some rods of the Liberty tree ;
And with them they lashed other folk out to sea
  To fight the brave tars of old England,
  To fight with the brave British tars.

Spanish dons in great force of big ships they were
   seen,
But Jervis and Nelson to fight them were keen,
So they fought and they beat twenty-sevèn with
   fifteen,
  Mann'd by the brave tars of old England,
  Mann'd by the old bold British tars.

Then the French crammed their principles down
   the Dutch throats,
And forced the Mynheers for to alter their notes,
And to don the red cap and become Sans Cullotes,
  And to fight the brave tars of old England,
  And to fight with the bold British tars.

To recover their Cape soon a squadron was found,
They split us, and there they got safely and sound,
But Elphinstone showed they'd got into Lob's
   Pound,
  They were nabbed by the tars of old England,
  They were nabbed by the bold British tars.

Then says Monsieur, " As, Mynheer, your trade
   is all lost,

THE BRAVE TARS OF OLD ENGLAND

Rig a fleet, and come out, we'll invade Britain's coast,"
But this reck'ning they made without minding their host,
  Without thinking of tars of old England,
  Without thinking of bold British tars.

For to block up Brest harbour Lord Bridport set sail,
And the mouth of the Texel our fleet did not fail,
To shut up and keep the Dutch rogues in their jail;
  Hemmed in by the tars of old England,
  Hemmed in by the bold British tars.

Our fleet to refit it had just sailed away,
When, the cat being gone, the mouse came out to play;
But this play it became woeful earnest that day,
  Laid on by the tars of old England,
  Laid on by the bold British tars.

For the news of their sailing had scarce reached our ears,
When our anchors flew up to the sound of three cheers;
And away to the Texel to fight the Mynheers,
  Away went the tars of old England,
  Away went the bold British tars.

With their Liberty hulks to sheer off was in vain,
For, as we got between, they their port could not gain,
So they took the resolve a hard fight to maintain,
  Against the brave tars of old England,
  Against the old bold British tars.

'Twas twelve when the signal for action was given,
Our guns opened fire like the thunder from heaven;
And by three the Dutch fleet off the water was driven,
   Smashed to pieces by tars of old England,
   Smashed to pieces by bold British tars.

Their hulks were a riddle, their canvas a rag,
Ten struck with their Vice and their Admiral's flag;
Their friends on the shore had no reason to brag
   Of success against tars of old England,
   Of success against bold British tars.

Then Gallia, exerting the strength of her power,
Sent a fleet out a-skulking to Africa's shore,
To plunder and rob the Egyptian store,
   And elude the brave tars of old England,
   And to bilk all the brave British tars.

But Nelson, that bold British Boy did set sail,
And in their concealment the Frenchmen did nail,
He destroyed their fine scheme, pulled the sting from their tail,
   And played them the tars of old England,
   To the tune of the bold British tars.

On their ships and their batteries, so fierce did he fall,
That he burnt, sunk, and took and destroyed them all.
A piping hot supper of powder and ball
   They received from the tars of old England,
   Piping hot from the bold British tars.

Britannia's high trident, still waving on high,
Bids her tars all be true, and their foes all defy;

To avenge all her wrongs they will conquer or die,
　　Like brave jolly tars of old England,
　　The conquering brave British tars.

Now fill up a glass, while a bumper we have,
To Howe, Jervis, Duncan, and Nelson the Brave;
To the bold British tars, who now rule on the wave,
　　Huzza for the bulwarks of England,
　　And health to each bold British tar.

Trafalgar

1805

'Twas at the close of that dark morn
　　On which our Hero, conquering, died,
That every seaman's heart was torn
　　By strife of sorrow and of pride;—

Of pride, that one short day would show
　　Deeds of eternal splendour done,
Full twenty hostile ensigns low,
　　And twenty glorious victories won—

Of grief, of deepest, tenderest grief,
　　That He, on every sea and shore,
Their brave, beloved, unconquer'd Chief,
　　Should wave his victor-flag no more.

Sad was the eve of that dire day:
　　But sadder, direr was the night,
When human rage had ceased the fray,
　　And elements maintain'd the fight.

All shaken in the conflict past,
　　The navies fear'd the tempest loud—

The gale, that shook the groaning mast—
   The wave, that climb'd the tatter'd shroud.

By passing gleams of sullen light,
   The worn and weary seamen view'd
The hard-earn'd prizes of the fight
   Sink, found'ring, in the midnight flood:

And oft, as drowning screams they heard,
   And oft, as sank the ships around,
Some British vessel lost they fear'd,
   And mourn'd some British brethren drown'd.

And oft they cried (as memory roll'd
   On Him, so late their hope and guide,
But now a bloody corse and cold),
   " Was it for this that NELSON died?"

For three short days, and three long nights,
   They wrestled with the tempest's force;
And sank the trophies of their fights,—
   And thought upon that bloody corse!—

But when the fairer morn arose
   Bright o'er the yet-tumultuous main,
They saw no wreck but that of foes,
   No ruin but of France and Spain:

And victors now of winds and seas,
   Beheld the British vessels brave,
Breasting the ocean at their ease,
   Like sea-birds on their native wave:

And now they cried (because they found
   Old England's fleet in all its pride,
While Spain's and France's hopes were drown'd),
   " It was for this that NELSON died!"

He died, with many an hundred bold
  And honest hearts as ever beat !—
But where's the British heart so cold
  That would not die in such a feat ?

Yes ! by their memories ! by all
  The honours which their tomb surround !
Theirs was the noblest, happiest fall
  Which ever mortal courage crown'd.

Then bear them to their glorious grave
  With no weak tears, no woman's sighs ;
Theirs was the deathbed of the brave,
  And manly be their obsequies.

Haul not your colours from on high,
  Nor down the flags of victory lower :—
Give every streamer to the sky,
  Let all your conqu'ring cannon roar ;

That every kindling soul may learn
  How to resign its patriot breath ;
And from a grateful country, earn
  The triumphs of a trophied death.

The Battle of Trafalgar

Arise, ye Sons of Britain, in chorus join and sing,
Great and joyful news is come unto our Royal King.
  An engagement we have had by sea
  With France and Spain, our enemy,
  And we've gained a glorious victory
    Again, my brave boys.

On the twenty-first of October, at the rising of
  the sun

We form'd the line for action, every man to his gun.
    Brave Nelson to his men did say,
    " The Lord will prosper us this day,
    Give them a broadside, fire away,
        My true British boys."

Broadside after broadside, our cannon balls did fly,
The small shot, like hailstones, upon the deck did lie.
    Their masts and rigging we shot away,
    Besides some thousands on that day
    Were killed and wounded in the fray
        On both sides, brave boys.

Lord reward brave Nelson, and protect his soul,
Nineteen sail the combin'd fleets lost in the whole ;
    The *Achille* blew up amidst them all,
    Which made the French for mercy call ;—
    Nelson was slain by a musket-ball,
        Mourn, Britons, Mourn.

Each brave commander in tears did shake his head,
Their grief was no relief when Nelson he was dead ;
    It was by a fatal musket-ball,
    Which caus'd our Hero for to fall,
    He cried, " Fight on, God bless you all,
        My brave British Tars."

Huzza, my valiant Seamen, huzza, we gain'd the day,
But lost a brave commander, bleeding on the lay ;
    With joy we'd gain'd the victory,
    Before his death, he did plainly see,
    " I die in peace, bless God," said he,
        " The victory is won."

I hope this glorious victory will bring a speedy
    peace,
That all trade in England may flourish and
    increase,
  And our ships from port to port go free
  As before, let us with them agree,
  May this turn the heart of our Enemy.
    Huzza, my brave boys.

Victoria

(June 22nd, 1893)

"There was absolutely no panic, no shouting, no rushing aimlessly about. The officers went quietly to their stations. Everything was prepared, and the men were all in their positions. . . . I can further testify to the men below in the engine-rooms. . . . In all the details of this terrible accident one spot especially stands out, and that is the heroic conduct of those who to the end remained below, stolidly yet boldly, at their place of duty."—*Captain Bourke's Statement.*

Queen! What is this that comes
Borne on thy rolling drums
At sunrise from the far
    Syrian borders?
—Sped from the flags that fly
Half-mast at Tripoli,
Where float the ships of war,
    Thy Virgin warders?

Where tarries she who should
Captain that sisterhood,
Named with thy name, and own
    Offspring of victory?

Deep, eighty fathoms deep,
She, with her crew asleep,
Recks not the signal flow,
   Vain, valedictory.

Not in thy day of wrath,
Lord God of Sabaoth,
Nor upon rock or sand
   Hemmed with thy breath round;
But leading tranquilly,
Upon a tranquil sea,
Swift at a sister's hand
   Took she her death-wound.

Launched on the fatal curve,
Too late to stay or swerve,
Starkly the *Camperdown*
   Rounded, descended,
Struck—saw, and backward reeled,
As he who on the field
By Oxus smote his own
   Sohrab, the splendid.

But She, the stricken hull,
The doomed, the beautiful,
Proudly to fate abased
   Her brow Titanic.
Praise now her multitude
Who, nursed in fortitude,
Fell in on deck and faced
   Death without panic.

Heaven, that to admirals,
Assigns their funerals,
To some the battle's ridge
   Full-starred, to die on—

VICTORIA

Took not the spirit proud
From him she less allowed.
—Calm, cool, upon the bridge,
　Sank the brave Tryon !

Now for the seamen whom
Thy not degenerate womb
Gave thus to die for thee,
　England, be tearless :
Rise, and with front serene
Answer, thou Spartan queen.
" Still God is good to me :
　My sons are fearless."

Back to the flags that fly
Half-mast at Tripoli,
Back on the sullen drum
　Mourning *Victoria*,
Loud, ay, and jubilant,
Hurl thine imperial chant—
" *In morte talium
　Stat matris gloria !* "

A. T. QUILLER-COUCH

POEMS OF SAILORS AND OF LIFE AT SEA

The Shipman

A SCHIPMAN was ther, wonying fer by weste:
For ought I woot, he was of Dertemouthe.
He rood upon a rouncy as he couthe,
In a gowne of faldying to the kne.
A dagger hanging on a laas hadde he
Aboute his nekke under his arm adoun.
The hoote somer had maad his hew al broun;
And certainly he was a good felawe.
Ful many a draught of wyn had he drawe
From Burdeux-ward, while that the chapman sleep.
Of nyce conscience took he no keep.
If that he foughte, and hadde the heigher hand,
By water he sente hem hoom to every land.
But of his craft to reckon well the tydes,
His stremes, and his dangers him besides,
His herbergh, and his mone, his lodemenage,
Ther was non such from Hulle to Cartage.
Hardy he was, and wys to undertake;
With many a tempest hadde his berd ben shake
He knew wel al the havenes, as thei were,
From Scotland to the Cape of Fynestere,
And every cryk in Bretayne and in Spayne;
His barge y-clepud was the *Magdelayne*.

GEOFFREY CHAUCER

The Sailing of the Pilgrims from Sandwich Towards St. James of Compostella

A POEM OF THE EARLY 15TH CENTURY

Men may leve all gamys
That saylem to Sent Jamys;
For many a man hit gramys;[1]
    When they begyn to sayle.

For when they have take the see,
At Sandwyche, or at Wynchylsee,
At Bristow, or where that hyt bee,
    Theyr herts begyn to fayle.

Anone the mastyr commaundeth fast
To hys shyp-men in all the hast,
To dresse hem sone about the mast,
    Theyr takelyng to make.

With " howe! hissa! " then they cry,
" What, hoist! mate thow stondst to ny,[2]
Thy felow may nat hale the by; "
    Thus they begyn to crake.

A boy or tweyne anone up-styen,
And overthwarte the sayle-yerde lyen;—
" Y how! taylia! "[3] the remenaunte cryen,
    And pull with all theyr myght.

" Bestowe the boote,[4] bote-swayne, anon,
That our pylgryms may pley thereon;
For som ar lyke to cowgh and grone,
    Or hit be full mydnyght."

[1] *Gramys*, troubles.
[2] *Ny*, too near, too close, so that the next man cannot haul.
[3] *Taylia*, O, tally on, take hold and haul.
[4] *Boote*, ship's boat.

"Hale the bowelyne ! now, vere the shete !
Cooke, make redy anoone our mete,
Our pylgryms have no lust to ete,
    I pray God yeve him rest."

" Go to the helm ! what, howe ! no nere ? [1]
Steward, felow ! a pot of bere ! "
" Ye shall have, sir, with good chere,
    Anone all of the best."

" Y howe ! trussa ! [2] hale in the brayles !
Thow halest nat, be God, thow fayles,
O se how well owre good shyp sayles ! "
    And thus they say among.

" Hale in the Wartake ! " [3] " Hit shall be done."
" Steward ! cover the boorde anone,
And set bred and salt thereone,
    And tarry nat to long."

Then cometh oone and seyth, " Be mery ;
Ye shall have a storme or a pery." [4]
" Hold thow thy pese ! thow canst no whery,
    Thow medlyst wondyr sore."

Thys menewhyle the pylgryms ly,
And have theyr bowlys fast them by,
And cry afthyr hote malvesy,
    " Thow helpe for to restore."

And som wold have a saltyd tost,
For they myght ete neyther sode ne rost
A man myght sone pay for theyr cost,
    As for oo day or twayne.

---

[1] *No nere*, steer no nearer the wind.
[2] *Trussa*, a call or hauling shout. " O truss her up."
[3] A warp.
[4] *A pery*, a danger.

Som layde theyr bookys on theyr kne,
And rad so long they myght nat se ;—
" Allas ! myne hede woll cleve on thre ! "
    Thus seyth another certayne.

Then commeth oure owner lyke a lorde,
And speketh many a royall worde,
And dresseth hym to the hygh borde
    To see all thyng be well.

Anone he calleth a carpentere,
And biddyth hym bryng with hym hys gere,
To make the cabans here and there,
    With many a febyl cell.

A sak of strawe werr there ryght good
For som must lyg them in theyr hood,
I had as lefe be in the wood,
    Without mete or drynk.

For when that we shall go to bedde,
The pumpe was nygh our bedde hede,
A man were as good to be dede,
    As smell thereof the stynk.[1]

Sir Patrick Spens

THE King sits in Dunfermline town,
    Drinking the blude-red wine :
" O whaur will I get a skeely skipper
    To sail this new ship o' mine ? "

---

[1] The water which leaks into a tight wooden ship generally rots in the bilges. The smell of this rotten water is abominable, but the presence of the smell indicates that the leak is inconsiderable.

O up and spake an eldern knight,
  Sat at the King's right knee :
" Sir Patrick Spens is the best sailor
  That ever sailed the sea."

Our King has written a braid letter
  And sealed it wi' his hand,
And sent it to Sir Patrick Spens,
  Was walking on the strand.

" To Noroway, to Noroway,
  To Noroway o'er the faem ;
The King's daughter to Noroway,
  'Tis thou maun bring her hame."

The first word that Sir Patrick read,
  Sae loud, loud lauchèd he ;
The neist word that Sir Patrick read,
  The tear blinded his ee.

" O wha is this has done this deed,
  And tauld the King of me,
To send us out at this time o' year
  To sail upon the sea ?

" Be it wind, be it weet, be it hail, be it sleet,
  Our ship must sail the faem ;
The King's daughter to Noroway,
  'Tis we must bring her hame."

They hoysed their sails on Monday morn
  Wi' a' the speed they may ;
They hae landed in Noroway
  Upon a Wodensday.

They hadna been a week, a week,
  In Noroway, but twae,

SIR PATRICK SPENS

When that the lords o' Noroway
  Began aloud to say :

" Ye Scottishmen spend a' our King's goud
  And a' our Queenis fee."
" Ye lie, ye lie, ye liars loud,
  Fu' loud I hear ye lie !

" For I brought as mickle white monie
  As gane my men and me,
And I brought a half-fou o' gude red goud
  Out o'er the sea wi' me.

" Mak' ready, mak' ready, my merry men a' !
  Our gude ship sails the morn."
" Now, ever alake, my master dear,
  I fear a deadly storm.

" I saw the new moon late yestreen
  Wi' the auld moon in her arm ;
And, if we gang to sea, master,
  I fear we'll come to harm."

They hadna sailed a league, a league,
  A league but barely three,
When the lift grew dark, and the wind blew loud,
  And gurly grew the sea.

" O where will I get a gude sailor
  To tak' my helm in hand,
Till I gae up to the tall topmast
  To see if I can spy land ? "

" O here am I, a sailor gude,
  To tak' the helm in hand,
Till you gae up to the tall topmast ;
  But I fear you'll ne'er spy land."

He hadna gane a step, a step,
  A step but barely ane,
When a bolt flew out o' our goodly ship,
  And the salt sea it came in.

" Gae fetch a web o' the silken claith,
  Anither o' the twine,
And wap them into our ship's side,
  And letna the sea come in."

They fetched a web o' the silken claith,
  Anither o' the twine,
And they wapped them round that gude ship's side,
  But still the sea cam' in.

O laith, laith were our gude Scots lords
  To weet their milk-white hands;
But lang ere a' the play was ower
  They wat their gowden bands.

O laith, laith were our gude Scots lords
  To weet their cork-heeled shoon;
But lang ere a' the play was played
  They wat their hats aboon.

O lang, lang may the ladies sit
  Wi' their fans intill their hand,
Before they see Sir Patrick Spens
  Come sailing to the strand !

And lang, lang may the maidens sit
  Wi' their goud kaims in their hair,
A' waiting for their ain dear loves !
  For them they'll see nae mair.

Hauf ower, hauf ower to Aberdour,
  It's fifty fathoms deep,
And there lies gude Sir Patrick Spens
  Wi' the Scots lords at his feet.

From " The Tempest "

ACT I

SCENE I.—On a Ship at Sea. A tempestuous noise of Thunder and Lightning heard.

Enter a Ship-Master and a Boatswain.

Master. Boatswain!
Boats. Here, master: what cheer?
Mast. Good, speak to the mariners: fall to 't yarely, or we run ourselves aground: bestir, bestir.   [*Exit.*

Enter Mariners.

Boats. Heigh, my hearts; cheerly, cheerly, my hearts; yare, yare. Take in the topsail; tend to the master's whistle.—Blow till thou burst thy wind, if room enough!

Enter ALONSO, SEBASTIAN, ANTONIO, FERDINAND, GONZALO, *and others*.

Alon. Good boatswain, have care. Where's the master? Play the men.
Boats. I pray now, keep below.
Ant. Where is the master, boatswain?
Boats. Do you not hear him? You mar our labour. Keep your cabins; you do assist the storm.
Gon. Nay, good, be patient.

Boats. When the sea is. Hence! What care these roarers for the name of king? To cabin: silence! trouble us not.

Gon. Good, yet remember whom thou hast aboard.

Boats. None that I more love than myself. You are a counsellor: if you can command these elements to silence, and work the peace of the present, we will not hand a rope more; use your authority: if you cannot, give thanks you have lived so long, and make yourself ready in your cabin for the mischance of the hour, if it so hap.— Cheerly, good hearts!—Out of our way, I say.

[*Exit.*

Gon. I have great comfort from this fellow: methinks he hath no drowning mark upon him; his complexion is perfect gallows. Stand fast, good Fate, to his hanging! make the rope of his destiny our cable, for our own doth little advantage: if he be not born to be hanged, our case is miserable. [*Exeunt.*

Re-enter Boatswain.

Boats. Down with the topmast: yare; lower, lower. Bring her to try with main-course. [*A cry within.*] A plague upon this howling! they are louder than the weather, or our office.—

Re-enter SEBASTIAN, ANTONIO, *and* GONZALO.

Yet again? what do you here? Shall we give o'er, and drown? Have you a mind to sink?

Seb. A pox o' your throat, you bawling, blasphemous, incharitable dog!

Boats. Work you, then.

Ant. Hang, cur, hang, you whoreson, insolent

noisemaker, we are less afraid to be drowned than thou art.

Gon. I'll warrant him for drowning, though the ship were no stronger than a nutshell, and as leaky as an unstanched wench.

Boats. Lay her a-hold, a-hold! Set her two courses; off to sea again; lay her off.

Enter Mariners, wet.

Mar. All lost! to prayers, to prayers! all lost!
[*Exeunt.*
Boats. What, must our mouths be cold?
Gon. The king and prince at prayers; let's assist them,
For our case is as theirs.
Seb. I am out of patience.
Ant. We are merely cheated of our lives by drunkards.—
This wide-chopped rascal,— 'would, thou might'st lie drowning,
The washing of ten tides!
Gon. He'll be hanged yet,
Though every drop of water swear against it,
And gape at wid'st to glut him.
[*A confused noise within.*] Mercy on us!—
We split, we split!—Farewell, my wife and children!—
Farewell, brother!—We split, we split, we split!—
Ant. Let's all sink with the king. [*Exit.*
Seb. Let's take leave of him. [*Exit.*
Gon. Now would I give a thousand furlongs of sea for an acre of barren ground; long heath, brown furze, anything. The wills above be done, but I would fain die a dry death. [*Exit.*

WILLIAM SHAKESPEARE

The Saylor's Song

We Seamen are the bonny boys
　That fear no storms nor rocks-a,
Whose music is the Cannon's noise,
　Whose sporting is with knocks-a.

'Tis brave to see a ship to sail
　With all her trim gear on-a,
As though the Devil were at her tail
　She with the wind will run-a.

Come let us reck'n what ships are ours,
　The *Gorgon*, and the *Dragon*;
The *Lion*, which in fight is bold
　The *Bull* with bloody flag on.

The *Bear*, the *Dog*, the *Fox*, the *Kite*;
　That stuck fast to the *Rover*,
They chased the Turk in a day and night
　From Scanderoon to Dover.

A health to brave sea-soldiers all,
　Let cans a-piece go round-a;
Pell-mell let's to the battle fall
　And lofty music sound-a.
　　　　　　(From *Wit and Drollery*, 1682)

A Ballad of Sea Fardingers, Describing Evil Fortune

What pen can well report the plight
Of those that travel on the sea?
To pass the weary winter's night
With stormy clouds wishing for day,
With waves that toss them to and fro,—
Their poor estate is hard to show

A BALLAD OF SEA FARDINGERS

When boistering winds begin to roar
On cruel coasts, from haven we,
The foggy mists so dims the shore,
The rocks and sands we may not see,
Nor have no room at sea to try,
But pray to God, and yield to die.

When shoals and sandy banks appear,
What pilot can direct his course?
When foaming tides drive us so near,
Alas! what fortune can be worse?
Then anchor's hold must be our stay,
Or else we fall into decay.

We wander still from luff to lie,
And find no steadfast wind to blow;
We still remain in jeopardy,
Each perilous point is hard to show;
In time we hope to find redress,
That long have lived in heaviness.

O pinching, weary, loathsome life,
That travel still in far exile,
The dangers great on seas be rife
Whose recompense doth yield but toil.
O Fortune, grant me my desire,—
A happy end I do require.

When frets and storms have had their fill,
And gentle calm the coast will clear,
Then haughty hearts shall have their will,
That long hast wept with mourning cheer;
And leave the seas with their annoy,
At home at ease to live in joy.

(Sloane MS. 2497 fol. 47)

Sir Walter Raleigh Sailing in the Lowlands

(To the tune of " Sailing in the Lowlands of Holland ")

Showing how the famous Ship called the *Sweet Trinity* was taken by a false Galley, and how it was again restored by the craft of a little Sea-boy, who sunk the Galley; as the following Song will declare.

SIR WALTER RALEIGH has built a Ship, in the Netherlands;
Sir Walter Raleigh has built a Ship, in the Netherlands;
And it is called the *Sweet Trinity*,
And it was taken by the false Gallaly, sailing in the Lowlands.

" Is there never a Seaman bold in the Netherlands;
Is there never a Seaman bold in the Netherlands;
That will go take this false Gallaly,
And to redeem the *Sweet Trinity*, sailing in the Lowlands ? "

Then spoke the little Ship-boy, in the Netherlands;
Then spoke the little Ship-boy, in the Netherlands;
" Master, what will you give me, and I take this false Gallaly,
And release the *Sweet Trinity*, sailing in the Lowlands ? "

" I'll give thee gold, and I'll give thee fee, in the Netherlands;
I'll give thee gold, and I'll give thee fee, in the Netherlands;
And my eldest daughter, thy wife shall be, sailing in the Lowlands."

He set his breast, and away he did swim, in the Netherlands;

SIR WALTER RALEIGH

He set his breast, and away he did swim, in the Netherlands,
Until he came to the false Gallaly, sailing in the Lowlands.

He had an Augur fit for the nonce, in the Netherlands;
He had an Augur fit for the nonce, in the Netherlands,
The which will bore fifteen good holes at once, sailing in the Lowlands.

Some were at Cards, and some at Dice, in the Netherlands;
Some were at Cards, and some at Dice, in the Netherlands,
Until the salt water flashed in their eyes, sailing in the Lowlands.

Some cut their hats, and some cut their caps, in the Netherlands;
Some cut their hats, and some cut their caps, in the Netherlands,
For to stop the salt water gaps, sailing in the Lowlands.

He set his breast, and away did swim, in the Netherlands;
He set his breast, and away did swim, in the Netherlands,
Until he came to his own ship again, sailing in the Lowlands.

" I have done the work I promised to do, in the Netherlands;
I have done the work I promised to do, in the Netherlands.

I have sunk the false *Gallaly*, and released the
Sweet Trinity, sailing in the Lowlands.

"You promised me gold, and you promised me
    fee, in the Netherlands ;
You promised me gold, and you promised me fee,
    in the Netherlands ;
Your eldest daughter my wife she must be, sailing
    in the Lowlands."

"You shall have gold, and you shall have fee, in
    the Netherlands ;
You shall have gold, and you shall have fee, in
    the Netherlands ;
But my eldest daughter your wife shall never be,
    sailing in the Lowlands."

"Then fare you well, you cozening Lord, in the
    Netherlands ;
Then fare you well, you cozening Lord, in the
    Netherlands ;
Seeing you are not so good as your word, sailing
    in the Lowlands."

And thus I shall conclude my Song of the sailing
    in the Lowlands ;
Wishing all happiness to all Seamen both old and
    young,
In their sailing in the Lowlands.

The *Goulden Vanitee*

THERE was a gallant ship, and a gallant ship was she,
    Ik iddle du, and the Lowlands low ;
And she was called the *Goulden Vanitee*,
    As she sailed to the Lowlands low.

THE *GOULDEN VANITEE* 173

She had not sailed a league, a league but only three,
   Ik iddle du, and the Lowlands low ;
When she came up with a French gallee,
   As she sailed to the Lowlands low.

Out spoke the little cabin boy, out spoke he,
   Ik iddle du, and the Lowlands low ;
" What will you give if I sink that French gallee,
   As ye sail to the Lowlands low ? "

Out spoke the Captain, out spoke he,
   Ik iddle du, and the Lowlands low ;
" We'll give ye an estate in the North countree,
   As ye sail to the Lowlands low."

" Then row me up tight in a black bull's skin,
   Ik iddle du, and the Lowlands low ;
And throw me o'er deck-board, sink I or swim,
   As ye sail to the Lowlands low."

So they sewed him up tight in a black bull's skin,
   Ik iddle du, and the Lowlands low ;
And threw him over deck-board, sink he or swim,
   As they sail to the Lowlands low.

About and about and about went he,
   Ik iddle du, and the Lowlands low ;
Until he had swam to the French gallee,
   As she sailed to the Lowlands low.

O some were playing cards, and some were playing
   dice,
   Ik iddle du, and the Lowlands low ;
When he took out an augur, bored thirty holes at
   twice,
   As she sailed to the Lowlands low.

And some they ran with cloaks, and some they ran with caps,
 Ik iddle du, and the Lowlands low;
To try if they could stop the salt water drops,
 As she sailed to the Lowlands low.

About and about and about went he,
 Ik iddle du, and the Lowlands low;
Until he came back to the *Goulden Vanitee*,
 As she sailed to the Lowlands low.

"Now heave me o'er a rope, and sway me up aboard,
 Ik iddle du, and the Lowlands low;
And give me the farm land, as good as your word,
 As ye sail to the Lowlands low."

"We'll heave you no rope, nor sway you up aboard,
 Ik iddle du, and the Lowlands low;
Nor give you an estate, as good as our word,
 As we sail to the Lowlands low."

Out spoke the little cabin-boy, out spoke he,
 Ik iddle du, and the Lowlands low;
"I'll sink ye as I sunk the French gallee,
 As ye sail to the Lowlands low."

They hove him o'er a rope, and they swayed him up aboard,
 Ik iddle du, and the Lowlands low;
And they have proved to him much better than their word,
 As they sailed to the Lowlands low.

The *Golden Vanity*

MODERN VERSION[1]

A SHIP I have in the North countree,
She goes by the name of the *Golden Vanity*,
I fear she will be taken by a Turkish galla-lee,
  As she sails by the Lowlands low.

Then up and says our little cabin-boy,
" What gold will you give me if I do them destroy ?
If I sink her in the seas that she never more annoy,
  As we sail by the Lowlands low ? "

" I will give you red gold, and silver good store,
And of acres of corn-land I'll give to you a score,
And my daughter to marry, if we ever come ashore,
  If you sink her in the Lowlands low."

The Boy he bent his breast, and away he jumpt in.
He swam till he came to the Turkish galley-in,
And the salt sea water was cold upon his skin,
  As he swam by the Lowlands low.

And out he took an augur, and bored holes thrice,
And some were playing cards, and some were playing dice,
When the water flowed in, it dazzled their eyes,
  And they sank by the Lowlands low.

The Boy he bent his breast, and he swam back again,
And the salt sea water was cold upon his brain,
And he cried, " O take me up, or I shall be slain,
  I am drowning in the Lowlands low."

[1] There are countless other versions of this old ballad ; and perhaps every village in Devon and Cornwall would furnish variation from the beautiful original.

"I'll not take you up, you can climb up her side,
I will not take you up," the master replied;
"I will kill you, I will shoot you," the cruel master cried,
  "*You may sink in the Lowlands low.*"

The Boy he swam round all by the starboard side
And they laid him on the deck, and there he soon died,
And they sewed him up tight in a black bull's hide,
And they hove him into the sea to go down with the tide,
  And sunk him in the Lowlands low.

The Storm

. . . . . .

ENGLAND, to whom we owe what we be and have,
Sad that her sons did seek a foreign grave,
— For Fate's or Fortune's drifts none can soothsay:
Honour and misery have one face, and way—
From out her pregnant entrails sighed a wind,
Which at the air's middle marble room did find
Such strong resistance, that itself it threw
Downward again; and so when it did view
How in the port our fleet dear time did leese,
Withering like prisoners, which lie but for fees,
Mildly it kiss'd our sails, and fresh and sweet
—As to a stomach starved, whose insides meet,
Meat comes—it came; and swole our sails, when we
So joy'd, as Sarah her swelling joyed to see.
But 'twas but so kind as our countrymen,
Which bring friends one day's way, and leave them then.
Then like two mighty kings, which dwelling far
Asunder, meet against a third to war.

THE STORM

The south and west winds joined, and, as they blew,
Waves like a rolling trench before them threw.
Sooner than you read this line, did the gale,
Like shot, not feared till felt, our sails assail;
And what at first was called a gust, the same
Hath now a storm's, anon a tempest's name.
Jonas, I pity thee, and curse those men
Who, when the storm raged most, did wake thee then.
Sleep is pain's easiest salve, and doth fulfil
All offices of death except to kill.
But when I waked, I saw that I saw not;
Ay, and the sun, which should teach me, had forgot
East, west, day, night; and I could only say,
If the world had lasted, now it had been day.
Thousands our noises were, yet we 'mongst all
Could none by his right name, but thunder, call.
Light'ning was all our light, and it rained more
Than if the sun had drunk the sea before.
Some coffin'd in their cabins lie, equally
Grieved that they are not dead, and yet must die;
And as sin-burdened souls from grave will creep
At the last day, some forth their cabins peep,
And trembling ask, "What news?" and do hear so,
As jealous husbands, what they would not know.
Some, sitting on the hatches, would seem there
With hideous gazing to fear away fear.
Then note they the ship's sicknesses, the mast
Shaked with an ague, and the hold and waist
With a salt dropsy clogged, and all our tacklings
Snapping, like too-too-high-stretched treble strings
And from our tattered sails rags drop down so,
As from one hanged in chains a year ago.
Even our ordnance, placed for our defence,
Strives to break loose, and 'scape away from thence
Pumping hath tired our men, and what's the gain?

Seas into seas thrown, we suck in again;
Hearing hath deaf'd our sailors, and if they
Knew how to hear, there's none knows what to say.
Compared to these storms death is but a qualm,
Hell somewhat lightsome, the Bermudas calm.
Darkness, light's eldest brother, his birthright
Claims o'er the world, and to heaven hath chased
   light.
All things are one, and that one none can be,
Since all forms uniform deformity
Doth cover; so that we, except God say
Another Fiat, shall have no more day.
So violent, yet long, these furies be.

JOHN DONNE

Shortening Sail

As the proud horse, with costly trappings gay,
Exulting prances to the bloody fray;
Spurning the ground, he glories in his might,
But reels tumultuous in the shock of fight;
E'en so, caparison'd in gaudy pride,
The bounding vessel dances on the tide.
Fierce and more fierce the southern demon blew,
And more incens'd the roaring waters grew.
The ship no longer can her topsails spread,
And every hope of fairer skies is fled.
Bowlines and halliards are relax'd again;
Clue-lines haul'd down, and sheets let fly amain;
Clu'd up, each topsail, and by braces squar'd;
The seamen climb aloft on either yard.
They furl the sail, and pointed to the wind
The yard, by rolling tackles [1] then confin'd.

[1] *The rolling tackle* is an assemblage of pullies used to confine the yard to the weather side of the mast, and prevent the former from rubbing against the latter by the fluctuating motion of the ship.

SHORTENING SAIL

While o'er the ship the gallant boatswain flies,
Like a hoarse mastiff, thro' the storm he cries :
Prompt to direct the unskilful still appears ;
Th' expert he praises, and the fearful cheers.
Now some to strike top-gallant yards[1] attend ;
Some travellers [2] up the weather back-stays [3] send ;
At each mast-head the top-ropes[4] others bend.
The youngest sailors from the yards above
Their parrels,[5] lifts,[6] and braces soon remove ;
Then topt an end, and to the travellers tied,
Charg'd with their sails, they down the back-stays slide.
The yards secure along the booms[7] reclin'd ;
While some the flying cords aloft confin'd.
Their sails reduc'd, and all the rigging clear,
Awhile the crew relax from toils severe.
Awhile their spirits, with fatigue opprest,
In vain expect th' alternate hour of rest :

[1] It was usual to send down the top-gallant yards on the approach of a storm.

[2] *Travellers* were slender iron rings encircling the back-stays, and used to facilitate the hoisting or lowering of the top-gallant yards, by confining them to the back-stays, in their ascent or descent, so as to prevent them from swinging about by the agitation of the vessel.

[3] *Back-stays* are long ropes extending from the right and left side of the ship to the mast heads, which they are intended to secure, by counteracting the efforts of the wind upon the sails.

[4] *Top-ropes* are the cords by which the top-gallant yards were hoisted up from the deck, or lowered again in stormy weather.

[5] *The parrel*, which is usually a movable band of rope, is employed to confine the yard to its respective mast.

[6] *Lifts* are ropes extending from the head of any mast to the extremities of its particular yard, to support the weight of the latter ; to retain it in balance ; or to raise one yard-arm higher than the other, which is accordingly called topping.

[7] *The booms* in this place imply masts or yards lying on the deck in reserve, to supply the place of others which may be carried away.

But with redoubling force the tempests blow,
And watery hills in fell succession flow.
A dismal shade o'ercasts the frowning skies ;
New troubles grow ; new difficulties rise.
No season this from duty to descend !
All hands on deck, th' eventful hour attend,
His race perform'd, the sacred lamp of day
Now dipt in western clouds his parting ray ;
His sick'ning fires, half-lost in ambient haze,
Refract along the dusk a crimson blaze ;
Till deep immerg'd the languid orb declines,
And now to cheerless night the sky resigns !
Sad evening's hour, how different from the past !
No flaming pomp, no blushing glories cast ;
No ray of friendly light is seen around :
The moon and stars in hopeless shade are drown'd.
The ship no longer can her courses[1] bear ;
To reef the courses is the master's care :
The sailors summon'd aft, a daring band !
Attend th' unfolding brails at his command.
But here the doubtful officers dispute,
Till skill and judgment prejudice confute.
Rodmond, whose genius never soar'd beyond
The narrow rules of art his youth had conn'd,
Still to the hostile fury of the wind
Releas'd the sheet, and kept the tack confin'd ;
To long tried practice obstinately warm,
He doubts conviction, and relies on form ;
But the sage master this advice declines ;
With whom Arion in opinion joins.
The watchful seaman, whose sagacious eye
On sure experience may with truth rely,
Who from the reigning cause foretels th' effect.

[1] *The courses* are generally understood to be the mainsail, foresail, and mizzen, which are the largest and lowest sails on their several masts.

SHORTENING SAIL

This barbarous practice ever will reject.
For, fluttering loose in air, the rigid sail
Soon slits to ruins in the furious gale !
And he who strives the tempest to disarm,
Will never first embrail the lee yard-arm.
The master said ; obedient to command
To raise the tack the ready sailors stand.[1]
Gradual it loosens, while th' involving clue,
Swell'd by the wind, aloft unruffling flew.
The sheet and weather-brace they now stand by ;[2]
The lee clue-garnet and the bunt-lines ply.
Thus all prepar'd, " Let go the sheet," he cries ;
Impetuous round the ringing wheels it flies :
Shivering at first, till, by the blast impell'd,
High o'er the lee yard-arm the canvas swell'd ;
By spilling-lines [3] embrac'd with brails confin'd
It lies at length unshaken by the wind.
The fore-sail then secur'd, with equal care
Again to reef the main-sail they repair.
While some high mounted over-haul the tye,
Below the down haul-tackle [4] others ply.
Jears,[5] lifts, and brails, a seaman each attends ;

[1] It has been remarked, the tack is always fastened to windward : accordingly as soon as it is cast loose, and the clue-garnet hauled up, the weather clue of the sail mounts to the yard.

[2] It is necessary to pull in the weather brace whenever the sheet is cast off, to preserve the sail from shaking violently.

[3] *The spilling lines*, which are only used on particular occasions in tempestuous weather, are employed to draw together and confine the belly of the sail when it is inflated by the wind over the yard.

[4] The violence of the wind forces the yard so much outward from the mast on these occasions, that it cannot be easily lowered so as to reef the sail, without applying a tackle to haul it down on the mast. This is afterwards converted into rolling tackle.

[5] *Jears* are the same to the mainsail, foresail, and mizzen, as the halliards are to all the inferior sails.

Along the mast the willing yard descends.
When lower'd sufficient they securely brace,
And fix the rolling-tackle in its place.
The reef-lines [1] and their earings now prepar'd,
Mounting on pliant shrouds, [2] they man the yard.
Far on th' extremes two able hands appear,
Arion there, the hardy boatswain here;
That in the van to front the tempest hung;
This round the lee yard-arm, ill-omen'd! clung:
Each earing to his station first they bend;
The reef band [3] then along the yard extend:
The circling earings, round th' extremes entwin'd,
By outer and by inner turns [4] they bind.
From hand to hand, the reef-lines next receiv'd,
Thro' eye-let holes and robin-legs were reev'd.
The reef in double folds involv'd they lay;
Strain the firm cord, and either end belay.

Hadst thou, Arion, held the leeward post,
While on the yard by mountain billows tost;
Perhaps oblivion o'er our tragic tale
Had then for ever drawn her dusky veil;

---

[1] *Reef lines* are only used to reef the mainsail and foresail. They are passed in spiral turns through the eyelet holes of the reef, and over the head of the sails between the rope band legs, till they reach the extremities of the reef, to which they are firmly extended, so as to lace the reef close up to the yard.

[2] *Shrouds* are thick ropes stretching from the mastheads downwards to the outside of the ship, serving to support the masts. They are also used as a range of rope-ladders, by which the seamen ascend or descend to perform whatever is necessary about the sails and rigging.

[3] *The reef band* is a long piece of canvas sewed across the sail, to strengthen the canvas in the place where the eye-let holes of the reef are formed.

[4] The outer turns of the earing serve to extend the sail along the yard; and the inner turns are employed to confine its head rope close to its surface.

But ruling Heav'n prolong'd thy vital date,
Severer ills to suffer and relate.

For, while their orders those aloft attend,
To furl the mainsail, or on deck descend,
A sea [1] upsurging, with tremendous roll,
To instant ruin seems to doom the whole.
" O friends, secure your hold ! "   Arion cries ;
It comes all dreadful, stooping from the skies !
Uplifted on its horrid edge, she feels
The shock, and on her side half-bury'd reels :
The sail, half-bury'd in the whelming wave,
A fearful warning to the seamen gave :
While from its margin, terrible to tell,
Three sailors with their gallant boatswains fell.
Torn with restless fury from their hold,
In vain their struggling arms the yard enfold ;
In vain to grapple flying cords they try ;
The cords, alas ! a solid gripe deny !
Prone on the midnight surge, with panting breath
They cried for aid, and long contend with death.
High o'er their heads the rolling billows sweep,
And down they sink in everlasting sleep.

       From WILLIAM FALCONER'S " Shipwreck."

The Calm

OUR storm is past, and that storm's tyrannous rage
A stupid calm, but nothing it doth 'suage.
The fable is inverted, and far more
A block afflicts, now, than a stork before.
Storms chafe, and soon wear out themselves or us ;

[1] *A sea* is the general name given by sailors to a single wave ; when a wave bursts over the deck, the vessel is said to have shipped a sea.—(*The notes are Falconer's*.)

In calms, Heaven laughs to see us languish thus.
As steady as I could wish my thoughts were,
Smooth as thy mistress' glass, or what shines there,
The sea is now, and, as these isles which we
Seek, when we can move, our ships rooted be.
As water did in storms, now pitch runs out;
As lead, when a fired church becomes one spout.
And all our beauty and our trim decays,
Like courts removing, or like ended plays.
The fighting-place now seamen's rags supply;
And all the tackling is a frippery.
No use for lanthorns; and in one place lay
Feathers and dust, to-day and yesterday.
Earth's hollowness, which the world's lungs are,
Have no more wind than th' upper vault of air.
We can nor lost friends nor sought foes recover,
But meteor-like, save that we move not, hover.
Only the calenture together draws
Dear friends, which meet dead in great fishes maws;
And on the hatches, as on altars, lies
Each one, his own priest and own sacrifice.
Who live that miracle do multiply,
Where walkers in hot ovens do not die.
If in despite of these we swim, that bath
No more refreshing than a brimstone hath;
But from the sea into the ship we turn,
Like parboil'd wretches on the coals to burn.
Like Bajazet encaged, the shepherd's scoff,
Or like slack-sinew'd Samson, his hair off,
Languish our ships. Now as a myriad
Of ants durst th' emperor's loved snake invade,
The crawling gallies, sea-gulls, finny chips,
Might brave our pinnaces, now bed-rid ships.
Whether a rotten state, and hope of gain,
Or to disuse me from the queasy pain

Of being beloved and loving, or the thirst
Of honour or fair death, out-push'd me first,
I lose my end ; for here, as well as I,
A desperate may live, and coward die.
Stag, dog, and all which from or towards flies,
Is paid with life or prey, or doing dies.
Fate grudges us all, and doth subtly lay
A scourge, 'gainst which we all forget to pray.
He that at sea prays for more wind, as well
Under the poles may beg cold, heat in hell,
What are we then ? How little more, alas,
Is man now, than, before he was, he was ?
Nothing for us, we are for nothing fit ;
Chance, or ourselves, still disproportion it.
We have no power, no will, no sense ; I lie,
I should not then thus feel this misery.

JOHN DONNE

Neptune's Raging Fury, or the Gallant Seaman's Sufferings

You Gentlemen of England,
That live at home at ease,
Full little do you think upon
The Dangers of the Seas :
Give ear unto the Mariners,
And they will plainly show,
The cares and the fears
  When the stormy winds do blow.

All you that will be Seamen,
Must bear a valiant heart,
For when you come upon the Seas,
You must not think to start :

Nor once to be faint-hearted,
In hail, or rain, or snow,
Nor to shrink, nor to shrink,
    When, etc.

The bitter storms and tempests
Poor seamen must endure,
Both day and night with many a fight,
We seldom rest secure :
Our sleep it is disturbed
With visions strange to know,
And with Dreams, on the Streams,
    When, etc.

In clasps of roaring thunder,
Which darkness doth enforce,
We often find our Ship to stray
Beyond our wonted course :
Which causes great distractions
And sinks our hearts full low,
'Tis in vain to complain
    When, etc.

Sometimes on *Neptune's* bosom,
Our Ship is lost in waves,
And every man expecting
The Sea to be their graves :
Then, up aloft she mounteth,
And down again so low,
'Tis with the waves, O with waves,
    When, etc.

Then down again we fall to prayer
With all our might and thought,
When refuge all doth fail us,
'Tis that must bear us out ;

NEPTUNE'S RAGING FURY

To God we call for succour,
For He it is, we know,
That must aid us and save us,
    When, etc.

The Lawyer and the Usurer,
That sit in gowns of Fur,
In closets warm, can take no harm,
Abroad they need not stir ;
When winter fierce, with cold doth pierce,
And beats with hail and snow,
We are sure to endure,
    When, etc.

We bring home costly merchandise,
And Jewels of great price,
To serve our *English* Gallantry,
With many a rare device :
To please the *English* Gallantry
Our pains we freely show,
For we toyl, and we moyl
    When, etc.

We sometimes sail to the *Indies*
To fetch home Spices rare,
Sometimes again, to *France* and *Spain*
For wines beyond compare ;
While gallants are carousing
In Taverns in a row,
Then we sweep o'er the deep,
    When, etc.

When tempests are blown over,
And greatest fears are past,
Ay, weather fair, and temperate air,
We straight lye down to rest ;

But, when the billows tumble,
And waves do furious grow,
Then we rouse, up we rouse,
    When, etc.

If enemies oppose us,
When *England* is at wars,
With any foreign Nations,
We fear not wounds and scars ;
Our roaring guns shall teach 'em
Our Valour for to know,
Whilst they reel, in the Keel,
    When, etc.

We are no cowardly shrinkers,
But *Englishmen* true bred,
We'll play our parts with valiant hearts,
And never fly for dread ;
We'll ply our business nimbly,
Where'er we come or go,
With our Mates to the Straights,
    When, etc.

Then courage, all brave Marriners,
And never be dismaid,
Whilst we have bold adventurers,
We ne'er shall want a trade ;
Our Merchants will imploy us,
To fetch them wealth, I know,
Then be bold, work for gold,
    When, etc.

When we return in safety,
With wages for our pains,
The Tapster and the Vintner
Will help to share our gains ;

We'll call for liquor roundly,
And pay before we go,
Then we'll roar on the shore,
   When the stormy winds do blow.

MARTYN PARKER

The Distressed Sailor's Garland

WHEN first I drew the breath of life,
'Twas in the merry month of June,
The fourteenth day as I am told,
When flowers they were in their bloom ;
It was in seventeen hundred and five,
(That was the very date of the year),
My parents did for me provide
The best of learning I declare.

When I grew up they asked me,
" What trade must we prepare for thee ? "
My answer was to them again,
" I mean to range the roaring sea ; "
My whimsical brain did falsely show
The pleasures men enjoy at sea,
But oh, the sorrow, grief, and woe,
They suffer in extremity.

If there be pleasure on the sea,
'Tis when the wind and weather's fair,
With a bowl of punch, " Here's to thee, Jack
" Thanks, Tom, let's drink to drown all care."
Hardships full well we know there be,
From which we dare not flinch, you know,
Dark dismal nights, and lofty sea,
Contrary winds, hail, rain, and snow.

When we are on the roaring main,
The wind right aft and a pleasant gale,
We have our wish and heart's desire,
'Tis then we spread a crowd of sail;
Our mainsail hauled up in the brails,
Our foresails drive us clearly through,
Main topsails and top-gallant sails
We'll hoist and make a gallant show.

Fore and fore topsail stunsails set,
So cheerily then we drive along;
When this is done then down we sit,
To a bowl of punch and a merry song:
We drink a health unto our wives,
The pretty girls our sweethearts, too,
The captain and the officers,
Our god-like ship and jovial crew.

The wind won't stand, I am afraid,
It beareth foreward still, I see,
Get the fore tack to the cat-head
And ride it down with a passaree;
Down studding sails, alow and aloft,
And lay them by in the tops a while,
And hoist your staysails fore and aft,
And trim your sails all to the wind.

Oh, now she'll hardly lie her course,
'Tis better get our tack on board,
Our sheets close aft and bowlines hauled,
And all things handily prepared;
We must expect to head the sea,
The foaming billows break and roar,
Like hills and death they look, you see,
And now our pleasant sailing's o'er.

It was " Steady, steady " ; now 'tis " Luff,"
And " Don't fall off," and " Thus, no near."
The grampus blows, the rigging squeaks,
The sky looks dismal, I declare.
So in top-gallant sails, my boys,
Haul down your topmast staysails, too,
We'll meet a tartar, I'm afraid,
We'll settle our three topsails now.

Come, boys, we'll reef whilst we have time,
Let go your topsail halliards now,
Your main and fore top bowlines are gone,
Let in your weather braces now ;
And spill the sails, my hearts of gold,
And haul out your reef-tackles too,
For it will blow, I plainly see,
So clew them up whilst you are below.

Three single reefs in each topsail,
And then we'll furl them, 'tis agreed,
So bear a hand, my hearts of gold,
And make haste down with a nimble speed ;
And see the gears cleared fore and aft,
The downhaul tackles hooked also,
And all things readily prepared
Both up aloft and here below.

Brail up the mizzen snug, my boys,
So, cheerily lower away the yard,
The petrel shows herself, I vow,
Which tells us plainly it will blow hard :
You nimble fellow at the helm,
Pray keep her under your command,
A good rack full and away with her,
" No near," my boys, " no near you can."

A good hand stand to the mainsheet,
And see all clear to let her fly ;
It looks as thick as buttermilk,
And will be with us by and by ;
So hard-a-weather goes the helm,
Let fly your main sheet now with speed,
The furious squall will soon be over,
It breaks apace you may perceive.

So gather aft your sheet again,
Look round, my boys, let's lose no ground,
The sky looks dark and dismal wet,
We'll surely lower our foreyard down.
So forward now, my hearts of gold,
See clear the lifts in the first place ;
A sturdy fellow to the geers,
Strength is required at the brace.

The downhaul tackles must be manned,
Clew garnets, bowlines, leech-lines too,
Loose off the sheet, let's rise the jack ;
Come now, my boys, and raise her clew ;
Belay the lifts, secure the yards,
And up aloft and furl him snug,
Coil up your ropes and then lay aft ;
We'll all hands tipple the nut-brown jug.

'Tis now our helm is lashed a-lee,
And all securely fast aloft :
You at the helm, pray mind the glass,
How she comes up, likewise falls off ;
The gale increases stronger still,
It blows a reef in our mainsail,
By one consent let us reef it now,
Let sailors' courage never fail.

So to your stations, now, my boys,
And stand by, sailors, every one,
So, cheerily lower away the yard,
Check in your brace, the bowline's gone;
When this is done, then down we come,
To see what more we have to do.
We'll lose our mizzen now, my boys,
We'll balance him and set him too.

Now it is balanced in a trice,
Sway up the yard, haul aft the sheet,
No sooner set but away she flies,
And leaves the bolt-rope in his stead.
Our ship lies-to most dangerously,
All in the trough of the roaring sea,
Which takes us on our broadside,
And over us makes a passage free.

The sea does run prodigiously,
For God's sake, boys, what must we do?
You see the danger we are in,
'Tis better sound than thus lie-to.
By one consent let it be agreed,
In readiness prepare all things,
And bunt the foresail securely fast,
And we will scud under our goose-wings.

THE SECOND PART

So hard a weather goes the helm;
Ho! Will she wear, or will she not?
Away she flies before the wind,—
She veers apace, thanks to Fortune kind;
Sway up the yard, haul aft the sheet,

Belay the braces, make all fast;
Two able sailors to the helm,
It blows a hurricane at last.

Steady, steady is the cry,
Pray mind your helm, and steady, starboard,
Away she flies, meet her again,
And stop her there, now, hard a-larboard:
Pray, mind the motion of her head
For your sake, boys, don't broach her to,
For all our lives lie at the stake,
Our goodly ship and jovial crew.

No sooner spoke, but to she flies,
Alas, we drove but all in vain.
She ships it green, and down she lies,
As if she'd never rise again:
And now, in all our great distress,
We cut our mizen mast away,
Thinking to right her once again.
'Tis all in vain, so down she lay.

The gale increases stronger still,
More grief to us it does afford;
To have our lives and goodly ship,
We cut our mainmast by the board:
The seas we shipped were wondrous high,
They staved our boat in pieces small,
Of all our lofty rearing masts,
Our foremast stood, and that was all.

THE THIRD PART

The wind is down, the weather's fair,
Oh, what a blessed change is this,

Strike open ports, let in the air,
Oh, sound and see what leak there is.
Oh, carpenter, come rig the pump.
'Tis nought, we'll quickly pump her free:
We'll dry our clothes by the galley-fire
After their soaking in the sea.

We are near to port, the sailors cry,
I see the spire beyond the rocks.
At anchor very soon we'll lie,
Delivered from the ocean's shocks.
With good rum punch we'll play our part,
With pretty girls we'll love to be.
We are never rightly satisfied
But when in their sweet company.

And to conclude, and make an end,
If I had known as much before,
I would have cried, " Sweep ! Chimney Sweep ! "
And " Black your Shoes," from door to door—
Before I had gone upon the sea,
Where foaming billows loud do roar ;
So all young men be warned by me,
And always live upon the shore.

A Gale of Wind

——Loud Boreas opened wide his mouth,
And puffed the Frigate toward the south,
Puff after puff grew more severe,
And still it thicken'd in the clear,
But while it for their course was fair,
One straw our Hero did not care ;
Tho' he was of another mind
When once they came to haul their wind.

'Twas his dog-watch from six to eight,
Relieved from deck, he turned in straight,
But such a screeching still did keep
The Beams and Guns, he could not sleep,
He yawned and turned times without number,
In feverish, restless, painful slumber ;
The 'tween-decks, too, was stifling hot,
And John a midship berth had got ;
Just o'er his head there was a leak
Which often dripped upon his cheek ;
Then water down the hatchways gushing,
And chests adrift athwart-ships rushing,
And clanking Pumps, and tones like thunder,
Exclaiming, " Bouse ! " or, " Stand from under ! "
Made up a concert so composing,
'Twas odd that John was shy of dozing ;
In short, to shorten much our tale,
We'll say at once, it blew a gale.—

At four o'clock, with great coat dripping,
The Quarter-Master came down tripping,
And by the head-clues holding on
To stay himself, awakened John.—
Quoth John—" Pray tell me, how's the weather ? "
—" It blows, rains, thunders, all together ;
You'd best heave out, Sir,—I expect
The hands will soon be called on deck ;
The Captain's there now—and the Master ;
The squalls come faster on, and faster ! "
Quoth John—" Tho' all night long this rout
Has kept me waking—here's turn out ! "—

When down on deck his feet he set,
Slap o'er his ankles came the wet ;
For all the steerage was on float ;

A GALE OF WIND

" Confound it all, where's my great coat ? "
John soon discover'd, to his cost,
That his warm Flushing Coat was lost ;
So, at the hazard of his neck,
He crawled up to the Quarter-deck,
There, by the life-lines held on fast,
And stared astonished and aghast ;
The foaming seas, the roaring wind,
The hail and lightning, all combined :
The ship that sometimes seemed to rise
As if she'd pierce the sable skies,
Now down the black abyss to glide,
Now hang suspended on its side,
Amazed him !—Every lurch she gave
The gangways rolled beneath the wave,

And large blue seas each other chased,
Cascading over down the waist.—
At every pitch he held his breath
As if he saw the face of death ;—
Amidst the roar there came a crash,—
" She's pitched away a Top-mast, smash ! '
All hands to clear away the wreck,
Were in an instant turned on deck ;
From hammock starting out alert,
Up flew each seaman in his shirt !
John said it really did him good
To see their reckless hardihood ;
—And up the straining shrouds they swarm,
Growling and swearing at the storm——
The wreck secured, or cut away,
She snug beneath a trysail lay.——

——At eight, in spite of John's alarm,
Breakfast he thought would do no harm,

But sorry was he, and surprised,
To find the Tea-kettle capsized.
The water pouring all about,
Had put the swinging stove quite out :
" 'Tis useless fretting," John did cry—
" We've got for Dinner a Sea-pie."——
At twelve o'clock, he hoped at last
To make a delicate repast.

The Peasebags, Ridgelines on the Table,
To save the Dishes scarce were able,
So Johnny, like his messmates, sate
With one hand holding fast his plate,
Himself beneath the Scuttle seating,
That he might see what he was eating ;
And faith he thought himself quite subtle,
To get a berth so near the scuttle.——

Down came the saucepan—John, we ween,
As any Tiger-cat was keen ;
But, oh ! his term of joy was soon up,
For scarcely had he ta'en his spoon up,
When, lo ! a sea with vengeful stroke
The scuttle glass to shivers broke !
One second filled the cabin brimming,
And set, like frogs, the Reefers swimming,
They soon escaped, but John was bother'd
So to get out, he was half smother'd.—
The Flushing coat he'd missed that morn,
Now reappeared on torrent borne,
From some dark nook it floated out,
All sopped, just like a large dish-clout,
And in the lieu of some old rug
Or swab, 'twas used for scuttle plug ;
In which capacity 'twas fated
To serve until it moderated.—

Drenched, hungry, tired John wished for close
Of day, that he might get repose ;
But when he did his hammock seek,
'Twas wringing wet through, from the leak.
——Nor ceased his fag, when daylight ceased,
The fury of the gale increased,
Until at length, as aft she *sent*,
The collar of the Forestay went ;
To save the masts while yet they stood,
Dale chose immediately to scud :
By much dexterity and care
They safely brought the ship to wear ;
Away ! she shot before the wind,
Fast followed by the surge behind.—

——All cold on deck—all wet below—
Our hero knew not where to go !
And in no enviable plight
You may believe he passed the night.—
   CAPT. JACK MITFORD, R.N.
(" Adventures of Johnny Newcome in the Navy.")

The *Benjamin's* Lamentations

FOR THEIR SAD LOSS AT SEA BY STORMS AND
TEMPESTS

CAPTAIN CHILVER'S gone to Sea,
 I Boys, O Boys,
With all his Company, I.
Captain Chilver's gone to Sea,
With all his Company,
 In the brave *Benjamin*, O.

Thirty Guns the Ship did bear,
 I Boys, O Boys,

They were bound for Venice fair, I.
Thirty guns his Ship did bear,
And a hundred men so dear,
    In the brave *Benjamin*, O.

But by ill Storms at Sea.
    I Boys, O Boys,
Which bred our Misery, I.
But by ill Storms at Sea,
We were drove out o' th' way,
    In the brave *Benjamin*, O.

We had more Wind than we could bear,
    I Boys, O Boys,
Our Ship it would not steer, I.
We had more Wind than we could bear,
Our Masts and Sails did tear
    In the poor *Benjamin*, O.

The first harm that we had,
    I Boys, O Boys,
It makes my heart so sad, I.
The first harm we had,
We lost our Fore-mast head,
    O, the poor *Benjamin*, O.

The Seas aloud did roar,
    I Boys, O Boys,
We being far from shore, I.
The Sea no favour shows
Unto Friends or Foes,
    O, the poor *Benjamin*, O.

The next harm that we spy'd,
    I Boys, O Boys,
Then we to Heaven cry'd, I.

Down fell our Main-mast head,
Which struck our senses dead,
   In the poor *Benjamin*, O.

Thus we with Seas were crost,
   I Boys, O Boys,
And on the Ocean tost, I.
Thus we with Seas were tost,
Many a brave man was lost,
   In the poor *Benjamin*, O.

The next harm that we had,
   I Boys, O Boys,
We had cause to be sad, I.
The next harm that we had,
We lost four men from the yard,
   In the poor *Benjamin*, O.

Disabled as I name,
   I Boys, O Boys,
We were drove on the Main, I.
So the next harm we had,
We lost our Rudder's head
   In the poor *Benjamin*, O.

Then we all fell to Prayer,
   I Boys, O Boys,
The Lord our lives would spare, I.
Then we fell to Prayer,
And He at last did hear,
   Us in the *Benjamin*, O.

Although we sail'd in fear,
   I Boys, O Boys,
The Lord our Ship did steer, I.
Our Prayers so fervent were,
That we had passage clear,
   Into brave Plymouth Sound, O.

We came to Plymouth Sound,
    I Boys, O Boys,
Our hearts did then resound, I.
When we came to Plymouth Sound
Our grief with joy was crown'd,
    In the poor *Benjamin*, O.

When we came all on shore,
    I Boys, O, Boys,
Every Man at his door, I.
When we came all on shore,
Our grief we did deplore,
    In the poor *Benjamin*, O.

You gallant Young-men all,
    I Boys, O Boys,
'Tis unto you I call, I.
Likewise brave Seamen all,
Lament the loss and fall,
    Of the poor *Benjamin*, O.

The Leadsman's Song

For England, when with favouring gale,
Our gallant ship up Channel steered,
And scudding, under easy sail,
The high blue western lands appeared.
To heave the lead the seaman sprang,
And to the pilot cheerly sang
    " By the deep—Nine."

And bearing up to gain the port,
Some well-known object kept in view,
An abbey tower, a ruined fort,
A beacon to the vessel true.

While oft the lead the seaman flung,
And to the pilot cheerly sung,
   " By the mark—Seven."

And as the much-loved shore we near,
With transport we behold the roof
Where dwelt a friend or partner dear,
Of faith and love and matchless proof.
The lead once more the seaman flung,
And to the watchful pilot sung,
   " Quarter less—Five."

Now to her berth the ship draws nigh,
With slackened sail she feels the tide,
Stand clear the cable is the cry,
The anchor's gone, we safely ride.
The watch is set, and through the night,
We hear the seaman with delight
   Proclaim—" All's well."

Christmas at Sea

THE sheets were frozen hard, and they cut the naked hand;
The decks were like a slide, where a seaman scarce could stand;
The wind was a nor'-wester, blowing squally off the sea;
And cliffs and spouting breakers were the only things a-lee.

They heard the surf a-roaring before the break of day;
But 'twas only with the peep of light we saw how ill we lay.

We tumbled every hand on deck instanter, with
    a shout,
And we gave her the maintops'l, and stood by to
    go about.

All day we tacked and tacked between the South
    Head and the North;
All day we hauled the frozen sheets, and got no
    further forth;
All day as cold as charity, in bitter pain and dread,
For very life and nature we tacked from head to head.

We gave the South a wider berth, for there the
    tide race roared;
But every tack we made brought the North Head
    close aboard:
So's we saw the cliffs and houses, and the breakers
    running high,
And the coastguard in his garden, with his glass
    against his eye.

The frost was on the village roofs as white as
    ocean foam;
The good red fires were burning bright in every
    'long shore home;
The windows sparkled clear, and the chimneys
    volleyed out;
And I vow we sniffed the victuals as the vessel
    went about.

The bells upon the church were rung with a mighty
    jovial cheer;
For it's just that I should tell you how (of all days
    in the year)
This day of our adversity was blessèd Christmas morn
And the house above the coastguard's was the
    house where I was born.

CHRISTMAS AT SEA

O well I saw the pleasant room, the pleasant faces there,
My mother's silver spectacles, my father's silver hair;
And well I saw the firelight, like a flight of homely elves,
Go dancing round the china plates that stand upon the shelves.

And well I knew the talk they had, the talk that was of me,
Of the shadow on the household and the son that went to sea ;
And O the wicked fool I seemed, in every kind of way,
To be here and hauling frozen ropes on blessed Christmas Day.

They lit the high sea-light, and the dark began to fall.
" All hands to loose topgallant sails," I heard the captain call.
" By the Lord, she'll never stand it," our first mate, Jackson, cried,
. . . " It's the one way or the other, Mr. Jackson," he replied.

She staggered to her bearings, but the sails were new and good,
And the ship smelt up to windward, just as though she understood.
As the winter's day was ending, in the entry of the night,
We cleared the weary headland, and passed below the light.

And they heaved a mighty breath, every soul on
    board but me,
As they saw her nose again pointing handsome
    out to sea;
But all that I could think of, in the darkness and
    the cold,
Was just that I was leaving home and my folks
    were growing old.

ROBERT LOUIS STEVENSON
("Ballads"[1])

The Whale

IT was in the year of ninety-four, in March the
    twentieth day,
Our gallant tars their anchors weigh'd, and for
    sea they bore away,
        Brave boys,
    And for sea they bore away.
Speedicut was our captain's name, our ship was
    the *Lyon* bold,
And we have gone to sea, brave boys, to face the
    storm and cold,
    To face the storm and the cold.

When that we came to the cold country where
    the frost and the snow did lie,
Where the frost, and the snow, and the whale-fish
    so blue, and the daylight's never gone,
        Brave boys,
    And the daylight's never gone.

---

[1] Published by Messrs. Chatto & Windus.

THE WHALE

Our boatswain went to topmast high, with his
  spy-glass in his hand,
"A whale, a whale, a whale," he did cry, "and
  she blows at every span,
    Brave boys,
      She blows at every span."

Our captain stood on the quarter-deck, and a clever
  little man was he,
"Overhaul, overhaul, let the wind-tackle fall,
  and to launch your boats so free,
    Brave boys,
      And to launch your boats so free!"

There's harpooneers, and line coilers, and line [1]
  colecks also,
There's boat-steerers and sailors brave,
To the whale, to where she blows, to the whale,
  to where she blows,
    Brave boys,
      To the whale, to where she blows.

We struck the whale, and away she went, casts
  a flourish with her tail,
But, oh, and alas, we've lost one man, and we
  did not kill that whale,
    Brave boys,
      And we did not kill that whale.

When that the news to our captain it did come,
  a sorrowful man was he,
For the losing of his 'prentice boy, and down his
  colours drew he,
    Brave boys,
      And down his colours drew he.

[1] So in my original.

Now, my lads, don't be amazed for the losing of
    one man;
For fortune it will take its place, let a man do all
    he can,
        Brave boys,
    Let a man do all he can.

Spanish Ladies

FAREWELL and adieu to you, fine Spanish ladies,
Farewell and adieu to you, ladies of Spain;
        For we have received orders
        For to sail to old England,
And perhaps we shall never more see you again.

We'll rant and we'll roar, like true British sailors,
We'll rant and we'll roar across the salt seas;
        Until we strike soundings
        In the Channel of old England,
From Ushant to Scilly 'tis thirty-five leagues.

We hove our ship to, with the wind at sou'west,
    boys,
We hove our ship to, for to strike soundings clear;
        Then we filled the main topsail
        And bore right away, boys,
And straight up the Channel our course we did
    steer.

And the first land we made, it is called the
    Deadman,
Next Ram Head, off Plymouth, Start, Portland,
    and the Wight;
        We sail-ed by Beachy,
        By Fairly and Dungeness,
And then bore away for the South Foreland Light.

Now the signal was made for the grand fleet to anchor,
All in the Downs that night for to meet;
    Then stand by your stoppers,
    See clear your shank painters,
Haul all your clew garnets, stick out tacks and sheets.

Now let every man take off his full bumper,
Let every man take off his full bowl;
    For we will be jolly.
    And drown melancholy,
With a health to each jovial and true-hearted soul.

The Greenwich Pensioner

'TWAS in the good ship *Rover*,
  I sailed the world all round,
And for three years and over
  I ne'er touched British ground,
At length in England landed,
  I left the roaring main,
Found all relations stranded,
  And went to sea again,
  And went to sea again.

That time bound straight for Portugal,
  Right fore and aft we bore,
But when we made Cape Ortegal,
  A gale blew off the shore;
She lay, so did it shock her,
  A log upon the main,
Till, saved from Davy's locker
  We put to sea again,
  We put to sea again

Next sailing in a frigate
  I got my timber toe.
I never more shall jig it
  As once I used to do ;
My leg was shot off fairly,
  All by a ship of Spain ;
But I could swab the galley,
  I went to sea again,
  I went to sea again

And still I am enabled
  To bring up in the rear,
Although I'm quite disabled
  And lie in Greenwich tier.
There's schooners in the river
  A riding to the chain,
But I shall never, ever
  Put out to sea again,
  Put out to sea again.

A Comfortable Song on the Poor Sailors

(1794)

How little do the landmen know,
  What we poor sailors feel,
When waves do mount and winds do blow
  But we have hearts of steel :
No danger can affright us,
  No enemy shall flout,
We'll make the Monsieurs right us,
  So toss the can about.

Stick close to orders, messmates,
  We'll plunder, burn, and sink,

Then, France, have at your first-rates,
  For Britons never shrink ;
We'll rummage all we fancy,
  We'll bring them in by scores,
And Moll and Kate and Nancy,
  Shall roll in louis d'ors.

While here at Deal we're lying,
  With our noble Commodore,
We'll spend our wages free, boys,
  And then to sea for more :
In peace we'll drink and sing, boys,
  In war we'll never fly,
Here's a health to George the King, boys,
  And the Royal Family.

Sailor's Delight

How happy are we now the wind is abaft,
And the Boatswain he pipes, "Haul both our sheets aft."
"Steady," says the Master, "it blows a fresh gale,
  We'll soon reach our port, boys,
  If the wind doth not fail."
    Then drink about, Tom,
    Although the ship roll,
  We'll save our rich liquor
    By slinging our bowl.

Port Admiral

'Twas at the landing-place that's just below Mount Wyse,
Poll lean'd against the sentry's box, a tear in both her eyes ;

Her apron twisted round her arms, all for to keep
    them warm,
Being a windy Christmas Day, and also a snow-
    storm.
    And Bet and Sue
    Both stood there too,
        A-shivering by her side ;
    They both were dumb,
    And both look'd glum,
        As they watch'd the ebbing tide.
Poll put her arms a-kimbo,
    At the admiral's house look'd she,
To thoughts before in limbo
    She now a vent gave free.
You have sent the ship in a gale to work,
    On a lee shore to be jamm'd,
I'll give you a piece of my mind, old Turk,
    Port Admiral. you be d——d.

Chorus

    We'll give you a piece of our mind, old Turk,
        Port Admiral, you be d——d.

Who ever heard in the sarvice of a frigate made to
    sail
On Christmas Day, it blowing hard, with sleet,
    and snow, and hail ?
I wish I had the fishing of your back that is so bent,
I'd use the galley poker hot unto your heart's
    content.
    Here Bet and Sue
    Are with me too,
        A-shivering by my side ;
    They both are dumb,
    And both look glum,
        And watch the ebbing tide

PORT ADMIRAL

Poll put her arms a-kimbo,
   At the admiral's house look'd she,
To thoughts that were in limbo
   She now a vent gave free.
You've got a roaring fire, I'll bet,
   In it your toes are jamm'd :
Let's give him a piece of our mind, my Bet,
   Port Admiral, you be d——d.

Chorus.

Let's give him a piece of our mind, my Bet,
   Port Admiral, you be d——d.

I had the flour and plums all pick'd, and suet all chopp'd fine,
To mix into a pudding rich for all the mess to dine ;
I pawn'd my ear-rings for the beef, it weigh'd at least a stone,
Now my fancy man is sent to sea, and I am left alone.
   Here's Bet and Sue
   Who stand here too.
     A-shivering by my side ;
   They both are dumb
   They both look glum,
     And watch the ebbing tide.
Poll put her arms a-kimbo,
   At the admiral's house look'd she,
To thoughts that were in limbo
   She now a vent gave free.
You've got a turkey, I'll be bound,
   With which you will be cramm'd ;
I'll give you a bit of my mind, old hound,
   Port Admiral, you be d——d.

Chorus.

I'll give you a bit of my mind, old hound,
    Port Admiral, you be d——d.

I'm sure that in this weather they cannot cook their meat,
To eat it raw on Christmas Day will be a pleasant treat ;
But let us all go home, girls ; it's no use waiting here,
We'll hope that Christmas Day to come they will have better cheer.
    So Bet and Sue,
    Don't stand here too,
      A-shivering by my side :
    Don't keep so dumb,
    Don't look so glum,
      Nor watch the ebbing tide.
Poll put her arms a-kimbo,
    At the admiral's house look'd she,
To thoughts that were in limbo
    She now a vent gave free.
So while they cut their raw salt junks,
    With dainties you'll be cramm'd,
Here's once for all my mind, old hunks,
    Port Admiral, you be d——d.

Chorus.

So once for all our mind, old hunks,
    Port Admiral, you be d——d.

FREDERICK MARRYAT

The Captain Stood on the Carronade

THE Captain stood on the carronade—"First lieutenant," says he,

"Send all my merry men aft here, for they must list to me :
I haven't the gift of the gab, my sons—because I'm bred to the sea ;
That ship there is a Frenchman, who means to fight with we.
   Odds blood, hammer and tongs, long as I've been to sea,
   I've fought 'gainst every odds—but I've gain'd the victory.

"That ship there is a Frenchman, and if we don't take *she*,
'Tis a thousand bullets to one, that she will capture *we* ;
I haven't the gift of the gab, my boys ; so each man to his gun ;
If she's not mine in half an hour, I'll flog each mother's son.
   Odds bobs, hammer and tongs, long as I've been to sea,
   I've fought 'gainst every odds—and I've gain'd the victory."

We fought for twenty minutes, when the Frenchmen had enough ;
"I little thought," said he, "that your men were of such stuff."
The captain took the Frenchman's sword, a low bow made to he ;
"I haven't the gift of the gab, monsieur, but polite I wish to be.
   Odds bobs, hammer and tongs, long as I've been to sea,
   I've fought 'gainst every odds—and I've gain'd the victory."

Our captain sent for all of us ; " My merry men,"
    said he,
" I haven't the gift of the gab, my lads, but yet I
    thankful be ;
You've done your duty handsomely, each man
    stood to his gun ;
If you hadn't, you villains, as sure as day, I'd have
    flogg'd each mother's son.
    Odds bobs, hammer and tongs, as long as I'm
        at sea,
    I'll fight 'gainst every odds—and I'll gain the
        victory."

FREDERICK MARRYAT

The Press-Gang

Here's the tender coming,
  Pressing all the men ;
    O, dear honey,
  What shall we do then ?
Here's the tender coming,
  Off at Shields Bar.
Here's the tender coming,
  Full of men of war.

Here's the tender coming,
  Stealing of my dear ;
    O dear honey,
They'll ship you out of here,
  They'll ship you foreign,
For that is what it means.
Here's the tender coming,
  Full of red marines.

Captain Bover

WHERE have you been, my canny honey?
Where have you been, my winsome man?
    I've been to the norrard,
    Cruizing back and forrard,
    I've been to the norrard,
      Cruizing sore and lang.
    I've been to the norrard,
    Cruizing back and forrard,
    But I dare not come ashore,
    For Bover and his gang.

The *Flash* Frigate

I SING of a frigate, a frigate of fame,
And in the West Indies she bore a great name
For cruel hard treatment of every degree.
Like slaves in the gallies we ploughed the salt sea.

At four in the morning our day's work's begun,
" Come lash up your hammocks, boys, ev-er-y one.'
Seven turns with the lashing so equal must show,
And all of one size through a hoop they must go.

The next thing we do is to holystone decks,
Mizzen-topmen from the fore-hatch their buckets must fetch;
And its " Fore and main-topmen," so loudly they bawl,
" Come broom after the sand with your squilgees and all."

The decks being scrubbed, and the rigging coiled down,
It is now, " Clean your bright work," which is found all around,

Your gun-caps and aprons so neatly must shine,
And in white frocks and trousers you must all toe a line.

The next thing we hear is " All hands to make sail,"
" Way aloft," and " lay out," and " let fall " is the hail,
O, your royals, and your skysails, and your moonsails so high,
At the sound of the call they must all be let fly.

But now, my brave boys, comes the best of the fun :
" All hands about ship and reef topsails," in one.
O, it's "lay aloft topmen," as the hellum goes down,
And it's " clew down your topsails," as the mainyard swings round.

" Trice up, and lay out, and take two reefs in one,"
And all in a moment this work must be done.
Then man your head-braces, topsail-halliards, and all,
And it's " hoist away topsails," as you " let go and haul."

Our senior lieutenant, you all know him well,
He comes upon deck, and he cuts a great swell.
O, it's " bear a hand here, boys," and " mind what you're at,"
And at the lee gangway he serves out the cat.

There is no games aboard her, and so you will find,
If you spit on her decks, why, your death-warrant's signed.
So all you bold seamen who sail the salt sea,
Beware of this frigate wherever you be.

The Man-o'-War

He that has sail'd upon the dark blue sea
Has view'd at times, I ween, a full fair sight;
When the fresh breeze is fair as breeze may be,
The white sail set, the gallant frigate tight;
Masts, spires, and strand retiring to the right,
The glorious main expanding o'er the bow,
The convoy spread like wild swans in their flight,
The dullest sailer wearing bravely now,
So gaily curl the waves before each dashing prow.

And oh, the little warlike world within!
The well-reeved guns, the netted canopy,
The hoarse command, the busy humming din,
When, at a word, the tops are manned on high:
Hark to the Boatswain's call, the cheering cry!
While through the seaman's hand the tackle glides;
Or schoolboy Midshipman that, standing by,
Strains his shrill pipe as good or ill betides,
And well the docile crew that skilful urchin guides.

White is the glassy deck, without a stain,
Where on the watch the staid Lieutenant walks:
Look on that part which sacred doth remain
For the lone chieftain, who majestic stalks,
Silent and fear'd by all—not oft he talks
With aught beneath him, if he would preserve
That strict restraint, which broken, ever balks
Conquest and fame: but Britons rarely swerve
From law, however stern, which tends their strength to nerve.

LORD BYRON
("Childe Harold's Pilgrimage.")

Jack Robinson

(To the tune of "College Hornpipe")

The perils and dangers of the voyage past,
And the ship to Portsmouth arrived at last;
The sails all furled, and the anchor cast,
The happiest of the crew was Jack Robinson.
For his Poll he had trinkets and gold galore,
Besides of prize-money quite a store;
And along with the crew he went ashore,
As coxwain to the boat, Jack Robinson.

He met with a man, and said, " I say,
Mayhap you may know one, Polly Gray?
She lives somewhere hereabouts : "—the man said, " Nay,
I do not, indeed," to Jack Robinson.
Says Jack to him, " I've left my ship,
And to my messmates given the slip,
Mayhap you'll partake of a good can of flip,
For you're a civil fellow," says Jack Robinson.

In a public-house then they both sat down,
And talked of Admirals of high renown,
And drank as much grog as came to half-a-crown,
This here strange man and Jack Robinson.
Then Jack called out the reckoning to pay,
The landlady came in, in fine array,
" My eyes and limbs, why, here's Polly Gray;
Who'd thought of meeting here?" says Jack Robinson.

The landlady staggered back against the wall,
And at first she said she knew him not at all;

"Shiver me," says Jack, "why, here's a pretty squall,
"*Damme, don't you know poor Jack Robinson?*
Don't you know this handkerchief you gave to me,
'Twas three years ago, before I went to sea;
Every day I look'd at it, and thought of thee,
Upon my soul, I have," says Jack Robinson.

Says the lady, says she, "I've changed my state."
"Why, you don't mean," says Jack, "that you've got a mate,
You know you promised me."—Says she, "I couldn't wait,
For no tidings could I gain of you, Jack Robinson.
And somebody one day came to me, and said,
That somebody else had somewhere read,
In some newspaper as how you was dead."
"*I've not been dead at all,*" says Jack Robinson.

Then he turned his quid and finished his glass,
And hitched up his trousers: "Alas, alas!
That ever I should live to be made such an ass,
To be bilked by a woman," says Jack Robinson.
"But to fret and stew about it much is all in vain,
I'll get a ship and go to Holland, France, and Spain,
No matter where, to Portsmouth, I'll never come again."
And he was off before they could say Jack Robinson.

THOMAS HUDSON

The Fight

THE look-out Seaman loudly bawled,
And Johnny to himself recalled!

To th' Officer the seaman said,
" I see a sail, Sir, right ahead !—
She's running large on t'other tack, Sir !—
She'll be on board us in a crack, Sir !—
She is, too," mutter'd low the Sailor,
" A *man-of-war*—or I'm a Tailor ! "

" Zounds ! " cried the other in a rout,
" Turn up the watch to go about !—
Young Gentlemen ! quick ! quick, Sir ! fly !
And tell the Captain what we spy."—
John soon returned, and took his place
As usual by the cross-jack brace—
Round came the ship, and when about,
The Captain bade them to hang out
Two Lanthorns of an equal height ;
The private signal for the night—
Which, plain 'twas, was not comprehended
By those for whom it was intended.—
The Drummer then to Quarters beat—
The Quarter-Masters fast and neat
Stowed all the Hammocks in the netting—
——" She's bearing up, and Studd'ng Sails setting ! "
The Look-outs cried—then growl'd—" And why !
Why, 'cause she is an Enemy !
What makes her else run down to leeward ? "
——The topsail sheets and yards secured ;
The fighting Lanthorns one by one
Disposed by every main-deck gun ;
The swabs, and sand in buckets ready,
The Decks to damp—and Footing steady ;
Each hatch close down—and woollen skreens
Nailed up to save the Magazines ;
The Surgeons in the Cockpit set

THE FIGHT

With Knife, and Saw, and Tourniquet;
And other duties numberless
Which we can't easily express,
Being all arranged in order due,
And duly all reported too;
Lieutenant Smart with satisfaction
Pronounced the Frigate fit for action;
Which having to the Captain stated,
He with his trumpet anxious waited.

Many a night-glass with keen intent
Upon the stranger had been bent;
She was a Rogue they did not doubt;
But then her force was not made out;
She might, for aught they could divine,
Be single deck'd, or of the Line.—
But they rejoiced when Captain Dale
Told Smart to wear and make all sail—
They knew their Captain was no starter,
Yet far too keen to catch a Tartar;
And therefore guessed he would not close
The Chase before the dawn arose.
But Mr. Smart, in far less time
Than we've been hammering out this rhyme,
Wore ship, made sail too in a trice,
Without once asking their advice.—

With little trouble, through the night
They kept the Stranger well in sight,
And towards morn found her, by the glass,
A Frigate of the largest class;
Yet very doubtful was the sequel,
Their rate of sailing seemed so equal;
Whene'er the wind appeared to die,
Away, the other seemed to fly;

But when it freshened up again,
They hoped their object to attain.

Just as the morning watch was done
A firm top-gallant breeze came on,
And 'twas no more a question called
If they the other overhauled;
Nay, 'twas so plain, that now the Chase,
To do things with a decent grace,
Since running could no more avail,
Haul'd close up, under easy sail.—

A Flag he hoisted at the Fore,
And at his Peak the Tricolor:
The *Capricorn's*, when up it went,
With three hurrahs their welcome sent:
Thought they—" *Jean Crappeau's* mighty stout,
He surely means to fight it out."—
Our Frigate's kites were just ta'en in,
When he thought proper to begin.—

His Broadside made a precious row,
As she bore down, against her bow;
But when she quietly had got
Her distance, scarce a pistol shot
Upon his weather beam, why then,
Our Frigate talked to him again.—

——Upon the Quarter-Deck stands John,
In quality of Aid-du-Camp—
We will not tell you how he feels,
Whether he stands on head or heels,
Just now 'twould puzzle him to tell—
Yet not through fear—we know full well,

THE FIGHT

It is not terror, but amaze
That makes him shake his ears and gaze—
He shakes himself to find out whether
His carcase yet sticks all together;
His gaze, too, is a gaze of wonder,
At all the havoc, smoke, and thunder;
Thought he—" Tho' I have heard on shore
Of Bullets' whiz, and Cannons' roar,
So piercing, spiteful, shrill a hiss
I ne'er supposed they had as this!"
Meanwhile they whistle closely past
His nose and ears, amazing fast—
Upon the deck before his eyes
A soldier knocked to pieces lies,
And as he turns round in the smother,
Against him wounded reels another;
He ne'er saw human blood before,
And it affected him the more—
But soon with orders to the Waist,
The Captain coolly bade him haste,
And there the Officers desire
A little to depress their Fire—
Not e'en in fancy, John had seen
Such sight as he saw then, we ween;
The Seamen toiling 'midst the clatter;
The carnage flowing like bilge water;
The Heat, the Noise, the Smoak, the Smell
Of Sulphur, much resembled Hell;
The Wounded lying shatter'd, jammed,
Writhing and howling like the Damned:
The *tout ensemble* of the fuss,
Reminded him of Tartarus.
The third Lieutenant next he found
Quite deafened by th' incessant sound,
So to John's mouth he clapped his ear

What he had got to say, to hear;
And as he stooped a wicked shot
Sent the Lieutenant's skull to pot,
Whose brains dislodged thus from their case,
Flew smoking hot in Johnny's face;
And those who witnessed the disaster,
Remark'd quite drily—" Tight work, Master ! "—
He looked about in rueful puzzle,
And mopped the plaister from his muzzle,
Till Shaughnessy observed him stare,
And guessed that he might orders bear—
Disburden'd of his missive load,
He turned back by a clearer road;
For on the Forecastle he skipped,
And aft along the gangway tripped—
When he regained the Quarter-Deck,
More dire had grown the strife and wreck;
For splinters flew and spars were falling
And every other man was sprawling.—

The Enemy, it since appears,
Had near an hundred Musqueteers
Beside his usual crew, and these
Poured in their small shot thick as peas.—
John missed his Captain—by ill luck
A splinter 'gainst his knee had struck—
He rested on the weather side
Abreast the wheel, on a Gun-slide,
Serenely viewed the hurly-burly,
And gave his orders not in surly,
But calm, and even cheerful tone,
As if he felt no broken bone—
John found him, and reported what
Had been the third Lieutenant's lot—
The Captain bade him near remain,

Until he wanted him again;
But scarcely was the sentence said,
Ere John was knocked heels over head!
In half a second up he jumped,
And first one leg, then t' other stumped
Upon the deck—then stretched each arm—
To find out where he'd got the harm—
'Twas either splinters, or the wind
Of bullet passing him behind
Which knocked him down; but in his fall
His side received a Musquet ball,
A flesh wound only—but the part
Began to bleed apace, and smart,
And when the blood began to trickle,
Thought John—" I'm in a pretty pickle!
It may be mortal—and if so,
I'll have a slap before I go!"

With that he snatch'd in anger keen
A musquet from a dead Marine.—
—" Before now I've knocked down a Partridge!
And if I can but find a cartridge,
I'll pepper yonder tatterdemalions—
Here's one—Have at ye! ye rascalions!"
With pouch and firelock in his hand,
He by the gangway took his stand,
And might and main began to bellows
In a blue fury at the Fellows;
While Shaughnessy, who stood below,
At every shot exclaimed " Bravo!"—

The French mainstay being cut at last,
Down staggering came the batter'd mast!
The Mizzen, too, to see it fall so,
Took huff, and therefore tumbled also—

" Well done, by Jasus ! "—bellowed Pat,
" Newcome, 'twas you knocked down all that ! "

Our Frigate forged ahead, and now
Lay right athwart the Frenchman's bow,
Who after a few broadsides more,
Was glad to give the business o'er.—

Along her bowsprit in procession
The English marched and took possession ;
And John ran too, with eager eyes
Among them, to explore the Prize.—

Her riven deck was sheeted o'er
Completely with a flood of gore ;
And every corner shew'd remains
Of legs, and arms, and hair, and brains ;
Nay, many by the Masts were crushed,
Whose blood in all directions gushed,
As when a man hath happed to place
His foot on one o' th' Beetle race !—

    CAPTAIN JACK MITFORD, R.N.
("Adventures of Johnny Newcombe in the Navy")

THE STORY OF JONAH. POEMS OF MERMAIDS AND OF THE SEA SPIRITS

The Story of Jonah

JONAH rose up to flee unto Tarshish from the presence of the Lord, and went down to Joppa; and he found a ship going to Tarshish: so he paid the fare thereof, and went down into it to go with them unto Tarshish from the presence of the Lord.

But the Lord sent out a great wind into the sea, and there was a mighty tempest in the sea, so that the ship was like to be broken.

Then the mariners were afraid, and cried every man unto his god, and cast forth the wares that *were* in the ship into the sea to lighten *it* of them. But Jonah was gone down into the sides of the ship; and he lay, and was fast asleep.

So the shipmaster came to him, and said unto him, "What meanest thou, O sleeper? Arise, call upon thy God, if so be that God will think upon us, that we perish not."

And they said every one to his fellow, "Come, and let us cast lots, that we may know for whose cause this evil *is* upon us; what *is* thine occupation? and whence comest thou? what *is* thy country? and of what people *art* thou?"

And he said unto them, "*I am* an Hebrew;

and I fear the Lord, the God of Heaven, which hath made the sea and the dry *land*."

Then were the men exceedingly afraid, and said unto him, " Why hast thou done this ? " For the men knew that he fled from the presence of the Lord, because he had told them.

Then said they unto him, " What shall we do unto thee, that the sea may be calm unto us ? " for the sea wrought, and was tempestuous.

And he said unto them, " Take me up, and cast me forth into the sea ; so shall the sea be calm unto you : for I know that for my sake the great tempest *is* upon you."

Nevertheless the men rowed hard to bring *it* to the land ; but they could not : for the sea wrought, and was tempestuous against them.

Wherefore they cried unto the Lord, and said, " We beseech Thee, O Lord, we beseech Thee, let us not perish for this man's life, and lay not upon us innocent blood : for thou, O Lord, hast done as it pleased Thee."

So they took up Jonah, and cast him forth into the sea ; and the sea ceased from her raging.

Then the men feared the Lord exceedingly, and offered a sacrifice unto the Lord, and made vows.

Now the Lord had prepared a great fish to swallow up Jonah. And Jonah was in the belly of the fish three days and three nights.

Captain Glen

THERE was a ship, and a ship of fame,
Launch'd off the stocks, bound to the main,
With a hundred and fifty brisk young men,
Was picked and chosen every one.

CAPTAIN GLEN

William Glen was their captain's name,
He was a brisk and a tall young man,
As bold a sailor as went to sea,
And he was bound for New Barbary.

The first of April we did set sail,
Blest with a pleasant prosperous gale;
And we were bound to New Barbary,
With all our whole ship's company.

We had not sailed a league or two,
Till all our whole ship's jovial crew,
They all fell sick but sixty-three,
As we went to New Barbary.

One night the captain he did dream,
There came a voice which said to him,
" Prepare, you and your company,
To-morrow night you must lodge with me."

This waked the captain in a fright,
It being the third watch of the night,
Then for his boatswain he did call,
And told to him his secrets all.

When I in England did remain,
The Holy Sabbath I did profane,
In drunkenness I took delight,
Which does my trembling soul affright.

There's one thing more I do rehearse,
Which I shall mention in this verse,
A squire I slew in Staffordshire,
All for the love of a lady fair.

" Now 'tis the ghost, I am afraid,
That hath in me such terror bred;
Although the King hath pardoned me,
He's daily in my company."

" O, worthy captain, since 'tis so,
No mortal of it e'er shall know ;
So keep this secret in your breast,
And pray to God to give you rest."

We had not sailed a league but three,
Till raging grew the roaring sea :
There rose a tempest in the skies,
Which filled our hearts with sad surmise.

Our mainmast sprung by break of day,
Which made our rigging all give way,
And did our seamen sore affright,
The terrors of that fatal night.

Up then spoke our foremast man,
As he did by the foreyard stand ;
He cried, " The Lord receive my soul,"
So to the bottom he did fall.

The sea did wash both fore and aft,
Till scarce one sail was left aloft ;
Our yards were sprung, our rigging tore,
The like you never saw before.

The boatswain straitly did declare
The captain was a murderer.
Which so enraged the whole ship's crew,
The captain overboard they threw.

Our treacherous captain being gone,
Immediately there was a calm ;
The winds did calm, and the raging sea,
As we went to New Barbary.

Now, when we came to the Spanish shore,
Our goodly ship for to repair,
The people all were amazed to see
Our dismal case and misery.

So when our ship was in repair,
To England then our ship did steer;
And when we came to London town,
Our dismal case we then made known.

For many wives their husbands lost,
Whom they lamented to their cost;
Which caused them to mourn bitterly,
These tidings from New Barbary.

A hundred and fifty brisk young men,
Did to our goodly ship belong;
Of all our whole ship's company
There now remained but sixty-three.

Now, seamen all, where'er you be,
I pray a warning take by me,
As you love your life, still have a care
You never sail with a murderer.

O, never more do I intend
For to cross o'er the raging main,
But live in peace in my own country,
And so I end my tragedy.

Brown Robyn's Confession

It fell upon a Wodensday
  Brown Robyn's men went to sea,
But they saw neither moon nor sun,
  Nor starlight wi' their ee.

" We'll cast Kevels us among,
  See who the unhappy man may be."
The Kevel fell on Brown Robyn
  The master-man was he.

"It is nae wonder," said Brown Robyn,
  "Altho' I dinna thrive,
For with my mither I had twa bairns
  And with my sister five.

"But tie me to a plank o' wood,
  And throw me in the sea;
And if I sink, ye may bid me sink,
  But if I swim, just let me be."

They've tied him to a plank of wood,
  And thrown him in the sea;
He didna sink, though they bade him sink:
  He swimd, and they bade let him be.

He hadna been into the sea
  An hour but barely three,
Till by it came Our Blessed Lady
  Her dear young Son her wi'.

"Will ye gang to your men again,
  Or will ye gang wi' me?
Will ye gang to the high heavens,
  Wi my dear Son and me?"

"I winna gang to my men again,
  For they would be feared at me;
But I would gang to the high heavens,
  With thy dear Son and thee."

"It's for nae honour ye did to me, Brown Robyn,
  It for nae good ye did to mee;
But a' is for your fair confession
  You've made upon the sea."

From William Grismond's Downfall
(1650)

THERE in the broom I killed her,
  With my accursed knife,

There hatefully I killed her,
  Who loved me as her life;
I cut her throat, I killed her,
  Who should have been my wife.
    And for mine offence I must die.

Three days she lay there murdered,
  Before that she was found,
But then the neighbours searching
  Within that broomy ground,
Did find her there uncovered,
  And with a bloody wound.
    And for mine offence I must die.

The neighbours having found her
  Where I did do this deed;
There in the broom they found her
  Where I her blood did shed;
But when I did perceive that,
  I ran away with speed.
    And for mine offence I must die.

No sooner had they found her,
  But away I did go,
And thought to go to Ireland,
  The very truth is so;
But God He would not suffer me
  To run my country through.
    And for mine offence I must die.

Yet I was got on ship-board,
  As you may understand,
But the ship was troubled,
  I must go back to land;
I could not get away so,
  With guilty heart and hand.
    And for mine offence I must die.

There is some wicked person
  The shipmen they did say,
Within the ship we know it,
  That cannot pass away ;
We must return to land here,
  And make no more delay.
      And for mine offence I must die.

Then near unto Westchester,
  I taken was at last,
And then in Chester prison
  I suddenly was cast ;
From thence brought unto Hereford,
  To answer what is past.
      And for mine offence I must die.

But then my loving father
  His gold he did not spare,
To save me from the gallows
  He had of me great care ;
But it would not be granted,
  The gallows was my share.
      And for mine offence I must die.

My fault it was so heinous
  It would not granted be,
I must for an example
  Hang on the gallows tree ;
God grant that I a warning
  For all young men may be.
      And for mine offence I must die.[1]

---

[1] He died for his offence at Leintwardine, in Herefordshire upon the scene of his crime, 1650.

The Rime of the Ancient Mariner

PART THE FIRST

It is an ancient Mariner,
And he stoppeth one of three,
" By thy long grey beard and glittering eye,
Now wherefore stopp'st thou me ?

" The Bridegroom's doors are opened wide,
And I am next of kin ;
The guests are met, the feast is set :
May'st hear the merry din."

He holds him with his skinny hand,
" There was a ship," quoth he.
" Hold off ! unhand me, grey-beard loon ! "
Eftsoons his hand dropt he.

He holds him with his glittering eye—
The Wedding-Guest stood still,
And listens like a three years' child :
The Mariner hath his will.

The Wedding-Guest sat on a stone,
He cannot choose but hear ;
And thus spake on that ancient man,
The bright-eyed Mariner.

The ship was cheered, the harbour cleared
Merrily did we drop
Below the kirk, below the hill,
Below the lighthouse top.

The Sun came up upon the left,
Out of the sea came he !

And he shone bright, and on the right
Went down into the sea.

Higher and higher every day,
Till over the mast at noon—
The Wedding-Guest here beat his breast,
For he heard the loud bassoon.

The bride hath paced into the hall,
Red as a rose is she;
Nodding their heads before her goes
The merry minstrelsy.

The Wedding-Guest he beat his breast,
Yet he cannot choose but hear,
And thus spake on that ancient man,
The bright-eyed Mariner.

And now the storm-blast came, and he
Was tyrannous and strong:
He struck with his o'ertaking wings,
And chased us south along.

With sloping masts and dipping prow,
As who pursued with yell and blow
Still treads the shadow of his foe,
And forward bends his head,
The ship drove fast, loud roared the blast
And southward aye we fled.

And now there came both mist and snow,
And it grew wondrous cold:
And ice, mast-high, came floating by,
As green as emerald.

And through the drifts the snowy clifts
Did send a dismal sheen :
Nor shapes of men nor beasts we ken—
The ice was all between.

The ice was here, the ice was there,
The ice was all around :
It cracked and growled, and roared and howled,
Like noises in a swound !

At length did cross an Albatross :
Through the fog it came ;
As if it had been a Christian soul,
We hailed it in God's name.

It ate the food it ne'er had eat,
And round and round it flew.
The ice did split with a thunder-fit ;
The helmsman steered us through !

And a good south wind sprung up behind ;
The Albatross did follow,
And every day, for food or play,
Came to the mariners' hollo !

In mist or cloud, on mast or shroud,
It perched for vespers nine ;
Whiles all the night, through fog-smoke white
Glimmered the white moon-shine.

" God save thee, ancient Mariner !
From the fiends, that plague thee thus !
Why look'st thou so ? "—With my cross-bow
I shot the albatross !

PART THE SECOND

The Sun now rose upon the right :
Out of the sea came he,
Still hid in mist, and on the left
Went down into the sea.

And the good south wind still blew behind,
But no sweet bird did follow,
Nor any day, for food or play,
Came to the mariners' hollo !

And I had done a hellish thing,
And it would work 'em woe ;
For all averred, I had killed the bird
That made the breeze to blow.
Ah wretch ! said they, the bird to slay
That made the breeze to blow !

Nor dim nor red, like God's own head,
The glorious Sun uprist :
Then all averred, I had killed the bird
That brought the fog and mist.
'Twas right, said they, such birds to slay,
That bring the fog and mist.

The fair breeze blew, the white foam flew,
The furrow streamed off free :
We were the first that ever burst
Into that silent sea.

Down dropt the breeze, the sails dropt down,
'Twas sad as sad could be ;
And we did speak only to break
The silence of the sea !

All in a hot and a copper sky,
The bloody Sun, at noon,
Right up above the mast did stand,
No bigger than the Moon.

Day after day, day after day,
We stuck, nor breath, nor motion ;
As idle as a painted ship
Upon a painted ocean.

Water, water, every where,
And all the boards did shrink ;
Water, water, every where,
Nor any drop to drink.

The very deep did rot : O Christ !
That ever this should be !
Yea, slimy things did crawl with legs
Upon the slimy sea.

About, about, in reel and rout
The death-fires danced at night ;
The water, like a witch's oils,
Burnt green, and blue and white.

And some in dreams assured were
Of the spirit that plagued us so :
Nine fathom deep he had followed us
From the land of mist and snow.

And every tongue, through utter drought,
Was withered at the root ;
We could not speak, no more than if
We had been choked with soot.

Ah! well-a-day! what evil looks
Had I from old and young!
Instead of the cross, the Albatross
About my neck was hung.

PART THE THIRD

There passed a weary time. Each throat
Was parched, and glazed each eye.
A weary time! A weary time!
How glazed each weary eye!
When looking westward, I beheld
A something in the sky.

At first it seemed a little speck,
And then it seemed a mist;
It moved and moved, and took at last
A certain shape, I wist.

A speck, a mist, a shape, I wist!
And still it neared and neared:
And as if it dodged a water-sprite,
It plunged and tacked and veered.

With throats unslaked, with black lips baked,
We could nor laugh nor wail;
Through utter drought all dumb we stood!
I bit my arm, I sucked the blood,
And cried, A sail! a sail!

With throats unslaked, with black lips baked,
Agape they heard me call:
Gramercy! they for joy did grin,
And all at once their breath drew in,
As they were drinking all.

See! see! (I cried) she tacks no more!
Hither to work us weal;
Without a breeze, without a tide,
She steadies with upright keel!

The western wave was all a-flame,
The day was well nigh done!
Almost upon the western wave
Rested the broad bright Sun;
When that strange shape drove suddenly
Betwixt us and the Sun.

And straight the Sun was flecked with bars,
(Heaven's Mother send us grace!)
As if through a dungeon grate he peered,
With broad and burning face.

Alas! (thought I, and my heart beat loud)
How fast she nears and nears!
Are those *her* sails that glance in the Sun,
Like restless gossameres?

Are those *her* ribs through which the Sun
Did peer, as through a grate?
And is that Woman all her crew?
Is that a DEATH? and are there two?
Is DEATH that woman's mate?

Her lips were red, her looks were free,
Her locks were yellow as gold;
Her skin was as white as leprosy,
The night-mare LIFE-IN-DEATH was she,
Who thicks man's blood with cold.

The naked hulk alongside came,
And the twain were casting dice;
" The game is done! I've won, I've won!'
Quoth she, and whistles thrice.

The Sun's rim dips ; the stars rush out :
At one stride comes the dark ;
With far-heard whisper, o'er the sea,
Off shot the spectre-bark.

We listened and looked sideways up !
Fear at my heart, as at a cup,
My life-blood seemed to sip !
The stars were dim, and thick the night,
The steersman's face by his lamp gleamed white
From the sails the dew did drip—
Till clomb above the eastern bar
The horned Moon, with one bright star
Within the nether tip.

One after one, by the star-dogged Moon,
Too quick for groan or sigh,
Each turned his face with a ghastly pang,
And cursed me with his eye.

Four times fifty living men,
(And I heard nor sigh nor groan)
With heavy thump, a lifeless lump,
They dropped down one by one.

The souls did from their bodies fly,—
They fled to bliss or woe !
And every soul, it passed me by,
Like the whiz of my cross-bow !

PART THE FOURTH

" I fear thee, ancient Mariner !
I fear thy skinny hand !
And thou art long, and lank, and brown,
As is the ribbed sea-sand.

THE ANCIENT MARINER

" I fear thee and thy glittering eye,
Thy skinny hand, so brown."—
Fear not, fear not, thou Wedding-Guest !
This body dropt not down.

Alone, alone, all, all alone,
Alone on a wide wide sea !
And never a saint took pity on
My soul in agony.

The many men, so beautiful !
And they all dead did lie ;
And a thousand thousand slimy things
Lived on ; and so did I.

I looked upon the rotting sea,
And drew my eyes away ;
I looked upon the rotting deck,
And there the dead men lay.

I looked to Heaven, and tried to pray ;
But or ever a prayer had gusht,
A wicked whisper came, and made
My heart as dry as dust.

I closed my lids, and kept them close,
And the balls like pulses beat ;
For the sky and the sea, and the sea and the sky
Lay, like a load on my weary eye,
And the dead were at my feet.

The cold sweat melted from their limbs,
Nor rot nor reek did they :
The look with which they looked on me
Had never passed away.

An orphan's curse would drag to Hell
A spirit from on high ;

But oh ; more horrible than that
Is the curse in a dead man's eye !
Seven days, seven nights, I saw that curse,
And yet I could not die.

The moving Moon went up the sky,
And no where did abide :
Softly she was going up,
And a star or two beside—

Her beams bemocked the sultry main,
Like April hoar-frost spread ;
But where the ship's huge shadow lay,
The charmed water burnt alway
A still and awful red.

Beyond the shadow of the ship,
I watched the water-snakes :
They moved in tracks of shining white,
And when they reared, the elfish light
Fell off in hoary flakes.

Within the shadow of the ship
I watched their rich attire :
Blue, glossy green, and velvet black,
They coiled and swam ; and every track
Was a flash of golden fire.

O happy living things ! no tongue
Their beauty might declare :
A spring of love gushed from my heart,
And I blessed them unaware :
Sure my kind saint took pity on me,
And I blessed them unaware.

The selfsame moment I could pray ;
And from my neck so free

THE ANCIENT MARINER

The Albatross fell off, and sank
Like lead into the sea.

PART THE FIFTH

Oh sleep ! it is a gentle thing,
Beloved from pole to pole !
To Mary Queen the praise be given !
She sent the gentle sleep from Heaven,
That slid into my soul.

The silly buckets on the deck,
That had so long remained,
I dreamt that they were filled with dew ;
And when I woke it rained.

My lips were wet, my throat was cold,
My garments all were dank ;
Sure I had drunken in my dreams,
And still my body drank.

I moved, and could not feel my limbs :
I was so light—almost
I thought that I had died in sleep,
And was a blessed ghost.

And soon I heard a roaring wind :
It did not come anear ;
But with its sound it shook the sails,
That were so thin and sere.

The upper air burst into life !
And a hundred fire-flags sheen,
To and fro they were hurried about ;
And to and fro, and in and out,
The wan stars danced between.

And the coming wind did roar more loud,
And the sails did sigh like sedge ;
And the rain poured down from one black cloud ;
The Moon was at its edge.

The thick black cloud was cleft, and still
The Moon was at its side ;
Like waters shot from some high crag,
The lightning fell with never a jag,
A river steep and wide.

The loud wind never reached the ship,
Yet now the ship moved on !
Beneath the lightning and the Moon
The dead men gave a groan.

They groaned, they stirred, they all uprose,
Nor spake nor moved their eyes ;
It had been strange, even in a dream,
To have seen those dead men rise.

The helmsman steered, the ship moved on ;
Yet never a breeze up blew ;
The mariners all 'gan work the ropes,
Where they were wont to do :
They raised their limbs like lifeless tools—
We were a ghastly crew.

The body of my brother's son
Stood by me, knee to knee :
The body and I pulled at one rope,
But he said nought to me.

" I fear thee, ancient Mariner ; "
Be calm, thou Wedding-Guest !

'Twas not those souls that fled in pain,
Which to their corses came again,
But a troop of spirits blest:

For when it dawned—they dropped their arms,
And clustered round the mast;
Sweet sounds rose slowly through their mouths,
And from their bodies passed.

Around, around, flew each sweet sound,
Then darted to the Sun;
Slowly the sounds came back again,
Now mixed, now one by one.

Sometimes a-dropping from the sky
I heard the sky-lark sing;
Sometimes all little birds that are,
How they seemed to fill the sea and air
With their sweet jargoning!

And now 'twas like all instruments,
Now like a lonely flute;
And now it is an angel's song,
That makes the heavens be mute.

It ceased; yet still the sails made on
A pleasant noise till noon,
A noise like of a hidden brook
In the leafy month of June,
That to the sleeping woods all night
Singeth a quiet tune.

Till noon we quietly sailed on,
Yet never a breeze did breathe:
Slowly and smoothly went the ship,
Moved onward from beneath.

Under the keel nine fathom deep,
From the land of mist and snow,
The spirit slid ; and it was he
That made the ship to go.
The sails at noon left off their tune,
And the ship stood still also.

The Sun, right up above the mast,
Had fixed her to the ocean ;
But in a minute she 'gan stir,
With a short uneasy motion—
Backwards and forwards half her length,
With a short uneasy motion.

Then like a pawing horse let go,
She made a sudden bound :
It flung the blood into my head,
And I fell down in a swound.

How long in that same fit I lay,
I have not to declare ;
But ere my living life returned,
I heard, and in my soul discerned
Two voices in the air.

" Is it he ? " quoth one, " is this the man ?
By Him who died on cross,
With his cruel bow he laid full low,
The harmless Albatross.

" The spirit who bideth by himself
In the land of mist and snow,
He loved the bird that loved the man
Who shot him with his bow."

The other with a softer voice,
As soft as honey-dew :
Quoth he, " The man hath penance done,
And penance more will do."

PART THE SIXTH
First Voice

But tell me, tell me ! speak again,
Thy soft response renewing—
What makes that ship drive on so fast ?
What is the ocean doing ?

Second Voice

Still as a slave before his lord,
The ocean hath no blast ;
His great bright eye most silently
Up to the Moon is cast—

If he may know which way to go ;
For she guides him smooth or grim,
See, brother, see ! how graciously
She looketh down on him.

First Voice

But why drives on that ship so fast,
Without or wave or wind ?

Second Voice

The air is cut away before,
And closes from behind.

Fly, brother, fly ! more high, more high !
Or we shall be belated :
For slow and slow that ship will go,
When the Mariner's trance is abated.

I woke, and we were sailing on
As in a gentle weather :
'Twas night, calm night, the Moon was high ;
The dead men stood together.

All stood together on the deck,
For a charnel-dungeon fitter :
All fixed on me their stony eyes,
That in the Moon did glitter.

The pang, the curse, with which they died,
Had never passed away :
I could not draw my eyes from theirs,
Nor turn them up to pray.

And now this spell was snapt : once more
I viewed the ocean green,
And looked far forth, yet little saw
Of what had else been seen—

Like one, that on a lonesome road
Doth walk in fear and dread,
And having once turned round, walks on,
And turns no more his head ;
Because he knows, a frightful fiend
Doth close behind him tread.

But soon there breathed a wind on me,
Nor sound nor motion made :
Its path was not upon the sea,
In ripple or in shade.

It raised my hair, it fanned my cheek
Like a meadow-gale of spring—
It mingled strangely with my fears,
Yet it felt like a welcoming.

THE ANCIENT MARINER

Swiftly, swiftly flew the ship,
Yet she sailed softly too :
Sweetly, sweetly blew the breeze—
On me alone it blew.

Oh ! dream of joy ! is this indeed
The lighthouse top I see ?
Is this the hill ? is this the kirk ?
Is this mine own countree ?

We drifted o'er the harbour-bar,
And I with sobs did pray—
O let me be awake, my God !
Or let me sleep alway.

The harbour-bay was clear as glass,
So smoothly it was strewn ;
And on the bay the moonlight lay,
And the shadow of the Moon.

The rock shone bright, the kirk no less,
That stands above the rock :
The moonlight steeped in silentness
The steady weathercock.

And the bay was white with silent light,
Till rising from the same,
Full many shapes, that shadows were,
In crimson colours came.

A little distance from the prow
Those crimson shadows were :
I turned my eyes upon the deck—
Oh, Christ ! what saw I there !

Each corse lay flat, lifeless and flat,
And, by the holy rood !

A man all light, a seraph-man,
On every corse there stood.

This seraph-band, each waved his hand :
It was a heavenly sight !
They stood as signals to the land,
Each one a lovely light :

This seraph-band, each waved his hand,
No voice did they impart—
No voice ; but oh ; the silence sank
Like music on my heart.

But soon I heard the dash of oars,
I heard the Pilot's cheer ;
My head was turned perforce away,
And I saw a boat appear.

The Pilot, and the Pilot's boy,
I heard them coming fast :
Dear Lord in Heaven ! it was a joy
The dead men could not blast.

I saw a third—I heard his voice ;
It is the Hermit good !
He singeth loud his godly hymns
That he makes in the wood.
He'll shrieve my soul, he'll wash away
The Albatross's blood.

PART THE SEVENTH

This Hermit good lives in that wood
Which slopes down to the sea.
How loudly his sweet voice he rears !
He loves to talk with marineres
That come from a far countree.

He kneels at morn, and noon, and eve—
He hath a cushion plump :
It is the moss that wholly hides
The rotted old oak stump.

The skiff-boat neared : I heard them talk,
" Why, this is strange, I trow !
Where are those lights so many and fair,
That signal made but now ? "

" Strange, by my faith ! " the Hermit said—
" And they answered not our cheer !
The planks looked warped ! and see those sails
How thin they are and sere !
I never saw aught like to them,
Unless perchance it were

Brown skeletons of leaves that lag
My forest-brook along :
When the ivy-tod is heavy with snow,
And the owlet whoops to the wolf below,
That eats the she-wolf's young."

" Dear Lord ! it hath a fiendish look "—
(The Pilot made reply)
" I am a-feared "—" Push on, push on ! "
Said the Hermit cheerily.

The boat came closer to the ship,
But I nor spake nor stirred ;
The boat came close beneath the ship,
And straight a sound was heard.

Under the water it rumbled on,
Still louder and more dread :
It reached the ship, it split the bay,
The ship went down like lead.

Stunned by that loud and dreadful sound,
Which sky and ocean smote,
Like one that hath been seven days drowned,
My body lay afloat;
But swift as dreams, myself I found
Within the Pilot's boat.

Upon the whirl, where sank the ship,
The boat spun round and round;
And all was still, save that the hill
Was telling of the sound.

I moved my lips—the Pilot shrieked
And fell down in a fit;
The holy Hermit raised his eyes,
And prayed where he did sit,

I took the oars: the Pilot's boy,
Who now doth crazy go,
Laughed loud and long, and all the while
His eyes went to and fro.
"Ha! ha!" quoth he, "full plain I see
The Devil knows how to row."

And now, all in my own countree,
I stood on the firm land!
The Hermit stepped forth from the boat,
And scarcely he could stand.

"O shrieve me, shrieve me, holy man!"
The Hermit crossed his brow.
"Say quick," quoth he, "I bid thee say—
What manner of man art thou?"

Forthwith this frame of mine was wrenched
With a woeful agony,

Which forced me to begin my tale ;
And then it left me free.

Since then, at an uncertain hour,
That agony returns ;
And till my ghastly tale is told,
This heart within me burns.

I pass, like night, from land to land ;
I have strange power of speech ;
That moment that his face I see,
I know the man that must hear me :
To him my tale I teach.

What loud uproar bursts from that door !
The wedding-guests are there ;
But in the garden-bower the bride
And bride-maids singing are ;
And hark the little vesper bell,
Which biddeth me to prayer !

O Wedding-Guest ! this soul hath been
Alone on a wide wide sea :
So lonely 'twas, that God himself
Scarce seemed there to be.

O sweeter than the marriage-feast,
'Tis sweeter far to me,
To walk together to the kirk
With a goodly company !—

To walk together to the kirk,
And all together pray,
While each to his great Father bends,
Old men, and babes, and loving friends,
And youths and maidens gay !

Farewell, farewell! but this I tell
To thee, thou Wedding-Guest!
He prayeth well, who loveth well
Both man and bird and beast.

He prayeth best who loveth best
All things both great and small;
For the dear God who loveth us,
He made and loveth all.

The Mariner, whose eye is bright,
Whose beard with age is hoar,
Is gone; and now the Wedding-Guest
Turned from the bridegroom's door.

He went like one that hath been stunned,
And is of sense forlorn:
A sadder and a wiser man,
He rose the morrow morn.

S. T. COLERIDGE

The Forsaken Merman

COME, dear children, let us away;
    Down and away below.
Now my brothers call from the bay;
Now the great winds shorewards blow;
Now the salt tides seawards flow;
Now the wild white horses play,
Champ and chafe and toss in the spray.
    Children dear, let us away!
        This way, this way!
Call her once before you go.
    Call once yet.

THE FORSAKEN MERMAN

In a voice that she will know:
    "Margaret! Margaret!"
Children's voices should be dear
(Call once more) to a mother's ear:
Children's voices, wild with pain.
    Surely she will come again.
Call her once, and come away.
       This way, this way.
"Mother dear, we cannot stay."
The wild white horses foam and fret.
    Margaret! Margaret!

Come, dear children, come away down.
    Call no more.
One last look at the white-walled town,
And the little grey church on the windy shore.
    Then come down.
She will not come though you call all day.
    Come away, come away.

Children dear, was it yesterday
We heard the sweet bells over the bay?
    In the caverns where we lay,
    Through the surf and through the swell.
The far-off sound of a silver bell?
Sand-strewn caverns, cool and deep,
Where the winds are all asleep;
Where the spent lights quiver and gleam;
Where the salt weed sways in the stream;
Where the sea-beasts, ranged all round,
Feed in the ooze of their pasture-ground;
Where the sea-snakes coil and twine,
Dry their mail and bask in the brine;
Where great whales come sailing by,
Sail and sail, with unshut eye,
Round the world for ever and aye?

When did music come this way?
Children dear, was it yesterday?
Children dear, was it yesterday
(Call yet once) that she went away?
Once she sate with you and me,
On a red gold throne in the heart of the sea,
And the youngest sate on her knee.
She combed its bright hair, and she tended it well,
When down swung the sound of the far-off bell.
She sighed, she looked up through the clear green sea.
She said : " I must go, for my kinsfolk pray
In the little grey church on the shore to-day.
'Twill be Easter-time in the world—ah me!
And I lose my poor soul, Merman, here with thee."
I said : " Go up, dear heart, through the waves;
Say thy prayer, and come back to the kind sea-caves!"
    She smiled, she went up through the surf in the bay.
Children dear, was it yesterday?

    Children dear, were we long alone?
" The sea grows stormy, the little ones moan;
Long prayers," I said, " in the world they say.
Come," I said, and we rose through the surf in the bay.
We went up the beach, by the sandy down
Where the sea-stocks bloom, to the white-walled town.
Through the narrow paved streets, where all was still,
To the little grey church on the windy hill.
From the church came a murmur of folk at their prayers,
But we stood without in the cold blowing airs.

THE FORSAKEN MERMAN

We climbed on the graves, on the stones, worn
  with rains,
And we gazed up the aisle through the small
  leaded panes.
  She sate by the pillar; we saw her clear:
  "Margaret, hist! come quick, we are here!
  Dear heart," I said, "we are long alone.
  The sea grows stormy, the little ones moan."
But, ah, she gave me never a look,
For her eyes were sealed to the holy book.
  "Loud prays the priest; shut stands the door."
Come away, children, call no more!
Come away, come down, call no more!

  Down, down, down.
  Down to the depths of the sea.
She sits at her wheel in the humming town,
  Singing most joyfully.
Hark what she sings: "O joy, O joy,
For the humming street, and the child with its toy.
For the priest, and the bell, and the holy well.
    For the wheel where I spun,
    And the blessed light of the sun!"
  And so she sings her fill,
  Singing most joyfully,
  Till the shuttle drops from her hand,
  And the whizzing wheel stands still.
She steals to the window, and looks at the sand;
  And over the sand at the sea;
  And her eyes are set in a stare;
  And anon there breaks a sigh,
  And anon there drops a tear
  From a sorrow-clouded eye,
  And a heart sorrow-laden,
    A long, long sigh

For the cold strange eyes of a little Mermaiden
    And the gleam of her golden hair.

    Come away, away children.
    Come children, come down.
    The hoarse wind blows colder ;
    Lights shine in the town.
    She will start from her slumber
    When gusts shake the door ;
    She will hear the winds howling,
    Will hear the waves roar.

    We shall see, while above us
    The waves roar and whirl,
    A ceiling of amber,
    A pavement of pearl.
    Singing : " Here came a mortal,
    But faithless was she.
    And alone dwell for ever
    The kings of the sea."

    But, children, at midnight,
    When soft the winds blow,
    When clear falls the moonlight ;
    When spring-tides are low :
    When sweet airs come seaward
    From heaths starred with broom ;
    And high rocks throw mildly
    On the blanched sands a gloom :
    Up the still, glistening beaches,
    Up the creeks we will hie ;
    Over banks of bright seaweed
    The ebb-tide leaves dry.
    We will gaze, from the sand-hills,
    At the white, sleeping town ;

At the church on the hill-side—
    And then come back down,
Singing : " There dwells a loved one,
But cruel is she.
She left lonely for ever
The kings of the sea."

                       MATTHEW ARNOLD

Dolor Oogo

THIRTEEN men by Ruan Shore
    —Dolor Oogo, Dolor Oogo—
Drowned men since 'eighty-four,
    Down in Dolor Oogo :
On the cliff against the sky,
Ailsa, wife of Malachi—
    That cold woman—
Sits and knits eternally.

By her silent husband's side
    —Dolor Oogo, Dolor Oogo—
Stretched awake, she hears the tide
    Moan in Dolor Oogo :
Till athwart the easter gale
Hark ! the merry dead men hail—
    " Thou cold woman,
Take the lantern from the nail ! "

Rising in her chilly sark
    —Dolor Oogo, Dolor Oogo—
Forth she fares by Behan Parc,
    Out to Dolor Oogo.
Kneeling there above the brink,
Lets her long red tresses sink
    —That cold woman—
For the sailor men to drink.

Then the sailor men beneath
    —Dolor Oogo, Dolor Oogo—
Take the ends between their teeth,
    Deep in Dolor Oogo.
  "Lusty blood is this to quaff:
  (So the merry dead men laugh)
    "O, cold woman,
  Hath thy man as good by half?"

"Drowned men by Ruan Shore
    —Dolor Oogo, Dolor Oogo—
Lost aboard the *Elsinore*
    Down by Dolor Oogo—
  If the gulls behind the share
  Yesterday had called "Beware,
    Thy cold woman!"
  Paler now had been my hair.

"Socks I knit you each a pair
    —Dolor Oogo, Dolor Oogo—
Half of yarn and half of hair,
    Over Dolor Oogo."
  "Dripping, dripping on the tide,
  What red dye thy hair hath dyed,
    Thou cold woman?"
  "It hath brushed upon his side."

Knitting with her double thread
    —Dolor Oogo, Dolor Oogo—
Half of black and half of red—
    Over Dolor Oogo,
  On the cliff against the sky,
  Ailsa, wife of Malachi,
    That cold woman,
  Wipes her hands incessantly.

                A. T. QUILLER-COUCH

Merman Rosmer

THERE dwells a lady in Denmark,
  Lady Hillers men her ca';
And she's gar'd bigg a new castell,
  That shines o'er Denmark a'.

Her daughter was stown awa frae her;
  She sought for her wide-where;
But the mair she sought, the less she fand;
  That works her mickle care.

And she's gar'd bigg a new ship,
  Wi' vanes o' flaming gold,
Wi' mony a knight and mariner,
  Sae stark in stour, bestowed.

She's followed her sons down to the strand
  And seen them sailing free,
And wull and waif for eight lang years
  They sailed upon the sea.

And eight years wull and waif, they sailed
  O' months that seemed sae lang;
Syne they sail'd afore a high castell,
  And to the land can gang.

And the young daughter Svanè lyle,
  In the bower that was the best,
Says, " Where frae come you foreign swains
  Wi' us this night to guest ? "

Then up and spak her youngest brither
  Sae wisely ay spak he;
" We are a widow's three poor sons,
  Lang wilder'd on the sea.

In Denmark were we born and bred,
  Lady Hillers was our mither ;
Our sister frae us was stown awa,
  We find na where nor whither."

" In Denmark were ye born and bred ?
  Was Lady Hillers your mither ?
I can nae longer hold frae thee,
  Thou art my youngest brither.

And hear ye this, my bonny boy,
  Why came ye o'er the faem ?
Thy bonny neckbone will be cut
  When my gudeman comes hame."

She's set him in the weirst nook
  She in the house can meet :
She's bidden him for the high God's sake
  Neither to laugh nor greet.

When Rosmer hame from Zeeland came,
  He took on to ban ;
" I smell fu' weel, by my right hand,
  That here is a Christian man."

" There cam a bird," quo' the Svanè lyle,
  " Wi' a man's bone in his mouth ;
He coost it in, and I cast it out,
  As fast as e'er I couth."

But wilily can she Rosmer win ;
  She claps him tenderly,
" It's here is come my sister's son ;
  Gin I lose him, I'll dee.

It's here is come my sister's son,
  Frae baith our father's land ;
And I ha'e pledged him faith and troth,
  That ye will not him ban."

" And is he come, thy sister's son,
  Frae thy father's land to thee ?
Then I will swear my highest aith
  He's dree nae scaith frae me."

'Twas then the high King Rosmer,
  He ca'd on pages twae :
" Ye bid Queen Svanè's sister's son
  To the chamber afore me gae."

When proud Queen Svanè's brither stood
  By the high King Rosmer's hand,
A strong quake quook in his blood,
  Sae as he scarce coud stand.

And Rosmer took the young wee lad
  Upo' his laidly knee ;
He clappit him sae luifsomely,
  He turned baith blue and blee.

And up and spak Queen Svanè lyle,
  " Sir Rosmer, ye're to learn,
That your ten fingers arena sma,
  To clap sae wee a bairn."

PART SECOND

He has stayed there till, the fifteenth year,
  He green'd for hame and land ;
With " Help me now, dear Svanè lyle,
  To be set on the white sand."

It was proud Lady Svanè lyle,
  Afore Rosmer doth stand :
"This lad sae lang i' the sea has been,
  He greens for hame and land."

" If the lad sae lang in the sea has been,
  And greens for hame and land,
Then I'll gie him a kist o' gold
  Sae fitting till his hand."

"And will ye gie him a kist o' gold,
  Sae fitting till his hand ?
Then hear ye, my noble heart's dear,
  Ye bear them baith to land."

Then wrought proud Lady Svanè lyle,
  What Rosmer little wist ;
For she's ta'en out the gold sae red,
  And laid herself in the kist.

He's ta'en the man upon his back ;
  The kist in his mouth took he ;
And he has gang the lang way up
  Frae the bottom of the sea.

" Now I ha'e borne thee to the land ;
  Thou seest baith sun and moon,
Thank Lady Svanè for the grace,
  I beg thee as a boon."

And Rosmer sprang i' the salt sea out,
  And jauped it up i' the sky ;
But when he cam to his castell hame
  Nae Svanè lyle could he spy.

When he cam till the castell in
  His dearest awa was gane ;
He stampit strang as he were thrang
  'Drew sparks frae the flint stane.

But blithe was the Lady Hillers' house,
  Wi' welcome joy and glee ;
Hame to their friends her bairns were come,
  That had been lang in the sea.

Ho, for Lubberland !

THERE is a ship, we understand,
  Now riding in the river ;
She is newly home from lubberland,
  The like I think was never.
" You that a lazy life do love,
  I'd have you now go over,
They say the land is not above
  Two thousand leagues from Dover."

The captain and the master, too,
  Do give us this relation ;
And so do all the whole ship's crew,
  Concerning this strange nation.
They say they scorn to tell you lies,
  That they are not mistaken,
But the streets are paved with pudding-pies
  Nay, powdered beef and bacon.

The King of Knaves and the Queen of Sluts
  Reign there in peace and quiet ;
There is good plum-porridge stored in butts,
  They have such store of diet.

There you may live released from care,
  Like hogs set up to fatten;
The garments that the people wear
  Are silver, silk, and satin.

The lofty buildings of this place
  For many years have lasted;
With nutmegs, pepper, cloves, and mace,
  The walls are there rough-casted.
In curious hasty-pudding boiled,
  And most ingenious carving;
Likewise they are with pancakes tiled,
  Sure, here's no fear of starving.

The captain says, " In every town,
  Hot roasted pigs will meet ye,
Then in the streets run up and down,
  Still crying out, *Come eat me.*"
Likewise he says, " At every feast,
  The very fowls and fishes,
Nay from the biggest to the least,
  Come tumbling to the dishes."

The rivers run with claret fine,
  The brooks with rich canary,
The ponds with other sorts of wine,
  To make your hearts full merry:
Nay more than this, you may behold
  The fountains flow with brandy,
The locks are like refined gold,
  The hills are sugar-candy.

Rose-water is the rain they have,
  Which comes in pleasant showers,
All places are adorned brave,
With sweet and fragrant flowers.

Hot custards grow on every tree,
　And jellies by the ditches ;
And the pebbles down beside the sea
　Are comely bacon-flitches.

There's nothing there but holy-days,
　With music out of measure ;
Who can forbear to speak the praise,
　Of such a land of pleasure ?
There you may lead a lazy life,
　Free from all kind of labour ;
And he that is without a wife,
　May borrow of his neighbour.

There is no law nor lawyer's fees,
　All men are free from fury,
For every one does what he please,
　Without a judge or jury.
The summer-time is warm, they say,
　The winter's ne'er the colder ;
They have no landlord's rent to pay,
　Each man is a freeholder.

You that are free to cross the seas,
　Make no more disputation ;
In Lubberland you'll live at ease,
　With pleasant recreation :
The captain waits but for a gale
　Of prosperous wind and weather,
And then they soon will hoist up sail,
　Make haste away together.

Ulysses and the Sirens

IN meantime flew our ships, and straight we fetch'd
The Sirens' isle ; a spleenless wind so stretch'd
Her wings to waft us, and so urged our keel,

But having reach'd this isle, we could not feel
The least gasp of it, it was stricken dead,
And all the sea in prostrate slumber spread,
The Sirens' devil charm'd all. Up then flew
My friends to work, struck sail, together drew,
And under hatches stow'd them, sat, and plied
The polished oars, and did in curls divide
The white head waters. My part then came on :
A mighty waxen cake I set upon,
Chopp'd it in fragments with my sword and wrought
With strong hand every piece, till all were soft.

The great power of the sun in such a beam
As then flew burning from his diadem,
To liquefaction helped us. Orderly
I stopp'd their ears ; and they as fair did ply
My feet and hands with cords, and to the mast
With other hawsers made me soundly fast.

Then took they seat, and forth our passage strook,
The foamy sea beneath their labour shook.
Row'd on, in reach of an erected voice,
The Sirens soon took note, without our noise,
Tuned those sweet accents that made charms so strong,
And these learn'd numbers made the Sirens' song :
> *Come here, thou worthy of a world of praise*
> *That dost so high the Grecian glory raise,*
> *Ulysses ! stay thy ship, and that song hear*
> *That none past ever but it bent his ear,*
> *But left him ravish'd, and instructed more*
> *By us, than any ever heard before,*
> *For we know all things whatsoever were*
> *In wide Troy labour'd ; whatsoever there*
> *The Grecians and the Trojans both sustain'd*
> *By those high issues that the Gods ordain'd.*

And whatsoever all the earth can show
T" inform a knowledge of desert, we know.
This they gave accent in the sweetest strain
That ever open'd an enamour'd vein.
                                GEORGE CHAPMAN

The Story of Ulysses

IN other thing who that recordeth
Like unto this sample accordeth,
Which in the tale of Troy I find.
Sirens of a wonder kind
Be monsters as the books tellen
And in the great sea they dwellen.
Of body both and of visage
Like unto women of young age
Up from the navel on high they be
And down beneath (as men may see),
They bear of fishes the figure.
And over this of such nature
They be, that with so sweet a steven
Like to the melody of heaven
In women's voice they sing,
With notes of so great liking,
Of such measure, of such musike
Whereof the ships they beswike,
That passen by the costes there.
For when the shipmen lay an ear
Unto the voice in their advice,
They ween it be a paradise:
Which after is to them a hell.
For reason may not with them dwell,
When they the great-lustes hear
They cannot their ships steer,
So busily upon the note
They harken, and in such wise assote,

That their right course and way
Forget, and to their ear obey,
And sailen, till it so befal
That they into the peril fall,
Where as the ships be to draw,
And they be with the monsters slaw.
But from this peril nevertheless,
With his wisdom King Ulysses
Escapeth, and it overpasseth
For he toforehand compasseth
That no man of his company
Hath power unto that folly
His ear for no lust to cast.
For he them stopped all so fast
That none of them may hear them sing.
So when they come forth sailing,
There was such governance on hand
That the monsters have withstand
And slew of them a great party.
Thus was he safe, with his navy,
This wise King, through governance.
JOHN GOWER

The Great Silkie of Sule Skerrie

An earthly nourrice [1] sit and sings,
And aye she sings, " Bye, lily wean,
Little ken I my bairnis' father,
Far less the land that he stops in."

Then one arose at her bed-foot,
And a grumly guest I'm sure was he;
" Here am I, thy bairnis' father,
Although that I be not comelie.

[1] *Nourrice*, a nurse.

I am a man, upon the land,
And I am a silkie[1] in the sea ;
And when I'm far and far frae land,
My dwelling is in Sule Skerrie."

" It was na weel," quoth the maiden fair,
" It was na weel, indeed," quoth she,
" That the Great Silkie of Sule Skerrie
Should hae come and aught a bairn to me."

Now he has ta'en a purse of gold,
And he has put it upon her knee,
Saying, " Gie to me my little young son,
And take thee up thy nourrice-fee.

It shall come to pass on a summer's day,
When the sun shines hot on every stane,
That I will take my little young son,
And teach him for to swim the faem.

And thou shalt marry a proud gunner,
And a proud gunner I'm sure he'll be,
And the very first shot that e'er he shoots,
He'll shoot both my young son and me."

The Daemon Lover

How a woman of Aberdeen, the wife of a ship-carpenter, was carried away by the spirit of a dead lover.

" O WHERE have ye been, my dearest dear,
  These seven long years and more ? "
" I am come to seek my former vows,
  That ye promised me before."

" Away with your former vows," she says,
  " Or else ye will breed strife ;

[1] *Silkie,* a seal.

Away with your former vows," she says,
  " For I am become a wife.

I am married to a ship-carpenter,
  A ship-carpenter he's bound ;
I would not he knew my mind this night,
  For twice five hundred pound."

.   .   .   .   *(Stanza lost)*

She has put her foot on good ship-board,
  And on ship-board she's gone,
And the veil that hung over her face
  Was all with gold begone.

She had not sailed a league, a league,
  A league but barely two,
Till she did mind on the husband she left,
  And her wee young son also.

" O, hold your tongue, my dearest dear,
  Let all your follies abee ;
I'll show where the white lilies grow,
  On the banks of Italie."

She had not sailed a league, a league,
  A league but barely three,
Till grim, grim grew his countenance,
  And gurly grew the sea.

" O, hold your tongue, my dearest dear,
  Let all your follies abee ;
I'll show where the white lilies grow,
  In the bottom of the sea ! "

He's taken her by the milk-white hand,
  And he's thrown her in the main ;
And full five-and-twenty hundred ships
  Sank all on the coast of Spain.

The Mermaid

On Friday morn as we set sail,
  It was not far from land,
O, there I spy'd a fair pretty maid,
  With a comb and a glass in her hand.
      The stormy winds did blow,
      And the raging seas did roar,
     While we poor sailors went to the top,
      And the land-lubbers laid below.

Then up spoke a boy of our gallant ship,
  And a well-speaking boy was he,
" I've a father and a mother in Portsmouth town,
  And this night they weep for me."
    The stormy, etc.

Then up spoke a man of our gallant ship,
  And a well speaking man was he,
" I married a wife in fair London town,
  And this night she a widow will be."
    The stormy, etc.

Then up spoke the Captain of our gallant ship,
  And a valiant man was he,
" For want of a boat we shall be drown'd,
  For she sunk to the bottom of the sea."
    The stormy, etc.

The moon shone bright, and the stars gave light,
  And my mother was looking for me,
She might look and weep with watery eyes,
  She might look to the bottom of the sea.
    The stormy, etc.

Three times round went our gallant ship,
  And three times round went she,
Three times round went our gallant ship,
  Then she sunk to the bottom of the sea.
    The stormy, etc.

POEMS OF LOVE AND THE AFFECTIONS

The Lass of Lochroyan

" O WHO will shoe my bonny foot ?
  And who will glove my hand ?
And who will bind my middle jimp,
  With a lang lang linen band ?

O who will comb my yellow hair,
  With a haw bay berry comb ?
And who will be my babe's father,
  Till Gregory come home ? "

" Thy father, he will shoe thy foot,
  Thy brother will glove thy hand,
Thy mother will bind thy middle jimp,
  With a long long linen band !

Thy sister will comb thy yellow hair,
  With a haw bay berry comb ;
The Almighty will be thy babe's father
  Till Gregory come home."

" And who will build a bonny ship,
  And set it on the sea ?
For I will go to seek my love,
  My own love Gregory."

Up then spake her father dear,
  A woeful man was he ;

THE LASS OF LOCHROYAN

" And I will build a bonny ship,
  And set her on the sea.

And I will build a bonny ship,
  And set her on the sea,
And ye shall go and seek your love,
  Your own love Gregory."

Then he's gar'd build a bonny ship,
  And set her on the sea,
With four-and-twenty mariners
  To bear her company.

O he's gar'd build a bonny ship
  To sail on the salt sea ;
The masts were of the good red gold,
  The sails of cramoisie.

O he's gar'd build a bonny ship,
  'Was fair with the pearl-shell ;
At every needle-tack was in't,
  There hung a silver bell.

Her sides were of the good stout oak,
  The deck of mountain pine,
The anchor of the silver sheen,
  The ropes of silken twine.

She had not sailed but twenty leagues
  But twenty leagues and three,
When she met with a rank rover,
  And all his company.

" Now are ye Queen of Heaven high,
  Come to pardon all our sin ?

Or are ye Mary Magdalene,
   Was born at Bethlehem ? "

" I'm not the Queen of Heaven high,
   Come to pardon ye your sin,
Nor am I Mary Magdalene,
   Was born in Bethlehem.

But I'm the lass of Lochroyan,
   That's sailing on the sea,
To see if I can find my love,
   My own love Gregory."

" O, see not ye yon bonny bower ?
   It's all covered o'er with tin ;
When thou hast sailed it round about
   Lord Gregory is within."

And when she saw the stately tower,
   Shining both clear and bright,
Which stood above the jawing wave,
   Built on a rock of height.

Says, " Row the boat, my mariners,
   And bring me to the land,
For yonder I see my love's castle,
   Close by the salt sea strand."

She sailed it round, and sailed it round,
   And loud and loud cried she,
" Now break, now break your fairy charms,
   And set my true-love free."

She's ta'en her young son in her arms,
   And to the door she's gone,

THE LASS OF LOCHROYAN

And long she knocked, and sore she called,
  But answer got she none

" O, open, open, Gregory !
  O, open, if ye be within ;
For here's the lass of Lochroyan,
  Come far from kith and kin.

O, open the door, Lord Gregory !
  O, open and let me in !
The wind blows loud and cold, Gregory,
  The rain drops from my chin.

The shoe is frozen to my foot,
  The glove unto my hand,
The wet drops from my yellow hair,
  No longer can I stand."

O, up then spake his ill mother,
  An ill-death may she die,
" Ye're no the lass of Lochroyan,
  She's far out o'er the sea.

Away, away, ye ill woman,
  Ye're not come here for good ;
Ye're but some witch or wild warlock,
  Or mermaid of the flood."

" I am neither witch nor wild warlock,
  Nor mermaid of the sea ;
But I am Annie of Lochroyan,
  O, open the door to me."

" If ye be Annie of Lochroyan,
  As I trow thou be not she,

Now tell me of some love-tokens
  That past 'tween thee and me."

O, dinna ye mind, love Gregory,
  As we sat at the wine,
We changed the rings from our fingers ?
  And I can show thee thine.

O yours was good and good enough,
  But ay the best was mine,
For yours was of the good red gold,
  But mine of the diamond fine.

Yours was of the good red gold,
  Mine of the diamond fine ;
Mine was of the purest troth,
  But thine was false within.

" If ye be the lass of Lochroyan,
  As I know not thou be,
Tell me some more of the love-tokens
  Past between thee and me."

" O do not ye mind, love Gregory,
  As we sat on the hill,
Thou twined me of my maidenhead,
  Right sore against my will ?

Now open the door, love Gregory,
  Open the door, I pray ;
For thy young son is in my arms,
  And will be dead ere day."

" Ye lie, ye lie, ye ill woman,
  So loud I hear ye lie ;
For Annie of the Lochroyan
  Is far out o'er the sea."

THE LASS OF LOCHROYAN

Fair Annie turned her round about :
  Well, since that it be so,
May never a woman that has borne a son
  Have a heart so full of woe.

Take down, take down, that mast of gold,
  Set up a mast of tree ;
It does not become a forsaken lady
  To sail so royally.

When the cock had crawn, and the day did dawn,
  And the sun began to peep,
Up then rose Lord Gregory,
  And sore, sore did he weep.

" O I have dreamed a dream, mother,
  I wish it may bring good—
That the bonny lass of Lochroyan
  At my bower-window stood.

O I have dreamed a dream, mother,
  The thought o't gars me greet,
That fair Annie of Lochroyan
  Lay dead at my bed feet."

" If it be for Annie of Lochroyan
  That you make all this moan,
She stood last night at your bower-door,
  But I have sent her home."

" O woe betide ye, ill woman,
  An ill death may ye die,
That would not open the door yourself,
  Nor yet would waken me."

O he's gone down to yon shoreside,
  As fast as he could dree,

And there he saw fair Annie's bark
　A-rowing o'er the sea.

" O Annie, Annie," loud he cried,
　" O Annie, O Annie, bide,"
But ay the more he cried Annie,
　The braider grew the tide.

" O Annie, Annie, dear Annie,
　Dear Annie, speak to me."
But ay the louder he gan call,
　The louder roared the sea.

The wind blew loud, the waves rose high,
　And dashed the boat on shore ;
Fair Annie's corpse was in the foam,
　The babe rose never more.

Lord Gregory tore his golden locks,
　And made a woeful moan ;
Fair Annie's corpse lay at his feet,
　His bonny son was gone.

" O cherry, cherry was her cheek,
　And golden was her hair,
And coral, coral were her lips,
　None might with her compare."

Then first he kissed her pale, pale cheek,
　And syne he kissed her chin,
And syne he kissed her wan, wan lips,
　There was no breath therein.

" O woe betide my ill mother,
　An ill death may she die,
She turned my true love from my door,
　Who came so far to me.

O woe betide my ill mother,
　An ill death may she die,
She has not been the death of one,
　She has been the death of three."

Then he's taken out a little dart,
　Hung low down by his gore,
He thrust it through and through his heart
　And words spake never more.

The Seaman's Happy Return

WHEN Sol did cast no light,
　Being darkened over,
And the dark time of night
　Did the skies cover.
Running a river by,
　There were ships sailing,
A maid most fair I spied,
　Crying and wailing.

Unto this maid I stept,
　Asking what grieved her,
She answered me and wept,
　Fates had deceived her:
" My love is prest," quoth she,
　" To cross the ocean,
Proud waves do make the ship
　Ever in motion.

We lov'd seven years and more,
　Both being sure,
But I am left on shore,
　Grief to endure.

He promised back to turn,
  If life was spared him,
With grief I daily mourn,
  Death hath debarred him."

Straight a brisk lad she spied,
  'Made her admire,
A present she received
  Pleased her desire.
" Is my love safe," quoth she,
  " Will he come near me ? "
The young man answer made,
  " Virgin, pray hear me :

Under one banner bright,
  For England's glory,
Your love and I did fight—
  Mark well my story :
By an unhappy shot
  We two were parted ;
His death's wound then he got
  Though valiant-hearted.

All this I witness can,
  For I stood by him,
For courage, I must say,
  None did outvie him :
He still would foremost be,
  Striving for honour ;
But Fortune is a whore,—
  Vengeance upon her.

But ere he was quite dead,
  Or his heart broken,
To me these words he said.
  ' Pray give this token

To my love, for there is
   Than she no fairer ;
Tell her she must be kind
   And love the bearer.'

Entombed he now doth lie,
   In stately manner,
'Cause he fought valiantly
   For love and honour.
The right he had in you,
   To me he gave it :
Now, since it is my due,
   Pray let me have it."

She, raging, fled away,
   Like one distracted,
Not knowing what to say,
   Nor what she acted.
So last she curst her fate,
   And showed her anger,
Saying, " Friend, you come too late,
   I'll have no stranger.

To your own house return,
   I am best pleased,
Here for my love to mourn,
   Since he's deceased.
In sable weeds I'll go,
   Let who will jeer me ;
Since Death has served me so,
   None shall come near me.

The chaste Penelope
   Mourned for Ulysses,

I have more grief than she,
  Robbed of my blisses.
I'll ne'er love man again,
  Therefore, pray hear me ;
I'll slight you with disdain
  If you come near me.

I know he loved me well,
  For when we parted,
None did in grief excel,—
  Both were true-hearted.
Those promises we made
  Ne'er shall be broken ;
Those words that then he said
  Ne'er shall be spoken."

He, hearing what she said,
  Made his love stronger,
Off his disguise he laid,
  And staid no longer.
When her dear love she knew,
  In wanton fashion
Into his arms she flew,—
  Such is love's passion.

He asked her how she liked
  His counterfeiting,
Whether she was well-pleased
  With such like greeting ?
" You are well versed," quoth she,
  " In several speeches ;
Could you coin money so,
  You might get riches."

O happy gale of wind
  That waft thee over,

May heaven preserve that ship
  That brought my lover.
"Come kiss me now, my sweet,
  True love's no slander;
Thou shalt my Hero be,
  I thy Leander.

Dido of Carthage queen
  Loved stout Eneas,
But my true love is found
  More true than he was.
Venus ne'er fonder was
  Of young Adonis,
Than I will be of thee,
  Since thy love her own is."

Then hand in hand they walk,
  With mirth and pleasure,
They laugh, they kiss, they talk—
  Love knows no measure.
Now both do sit and sing—
  But she sings clearest;
Like nightingale in Spring,
  Welcome my dearest.

An Admirable new Northern Story of Two Constant Lovers

(To the tune of " I would thou wert for Shrewsbury")

Two lovers in the north,
  Constance and Anthony,
Of them I will set forth
  A gallant history:

They loved exceeding well,
As plainly doth appear,
But that which I shall tell,
The like you ne'er did hear.
> Still she cries, *Anthony,*
> *My bonny Anthony,*
> *Gang thou by land or sea,*
> *I'll wend along with thee.*

Anthony must to sea,
His calling did him bind,
" My Constance dear," quoth he,
" I must leave thee behind :
I pr'y thee do not grieve,
Thy tears will not prevail ;
I'll think on thee, my sweet,
When the ship's under sail."
> But still she cries, *Anthony,*
> *My bonny Anthony, etc.*

" How may that be ? " said he,
" Consider well the case."
Quoth she, " Sweet Anthony,
I'll bide not in this place.
If thou gang, so will I,
Of the means do not doubt :
A woman's policy
Great matters may find out."
> Still she cries, *Anthony,*
> *My bonny Anthony, etc.*

" I would be very glad,
But pr'y thee tell me how ? "
" I'll dress me like a lad,
What say'st thou to me now ? "

TWO CONSTANT LOVERS

"The sea thou canst not brook."
"Yes, very well," quoth she,
"I'll scullion to the cook
For thy sweet company."
    Still she cries, Anthony,
    My bonny Anthony, etc.

Anthony's leave she had,
And dressed in man's array,
She seemed the blithest lad
Seen on a summer's day.
O see what Love can do,
At home she will not bide;
With her true love she'll go,
Let weal or woe betide.
    Still she cries, Anthony,
    My bonny Anthony, etc.

In the ship it was her lot
To be the Under-Cook;
And at the fire hot
Wonderful pains she took.
She served everyone
Fitting to their degree;
And now and then alone,
She kissed Anthony.
    Still she cries, Anthony,
    My bonny Anthony,
    Gang thou by land or sea,
    I'll wend along with thee.

THE SECOND PART

Alack and welladay!
In tempest on the Main,
Their ship was cast away
Upon the coast of Spain;

To the mercy of the waves,
They all committed were,
Constance herself she saves,
Then she cries for her dear.
> *My bonny Anthony,*
> *My bonny Anthony,*
> *Gang thou by land or sea,*
> *I'll wend along with thee.*

Swimming upon a plank,
At Bilboa she got ashore,
First she did Heaven thank,
Then she lamented sore.
" O woe is me," said she,
" The saddest lass alive,
My dearest Anthony,
Now on the sea doth drive."
> *My bonny Anthony,*
> *My bonny Anthony, etc.*

" What shall become of me ?
Why do I strive for shore ?
Sith my sweet Anthony,
I never shall see more ? "
Fair Constance, do not grieve,
The same good Providence
Hath saved thy lover sweet,
But he is far from hence.
> Still she cries, *Anthony,*
> *My bonny Anthony, etc*

A Spanish merchant rich,
Saw this fair-seeming lad,
That did lament so much,
And was so grievous sad.

TWO CONSTANT LOVERS

He had in England been,
And English understood,
He having heard and seen,
He in amazement stood.
    Still she cries, *Anthony*,
    My bonny Anthony, etc.

The Merchant asked her
What was that Anthony :
Quoth she, " My brother, sir,
Who came from thence with me.
He did her entertain,
Thinking she was a boy,
Two years she did remain.
Before she met her joy.
    Still she cries, *Anthony*,
    My bonny Anthony, etc.

Anthony up was ta'en
By an English renegade,
With whom he did remain
At the sea-roving trade :
In the nature of a slave
He did in the galley row,
Thus he his life did save,
But Constance did not know :
    Still she cries, *Anthony*,
    My bonny Anthony, etc.

Now mark what came to pass !
See how the Fates did work !
A ship that her Master's was,
Surprized this English Turk,
And to Bilboa brought
All that aboard her were ;

Constance full little thought
Anthony was so near.
    Still she cries, *Anthony,*
    My bonny Anthony, etc.

When they were come ashore,
Anthony and the rest,
She who was sad before,
Was now with joy possessed;
The merchant much did muse
At this so sudden change,
He did demand the news,
Which unto him was strange.
    Still she cries, *Anthony,*
    My bonny Anthony, etc.

Upon her knees she fell
Unto her master kind,
And all the truth did tell,
Nothing she kept behind:
At which he did admire,
And in the ship of Spain
Not paying for their hire,
He sent them home again.
    Now she cries, *Anthony,*
    My bonny Anthony, etc.

The Spanish merchant rich
Did of his bounty give
A sum of gold, on which
They now most bravely live.
They were joined hand in hand,
Constance and Anthony,
And now in Westmoreland,
They live in mirth and glee.

> Now she says, *Anthony,*
> *My bonny Anthony,*
> *God's Providence we see,*
> *Hath guarded thee and me.*

From "The Tragedy of Dido"

Aeneas. So much have I received at Dido's hands,
As, without blushing, I can ask no more:
Yet, Queen of Affrick, are my ships unrigged,
My sails all rent in sunder with the wind,
My oars broken, and my tackling lost,
Yea, all my navy split with rocks and shelves:
Nor stern, nor anchor, have our maimed fleet;
Our masts the furious winds strook overboard
Which piteous wants, if Dido will supply,
We will account her author of our lives.

Dido. Aeneas, I'll repair thy Trojan ships,
Conditionally that thou wilt stay with me,
And let Achates sail to Italy:
I'll give thee tackling made of rivelled gold,
Wound on the barks of odoriferous trees,
Oars of massy ivory, full of holes,
Through which the water shall delight to play:
Thy anchors shall be hewed from crystal rocks,
Which, if thou lose, shall shine above the waves
The masts, whereon thy swelling sails shall hang
Hollow pyramides of silver plate:
The sails of folded lawn, where shall be wrought
The wars of Troy, but not Troy's overthrow:
For ballast, empty Dido's treasury;
Take what ye will, but leave Aeneas here.
Meantime Achates thou shalt be so clad,

As seaborn Nymphs shall swarm about thy ships,
And wanton mermaids court thee with sweet songs.
    THOMAS NASHE AND CHRISTOPHER MARLOWE

Stephano's Song

THE master, the swabber, the boatswain and I,
    The gunner and his mate,
Loved Mall, and Meg, and Marian, and Margery,
    But none of us cared for Kate :
    For she had a tongue with a tang,
    Would cry to a sailor, *Go hang :*
She loved not the savour of tar nor of pitch,
Yet a tailor might scratch her where'er she did itch:
    Then to sea, boys, and let her go hang.
               WILLIAM SHAKESPEARE
                  (From "The Tempest ")

The Lowlands of Holland

" My love has built a bonny ship, and set her on the sea,
With seven score good mariners to bear her company ;
There's three score is sunk, and three score dead at sea,
And the Lowlands of Holland have twin'd my love and me.

My love he built another ship, and set her on the main,
And none but twenty mariners for to bring her hame ;

But the weary wind began to rise, and the seas
 began to rout,
My love then and his bonny ship turned withershins
 about.

There shall neither coif come on my head, nor
 comb come in my hair,
There shall neither coal nor candle light shine in
 my chamber mair;
Nor will I love another one until the day I dee,
For I never loved a love but one, and he's drowned
 in the sea."

" O hold your tongue, my daughter dear, be still
 and be content,
There are more lads in Galloway, ye need not so
 lament."
" O there is none in Galloway, there's none at all
 for me,
For I never loved a love but one, and he's drowned
 in the sea."

The Maydens of London's Brave Adventures

(To the tune of " A Taylor is a Man ")

COME all you very merry London girls, that are
 disposed to travel,
There is a voyage now at hand will save your feet
 from gravel.
If you have shoes you need not fear for wearing
 out the leather;
For why, you shall on shipboard go, like loving
 rogues together.

> *Some are already gone before, the rest must
> after follow,*
> *Then come away, and do not stay, your guide
> will be Apollo.*

Peg, Nell, and Sis, Kate, Doll, and Bess, Sue,
Rachel, and sweet Sara,
Joan, Prue, and Grace have took their place, with
Deborah, Jane, and Mary,
Fair Winifred, and Bridget bright, sweet Rose
and pretty Nanny,
With Ursula neat and Alice complete that had the
love of many.
> *All these brave girls, and others more,
> conducted by Apollo,*
> *Have ta'en their leaves and are gone before,
> and their Loves will after follow.*

Then why should those that are behind slink back
and dare not venture?
For you shall prove the seamen kind, if once the
ships you enter.
You shall be fed with good strong fare, according
to the season,
Biscuit, salt beef, and English beer, and pork well
boiled with peason.
> *And since that some are gone before, the rest
> with joy may follow,*
> *To bear each other company, conducted by
> Apollo.*

When you come to the appointed place, your minds
you need not trouble,
For every groat that you got here, you shall have
three times double.

For there are gold and silver mines and treasures
    much abounding,
As plenty as Newcastle coals, at some parts may
    be found in.
> *Then come away, make no delay, all you that*
>   *mean to follow ;*
> *The ships are ready bound to go, conducted*
>   *by Apollo.*

The Gallant Seaman's Resolution

(To the tune of "Think on thy Loving Landlady;")

A GALLANT youth at Gravesend lived, a seaman
    neither rich nor poor ;
But when his means were almost spent, he bravely
    went to sea for more.
> *Turn to thy love, and take a kiss, this gold*
>   *about thy wrist I'll tie,*
> *And always when thou look'st on this,*
> *Think on thy loving Landlady.*

His father being dead and gone, he loved his
    mother as his life,
And did maintain her gallantly, it was well known
    he had no wife.
> *Turn to thy love, etc.*

He was beloved of rich and poor, and still kept
    company with the best.
A gallant widow in the town her love unto him
    thus exprest ;
> *Turn to thy love, etc.*

Young man, could I thy favour win, or might thy
    company but crave,
To come and live at home with me, I'd make thee
    Lord of all I have.
> *Turn to thy love, etc.*

Fair Mistress, I am for the seas, here's gold and
    silver in my hand,
And when the drums and trumpets sound, I'll bid
    adieu to fair England.
> *And if thou wilt with patience stay,*
> *Till I from sea return again,*
> *For every kiss thou lendest me*
> *I will repay thee ten times ten.*

Do but resolve to stay at home, I'll put another in
    thy place.
No, that will be a shame, quoth he, and to my
    name a foul disgrace.
> *Turn to thy love, etc.*

I have five hundred pounds, at least, of silver which
    I never told,
Besides, I have in store for thee five hundred
    pounds in good red gold.
> *Turn to thy love, etc.*

If you could give me all the wealth that ever
    Europe did afford,
A faithful promise I have made, and I will not be
    worse than my word.
> *And if thou wilt with patience stay, etc.*

If neither strength nor policy can further me in
    my design,

THE GALLANT SEAMAN'S RESOLUTION

Remain a constant friend to me, and I for ever
  will be thine.
  Turn to thy love, etc.

And whilst that breath and life doth last, to me
  this thing I'll verify,
Though you at sea, and I on shore, I'll pray for
  thy prosperity.
  Turn to thy love, etc.

Heaven bless the ship thou sailest in, whether it
  swim with wind or tide,
And all that with thee comes or goes, I hope that
  Netpune will them guide.
  Turn to thy love, etc.

From pirates, blows, and bloody knocks, I pray
  great Mars protect thee still,
Nor may quick-sands or stony rocks have power
  to do thee any ill.
  Turn to thy love, etc.

And whilst thou art in foreign parts, in Holland,
  Flanders, France, or Spain,
As thou in safety didst launch forth, God bring
  thee safely home again.
  Turn to thy love, etc.

If I may speak without offence, my heart will
  never quiet be,
Till thou give me full recompense, and sayst that
  I thy wife shall be.
  Turn to thy love, etc.

Yet one thing here I beg of thee, before from me
 thou dost depart,
That thou wilt let no woman know the thoughts
 and secrets of thy heart.
> *Turn to thy love, etc.*

When thou art gone out of my sight, and com'st
 where pretty lasses are,
Thou'll fall in love with some of them; that is
 the thing I most do fear.
> *Turn to thy love, etc.*

If I should hear, in any case, that thou abroad
 should married be,
Then would I weep, lament and grieve, and break
 my heart for love of Thee.
> *Turn to thy love and take a kiss*
> *This gold about thy wrist I'll tie,*
> *And always when thou look'st on this,*
> *Think on thy loving landlady.*

The Seaman's Reply

HARK, hark, I hear the trumpet sound; it calleth
 me to come away,
Therefore in haste I must be gone, I can, nor will,
 no longer stay.
> *And if thou wilt in patience stay,*
> *Till I from sea return again,*
> *For every kiss thou lendest me*
> *I will repay thee ten times ten.*

Therefore sweet lady, now farewell, more than a
 thousand times adieu,

Where'er I pass, by land or sea, I'll still be faithful unto you.
> *And if thou wilt, etc.*

This golden ribbon which you tied about my wrist-band in pure love,
Shall be a token whilst I live, that I to you will constant prove.
> *And if thou wilt, etc.*

And when that I return again, if God affords me breath and life,
You that are now my landlady, shall then be made my wedded wife.
> *And if thou wilt, etc.*

The bells shall ring melodiously, the music shall most sweetly play,
And all our friends will then rejoice to see our happy wedding-day.
> *And if thou wilt with patience stay,*
> *Till I from sea return again,*
> *For every kiss thou lendest me*
> *I will return thee ten times ten.*

The Gallant Seaman's Return from the Indies

Observe this song, which is both neat and pretty,
'Tis on a seaman in his praise of Betty.

(To the tune of " Five Sail of Frigots," or " Shrewsbury for Me ")

I AM a stout seaman, and newly come on shore,
I have been a long voyage, where I never was before;

But now I am returned, I am resolved to see
My own dearest honey, whose name is Betty.

I have been absent from her full many a day,
But yet I was constant in every way;
Though many a beautiful dame I did see,
Yet none pleased me so well as Betty.

Now I am intended, whatever betide,
For to go and see her and make her my bride;
If that she and I can together agree,
I never will love none but pretty Betty.

The Gallant Seaman's Song at His Meeting of Betty

WELL met, pretty Betty, my joy and my dear,
I now am returned thy heart for to cheer;
Though long I have been absent, yet I thought on thee,
O my heart it was always with pretty Betty.

Then come, my own dearest, to tavern let's go,
Whereas we'll be merry for an hour or two;
Lovingly together we both will agree,
And I'll drink a good health to my pretty Betty.

I will kiss thee and hug thee all night in my arms,
I'll be careful of thee and keep thee from harms,
I will love thee dearly in every degree,
For my heart it is fixed on pretty Betty.

For thee I will rove and sail far and near,
The dangerous rough sea shall not put me in fear;

If I do get treasure I'll bring it to thee,
And I'll venture my life for my pretty Betty.

And more than all this, I can tell thee, my dear,
I will bring thee home some rich jewels to wear,
And many new fashions, I will provide thee,
So that none shall compare with pretty Betty.

Then come, my own dearest, and grant me thy love,
Both loyal and constant to thee I will prove ;
If that thou wilt put trust and belief in me,
I vow ne'er to love none but pretty Betty.

A Sailor

A SAILOR is blythe and bonny O,
His lips are sweet as honey O,
  O how happy am I,
  When my sailor is by,
And sings love-songs to his Molly O.

A sailor is full of bravery O
He knows not of rogues or knavery O ;
  When his prince doth him call,
  He mans the wooden wall,
That defends us from Popery and slavery O.

When my sailor goes to sea, and leaves me O,
Alas ! how it frets and grieves me O ;
  But when he doth come home,
  There's an end of all my moan,
For kisses from his lips do please me O.

Who would not be a sailor's lassy O,
Rather than a meagre lady O ;

He sails from east to west,
　　And brings home the best
Of jewels and silks to his deary O.

A soldier brags of his bravery O,
And says when he's by we're in safety O,
　　But the riches of Peru,
　　And the gold of Ophir, too.
Are brought by the sailor to his country O.

The wine that revives our spirits O (?)
We have by the sailor's merits O ;
　　How can they have chagrin
　　Or be troubled by the spleen,
That such blessings do inherit O.

O praise ye the jovial sailor O,
No red-coat, tinker, or tailor O,
　　Can e'er with him compare,
　　For liveliness and air,
And all we enjoy's through his labour O.

Now I must conclude my ditty O,
For want of words, it's a pity O,
　　But all your voices raise,
　　To sound a sailor's praise,
In country, town, and city O.

To All You Ladies

Song written at sea, in the first Dutch war, 1665, the night before an engagement.

To all you ladies now at land
　　We men at sea indite ;
But first would have you understand
　　How hard it is to write :

TO ALL YOU LADIES

The Muses now, and Neptune too,
We must implore to write to you,
   With a fa, la, la, la, la.

For though the Muses should prove kind,
   And fill our empty brain ;
Yet if rough Neptune rouse the wind,
   To wave the azure main :
Our paper, pen, and ink, and we,
Roll up and down our ships at sea.
   With a fa, etc.

Then, if we write not by each post,
   Think not we are unkind ;
Nor yet conclude our ships are lost
   By Dutchmen, or by wind :
Our tears we'll send a speedier way,
The tide shall bring 'em twice a day.
   With a fa, etc.

The king with wonder and surprise
   Will swear the seas grow bold ;
Because the tides will higher rise,
   Than e'er they used of old :
But let him know it is our tears
Bring floods of grief to Whitehall-stairs.
   With a fa, etc.

Should foggy Opdam chance to know
   Our sad and dismal story ;
The Dutch would scorn so weak a foe,
   And quit their fort at Goree ;
For what resistance can they find
From men who've left their hearts behind ?
   With a fa, etc.

Let wind and weather do its worst,
  Be you to us but kind ;
Let Dutchmen vapour, Spaniards curse,
  No sorrow we shall find ;
'Tis then no matter how things go,
Or who's our friend, or who's our foe.
    With a fa, etc.

To pass our tedious hours away,
  We throw a merry main ;
Or else at serious ombre play ;
  But why should we in vain
Each other's ruin thus pursue ?
We were undone when we left you.
    With a fa, etc.

But now our fears tempestuous grow,
  And cast our hopes away,
Whilst you, regardless of our woe,
  Sit careless at a play :
Perhaps permit some happier man
To kiss your hand, or flirt your fan.
    With a fa, etc.

When any mournful tune you hear,
  That dies in ev'ry note,
As if it sighed with each man's care,
  For being so remote ;
Think then how often love we've made
To you when all those tunes were play'd
    With a fa, etc.

In justice, you can not refuse,
  To think of our distress,
When we for hopes of honour lose
  Our certain happiness ;

All those designs are but to prove
Ourselves more worthy of your love.
    With a fa, etc.

And now we've told you all our loves,
    And likewise all our fears;
In hopes this declaration moves
    Some pity for our tears;
Let's hear of no inconstancy,
We have too much of that at sea.
    With a fa, la, la, la, la.
    CHARLES SACKVILLE EARL OF DORSET

The Seaman's Compass

A dainty new ditty composed and penned,
The deeds of brave seamen to praise and commend:
'Twas made by a Maid that to Gravesend did pass,
Now mark, and you quickly shall hear how it was.

(To the tune of " The Tyrant hath Stolen ")

As lately I travelled
Towards Gravesend,
I heard a fair Damsel
A Seaman commend;
And as in a tilt-boat
We passed along,
In praise of brave Seamen
She sung this new song:
Come Tradesman or Merchant,
Whoever he be,
    There's none but a Seaman
    Shall marry with me.

A seaman in promise
Is faithful and just,
Honest in carriage
And true to his trust:
Kind in behaviour
And constant in love,
Is firm in affection
As the turtle dove:
Valiant in action
In every degree.
 *O, none but a sailor
 Shall marry with me.*

The seamen adventure
Their lives on the seas,
Whilst landmen on shore
Take pleasure and ease;
The seamen at all times
Their business must ply,
In winter and summer,
In wet and in dry.
From toil and pains-taking
They seldom are free,
 *And none but a sailor
 Shall marry with me.*

Moreover, I'd have you
For to understand,
That seamen bring treasure
And profit to land;
Above and beneath ground
For wealth they have sought;
And when they have found it,
To England 'tis brought,

With hazard of lives,
By experience we see :
> *There's none but a sailor*
> *Shall marry with me.*

Seamen from beyond the seas
Bring silver and gold,
With pearls and rich jewels,
Most rare to behold ;
With silks and rich velvets,
Their credits to save,
Or else you gay ladies
Could not go so brave.
This makes my heart merry
As merry may be,
> *There's none but a seaman*
> *Shall marry with me.*

The seamen bring spices,
And sugar so fine,
Which serve the brave gallants
To drink with their wine,
With lemons and oranges
All of the best,
To relish their palates
When they make a feast ;
Sweet figs, prunes, and raisins,
By them brought home be.
> *There's none but a seaman*
> *Shall marry with me.*

To comfort poor people
The seamen do strive,
They bring in maintenance
To keep them alive,

As raw silk and cotton-wool
To card and to spin,
And so by their labours
Their livings come in :
Most men are beholding
To seamen we see.
> *And none but a seaman*
> *Shall marry with me.*

The mercer's beholding,
We know well enough,
For holland, lawn, cambric,
And other gay stuff,
That's brought from beyond seas
By seamen so bold,
The rarest that ever
Men's eyes did behold.
God prosper the seamen
Wherever they be.
> *There's none but a seaman*
> *Shall marry with me.*

The merchants themselves
Are beholding also
To honest seamen
That on purpose do go,
To bring them home profit
From other strange lands,
Or else their fine daughters
Must work with their hands,
The nobles and gentry
In every degree.
> *O, none but a sailor*
> *Shall marry with me.*

THE SEAMAN'S COMPAS

Thus for rich men and poor men
The seamen does good,
And sometimes comes off with
Loss of much blood:
If they were not a guard
And a defence for our land
Our enemies soon will get
The upper hand,
And then in a woeful case
Straight should we be.
> *There's none but a seaman*
> *Shall marry with me.*

To draw to conclusion
And so make an end,
I hope that great Neptune
My love will befriend,
And send him home safely
With health and with life,
Then shall I with joyfulness
Soon be his wife.
You maids, wives, and widows,
That seamen's loves be,
> *With hearts and with voices*
> *Join prayers with me.*

God bless all brave seamen
From quicksands and rocks,
From loss of their blood,
And from enemies' knocks,
From lightning and thunder,
And tempests so strong,
From shipwreck and drowning,
And all other wrong,

And they that to these words
Will not say amen,
   'Tis pity they should
   Ever speak word agen.

A Young Man's Fancy

ALL the sheets are clacking, all the blocks are whining,
The sails are frozen stiff, and the wetted decks are shining,
The reef's in the topsails, and it's coming on to blow,
And I think of the dear love I left long ago.

Grey were her eyes, and her hair was long and bonny,
Golden was her hair, like the wild bee's honey,
And I was but a dog, and a mad one, to despise
The gold of her hair and the grey of her eyes.

There's the sea before me, and my home behind me,
And beyond there the lands where nobody will mind me,
No one but the girls with the paint upon their cheeks,
Who sell away their beauty to whomsoever seeks.

There'll be drink and women there, and songs and laughter;
Peace from what is past, and from all that follows after;
And a fellow will forget how a woman lies awake
Lonely in the night-watch crying for his sake.

Black it blows, and bad, and it howls like slaughter,
And the ship she shudders as she takes the water,
Hissing flies the spindrift, like a wind-blown smoke,
And I think of a woman, and a heart I broke.

R. E. McGOWAN

The Fair Maid's Choice or the Seaman's Renown

BEING a pleasant song made of a sailor,
Who excels a soldier, miller, and a tailor,
Likewise brave gallants that go fine and rare,
None of them with a seaman can compare.

As lately I journeyed through Winchelsea town,
I spied a gallant lady in a brave golden gown;
Like a thrush upon a thornbush so sweetly sang she
O, of all sorts of tradesmen a sailor for me.

Of all sorts of gallants so gaudy and fine,
That with gold lace and silver so bravely do shine,
The seaman doth pass them in every degree,
And of all sorts of tradesmen a sailor for me.

For a seaman will venture his life and his blood,
For the sake of his King and his countrie's good;
He is valiant and gallant in every degree,
So of all sorts of tradesmen a sailor for me.

He ventures for traffic upon the salt seas,
To pleasure our gentry who live at their ease,
Through dangerous places right gaily goes he,
So of all sorts of tradesmen a sailor for me.

Amongst all your tradesmen and merchants so
   brave,
I can't set my fancy one of them to have ;
A seaman from Bristol my husband shall be,
For of all sorts of tradesmen a sailor for me.

With a scarlet coat soldier in a bold bandoleer,
Who fires a great musket for crusts and small beer,
With all such fierce firebloods I could not agree,
So of all sorts of tradesmen a sailor for me.

With a dusty-cap miller I will never deal,
For out of a bushel a peck he will steal ;
I will have no society with rogues such as he,
But of all sorts of tradesmen a sailor for me.

Also the carpenter and the shoemaker,
The blacksmith, the brewer, and likewise the baker,
Some of them use knavery, and some honesty,
But of all sorts of tradesmen a sailor for me.

For I love a seaman as I love my life,
And I am resolved to be a seaman's wife,
No man else in England my husband shall be,
For of all sorts of tradesmen a sailor for me.

Now I'll tell you why I love a seaman so dear,
I have to my sweetheart a seaman most rare,
He is a stout proper lad, as you shall see,
And of all sorts of tradesmen a sailor for me.

If that I were worth a whole ship-load of gold,
My love should possess it, and with it make bold,
I would make him the master of every penny,
For of all sorts of tradesmen a sailor for me.

THE SAILOR LADDIE

Through fire and water I would go, I swear,
For the sake of my true love whom I love so dear,
If I might have an earl, I'd forsake him for he;
Then of all sorts of tradesmen a sailor for me.

Here's a health to my dear, come pledge me who please,
To all gallant seamen that sail on the seas.
Pray God bless and keep them from all dangers free,
So of all sorts of tradesmen a sailor for me.

The Sailor Laddie

My love has been in London city,
My love has been at Port Mahon,
My love is away at Greenland,
I hope he will come back again.
  Oh! my bonny sailor laddie,
   Oh! my bonny sailor, he,
  Well I love my sailor laddie,
   Blythe and merry may he be.

Greenland altho' it is no City,
Yet it is a bonny place,
Soon will he come back to England,
Then to court his bonny lass.
  Oh! my bonny, etc.

Fisher lads go the fishing,
Bonny lasses to the braes,
Fisher lads come home at even,
Tell how their fishing goes.
  Oh! my bonny, etc.

Sailor lads come home at even,
Casting off their tarry cloaths,
Calling for their own true lovers,
And telling how their trading goes.
    Oh! my bonny, etc.

Sailor lads has gold and silver,
Fisher lads has nought but brass,
Well I love my sailor laddie,
Because I am a sailor's lass.
    Oh! my bonny, etc.

Our noble Captain's gone to London,
Oh! preserve them from the press,
Send him safely back to Terry,
There to court his bonny lass.
    Oh! my bonny, etc.

How can I be blythe and merry,
And my true love so far from me,
When so many pretty sailors,
Are prest, and taken to the sea.
    Oh! my bonny, etc.

When my love, he was in Terry,
He came and saw me once a night;
But now he's prest to the *St. Ann's*,
And is kept quite out of my sight.
  Oh! my bonny, etc.

Oh! I wish the press was over,
And all the wars was at an end;
Then every bonny sailor laddie
Would be merry with his friend.
    Oh! my bonnie, etc.

THE SAILOR LADDIE

Here has been so much disturbance,
Our sailor lads dare not look out,
For to drink with their own lasses,
Or to have a single rout.
    Oh! my bonny, etc.

My love, he's a bonny laddie,
Blythe and merry may he be,
If the wars were at an end,
He would come and marry me.
    Oh! my bonny, etc.

Some delight in jolly farmers,
Some delight in soldiers free;
But my delight's in a sailor laddie,
Blythe and merry may he be.
    Oh! my bonny, etc.

Oh, I wish the war was over,
And peace and plenty come again,
Then every bonny sailor laddie,
Would come sailing o'er the main.
    Oh! my bonny, etc.

If the wars they were all over,
And all our sailors were come home,
Then every lass would get her laddie,
And every mother get her son.
    Oh! my bonny, etc.

Come you by the Buoy and Nore,
Or come you by the Roperie,
Saw you of my love sailing,
Oh, saw you him coming home to me.
    Oh! my bonny sailor laddie,
      Oh! my bonny sailor, he,
     Well I love my sailor laddie,
       And my sailor he loves me.

Song to Mary

The topsails shiver in the wind,
    The ship she casts to sea;
But yet my soul, my heart, my mind,
    Are, Mary, moored with thee:
For, though thy sailor's bound afar,
Still love shall be his leading star.

Should landsmen flatter when we're sailed,
    O doubt their artful tales;
No gallant sailor ever failed,
    If Cupid filled his sails:
Thou art the compass of my soul
Which steers my heart from pole to pole.

Sirens in every port we meet,
    More fell than rocks and waves;
But sailors of the British fleet,
    Are lovers, and not slaves,
No foes our courage shall subdue,
Although we've left our hearts with you.

These are our cares; but, if you're kind,
    We'll scorn the dashing main,
The rocks, the billows, and the wind,
    The powers of France and Spain.
Now Britain's glory rests with you,
Our sails are full—sweet girls adieu.
                    CAPTAIN THOMSON

The North Country Collier

At the head of Wear Water, about twelve at noon,
I heard a maid a-talking and this was her tune,

There are all sorts of callings, in every degree,
But of all sorts of callings a collier for me.

You may know a jolly collier as he walks on the street,
His clothing is so handsome, and so neat are his feet,
With teeth as white as ivory, and his eyes as black as sloes,
You may know a jolly collier wherever he goes.

You may know a jolly collier : he's a swaggering, young blade,
When he goes a-courting of his buxom fair maid,
With his lips he so flatters her, and spends his money free,
You may know a jolly collier wheresoever that he be.

You may know a jolly collier as he sails the salt sea ;
As he ploughs the wide ocean he sets his sails three,
The foresail for to lift her, and the mainsail to drive,
And the little pretty crojick for to make her steer wild.

I'll build my jolly collier a castle on a hill,
Where neither Duke nor Squire can work me any ill,
For the Queen can but enjoy the King, and I can do the same,
And I am but a sheep-girl, and who can me blame ?

The Bold Privateer

O, FARE you well, my Polly dear, since you and I must part,

In crossing of the seas, my love, I'll pledge to you
    my heart ;
For our ship she lies waiting, so fare you well, my
    dear,
For I just now am going aboard of a bold privateer.

She said, "My dearest Jemmy, I hope you will
    forbear,
And do not leave your Polly in grief and in
    despair ;
You'd better stay at home with the girl you love
    so dear,
Than venture on the seas your life in a bold privateer.

You know, my dearest Polly, your friends they do
    me slight ;
Besides, you have two brothers would take away
    my life ;
And from them I must wander, myself to get me
    clear,
So I am just now going aboard of a bold privateer.

And when the wars are over, if God does spare
    our lives,
We will return safe back again to our sweethearts
    and our wives,
And then I will get married to my charming Polly,
    dear,
And forever bid adieu to the bold privateer.

Tom Bowling

HERE, a sheer hulk, lies poor Tom Bowling,
    The darling of our crew ;

TOM BOWLING

No more he'll hear the tempest howling,
   For death has broached him to.
His form was of the manliest beauty,
   His heart was kind and soft,
Faithful, below, he did his duty ;
   But now he's gone aloft.

Tom never from his word departed,
   His virtues were so rare ;
His friends were many and true-hearted,
   His Poll was kind and fair :
And then he'd sing so blithe and jolly,
   Ah, many's the time and oft !
But mirth is turned to melancholy,
   For Tom is gone aloft.

Yet shall poor Tom find pleasant weather,
   When He, who all commands,
Shall give, to call life's crew together,
   The word to pipe all hands.
Thus Death, who kings and tars despatches,
   In vain Tom's life has doff'd,
For, though his body's under hatches,
   His soul has gone aloft.

CHARLES DIBDIN

POEMS OF PIRATES AND SMUGGLERS

John Dory

As it fell on a holy day,
  And upon a holy tide-a,
John Dory bought him an ambling nag
  To Paris for to ride-a.

And when John Dory to Paris was come
  A little before the gate-a ;
John Dory was fitted, the porter was witted,
  To let him in thereat-a.

The first man that John Dory did meet,
  Was good King John of France-a :
John Dory could well of his courtesy,
  But fell down in a trance-a.

A pardon, a pardon, my liege and king,
  For my merry men and me-a :
And all the churls in merry England
  I'll bring them bound to thee-a,

And Nichol was then a Cornish man,
  A little beside Bohyde-a ;
And he manned forth a good black bark,
  With fifty good oars on a side-a.

Run up, my boy, into the main-top,
  And look what thou canst spy-a ;

Who ho, who ho, a good ship I do see,
  I trow it be John Dory-a.

They hoist their sails, both top and top,
  The mizzen and all was tried-a;
And every man stood to his lot,
  Whatever should betide-a.

The roaring cannons then were plied,
  And dub-a-dub went the drum-a;
The braying trumpets loud they cried,
  To courage both all and some-a.

The grappling hooks were brought at length,
  The brown bill and the sword-a;
John Dory [1] at length, for all his strength,
  Was clapt fast under board-a.

Henry Martyn

THERE were three brothers in merry Scotland,
  In merry Scotland there were three,
And each of these brothers they did cast lots
  To see which should rob the salt sea.

Then this lot did fall on young Henry Martyn,
  The youngest of these brothers three,
So now he's turned robber on all the salt seas,
  To maintain his two brothers and he.

He had not sailed one long winter's night,
  One cold winter's night before day,
Before he espied a rich merchant-ship,
  Come bearing straight down that way.

[1] One Nicholas, son to a widow near Foy, . . . fought bravely at sea with one John Dory (a Genowey, as I conjecture), set forth by John, the French king, and, after much bloodshed, . . . took and slew him."—Carew, "Survey of Cornwall."

"Who are you ? Who are you ? " said Henry Martyn,
　" Or how durst thou come so nigh ? "
" I'm a rich merchant-ship for old England bound,
　If you please, will you let me pass by ? "

" O no ! O no ! " cried Henry Martyn,
　" O no, that can never be,
Since I have turned robber all on the salt seas,
　To maintain my two brothers and me.

Now lower your topsails, you alderman bold,
　Come lower them under my lee !
Seeing I am resolved to pirate you here,
　To maintain my two brothers and me."

Then broadside to broadside to battle they went,
　For more than two hours or three ;
At last Henry Martyn gave her a death wound,
　And down to the bottom went she.

Bad news, bad news, to England has come,
　Bad news I will tell to you all,
'Twas a rich merchant-ship to England was bound,
　And most of her merry men drowned.

A Ballad of Dansekar the Dutchman

A LATE FAMOUS PIRATE

SING we seamen now and then
　Of Dansekar the Dutchman
Whose gallant mind hath won him great renown ;
　To live on land he counts it base,
　But seeks to purchase greater grace
By roving on the ocean up and down.

A BALLAD OF DANSEKAR

His heart is so aspiring,
 That now his chief desiring
Is for to win himself a worthy name;
 The land hath far too little ground,
 The sea is of a larger bound,
And of a greater dignity and fame.

And many a worthy gallant,
 Of courage now most valiant,
With him hath put his fortunes to the sea;
 All the world about have heard
 Of Dansekar and English Ward,
And of their proud adventures every day.

There is not any Kingdom,
 In Turkey or in Christendom,
But by these pirates have received loss;
 Merchantmen of every land,
 Do daily in great danger stand,
And much do fear the ocean main to cross.

They make children fatherless,
 Woeful widows in distress,
In shedding blood they took too much delight;
 Fathers they bereave of sons,
 Regarding neither cries nor moans,
So much they joy to see a bloody fight.

They count it gallant bearing,
 To hear the cannons roaring,
And musket shot to rattle in the sky;
 Their glories would be at the highest,
 To fight against the foes of Christ,
And such as do our Christian faith deny.

But their cursed villainies,
And their bloody piracies,
Are chiefly bent against our Christian friends;
Since Christians so delight in evils,
That they become the sons of devils,
And for the same have many shameful ends.

England suffers danger,
As well as any stranger,
Nations are alike unto this company;
Many English merchantmen,
And of London now and then,
Have tasted of their vile extremity.

London's *Elizabeth*,
Of late these rovers taken have,
A ship well laden with rich merchandize;
The nimble *Pearl* and *Charity*,
All ships of gallant bravery,
Are by these pirates made a lawful prize.

The *Trojan* of London,
With other ships many a one,
Hath stooped sail and yielded out of hand,
These pirates, they have shed their bloods,
And the Turks have bought their goods,
Being all too weak their power to withstand.

Of Hull the *Bonaventure*,
Which was a great frequenter,
And passer of the Straits to Barbary;
Both ship and men late taken were,
By the pirates Ward and Dansekar,
And brought by them into captivity.

A FAMOUS SEA FIGHT

SECOND PART

English Ward and Dansekar,
  Begin greatly now to jar,
About dividing their goods ;
  Both ships and soldiers gather head,
  Dansekar from Ward is fled,
So full of pride and malice are their bloods.

Ward doth only promise
  To keep about rich Tunis,
And be commander of those Turkish seas ;
  But valiant Dutch-land Dansekar,
  Doth hover near unto Argier,
And there his threat'ning colours now displays.

These pirates thus divided,
  By God is soon provided,
In secret sort to work each other's woe ;
  Such wicked courses cannot stand,
  The devil thus puts in his hand,
And God will give them soon an overthrow.

A Famous Sea Fight between Captain Ward and the *Rainbow*

Strike up, you lusty gallants,
  With music and sound of drum,
For we have descried a Rover
  Upon the sea is come ;
His name is Captain Ward,
  Right well it doth appear,
There has not been such a Rover
  Found out this thousand year :

For he hath sent unto the King,
  The sixth of January,
Desiring that he might come in
  With all his company;
And if your King will let me come,
  Till I my tale have told,
I will bestow for my ransom,
  Full thirty ton of gold.

"O nay, O nay," then said our King,
  "O nay, this must not be,
To yield to such a Rover,
  Myself will not agree:
He hath deceived the Frenchman,
  Likewise the King of Spain,
And how can he be true to me,
  That hath been false to twain?"

With that our King provided
  A ship of worthy fame,
Rainbow is she called,
  If you would know her name:
Now the gallant *Rainbow*
  She rows upon the sea,
Five hundred gallant seamen
  To bear her company.

The Dutchman and the Spaniard,
  She made them for to fly,
Also the bonny Frenchman,
  As she met him on the sea.
When as this gallant *Rainbow*
  Did come where *Ward* did lie
"Where is the Captain of this ship?"
  This gallant *Rainbow* did cry.

"O, that am I," says Captain Ward,
  "There's no man bids me lie,
And if thou art the King's fair ship,
  Thou art welcome to me."
"I'll tell thee what," says *Rainbow*,
  "Our King is in great grief,
That thou shouldst lie upon the sea,
  And play the arrant thief.

And will not let our merchants' ships
  Pass as they did before;
Such tidings to our King is come,
  Which grieves his heart full sore."
With that, this gallant *Rainbow*
  She shot, out of her pride,
Full fifty gallant brass pieces
  Charged on every side.

And yet these gallant shooters
  Prevailed not a pin,
Though they were brass on the outside,
  Brave Ward was steel within :
"Shoot on, shoot on," says Captain Ward,
  "Your sport well pleaseth me,
And he that first gives over,
  Shall yield unto the sea.

I never wronged an English ship,
  But the Turk and King of Spain,
And the jovial Dutchman,
  As I met on the Main ;
If I had known your King,
  But one two years before,
I would have saved brave Essex' life,
  Whose death did grieve me sore.

Go tell the King of England,
  Go tell him thus from me,
If he reigns King of all the land,
  I will reign King at sea."
With that the gallant *Rainbow* shot,
  And shot and shot in vain,
And left the Rover's company
  And return'd home again.

" Our Royal King of England,
  Your ship's returned again,
For Ward's ship is so strong
  It never will be ta'en."
" O everlasting ! " says our King,
  " I have lost jewels three,
Which would have gone unto the seas,
  And brought proud Ward to me.

The first was Lord Clifford,
  The Earl of Cumberland ;
The second was Lord Mountjoy
  As you shall understand ;
The third was brave Essex
  From field would never flee,
Which would have gone unto the seas,
  And brought proud Ward to me."

As We Were A-Sailing

As we were a-sailing unto the Spanish shore,
Where the drums they did beat, boys, and the guns they did roar,
We spied our lofty enemies come spooming down the main,
Which caused us to hoist our topsails again.

There was a gallant damsel, a damsel of fame,
She was daughter of the Captain, and Nancy was
  her name,
She stood on the deck, and gallantly she calls,
" O stand to your guns, boys, and load with
  cannon-balls."

O broadside to broadside to battle then we went,
To sink one another it was our intent ;
The very second broadside our captain got slain,
And the damsel she stood up there his place to
  maintain.

We fought for a watch, for a watch so severe,
We scarcely had a man left was able for to steer ;
We scarcely had a man left could fire off a gun,
And the blood from our deck like a river it did run.

For quarter, for quarter, the Spanish lads did cry,
" No quarter, no quarter," this damsel did reply ;
" You've had the best of quarter that I can afford,
You must fight, sink, or swim, my boys, or jump
  overboard."

So now the battle's over, we'll drink a can of wine,
And you will drink to your love and I will drink
  to mine ;
Good health unto the damsel who fought upon the
  main,
And here's to the royal ship the *Rainbow* by name.

The Salcombe Seaman's Flaunt to the Proud Pirate

A LOFTY ship from Salcombe came,
  Blow high, blow low, and so sailed we ;
She had golden trucks that shone like flame,
  On the bonny coasts of Barbary.

"Masthead, masthead," the captains hail,
Blow high, blow low, and so sailed we ;
"Look out and round ; d' ye see a sail ? "
On the bonny coasts of Barbary.

"There's a ship what looms like Beachy Head,"
Blow high, blow low, and so sailed we ;
"Her banner aloft it blows out red,"
On the bonny coasts of Barbary.

"Oh, ship ahoy, and where do you steer ? "
Blow high, blow low, and so sailed we ;
"Are you man-of-war, or privateer ? "
On the bonny coasts of Barbary.

"I am neither one of the two," said she,
Blow high, blow low, and so sailed we ;
"I'm a pirate, looking for my fee,"
On the bonny coasts of Barbary.

"I'm a jolly pirate, out for gold : "
Blow high, blow low, and so sailed we ;
"I will rummage through your after hold,"
On the bonny coasts of Barbary.

The grumbling guns they flashed and roared,
Blow high, blow low, and so sailed we ;
Till the pirate's mast went overboard,
On the bonny coasts of Barbary.

They fired shot till the pirate's deck,
Blow high, blow low, and so sailed we ;
Was blood and spars and broken wreck,
On the bonny coasts of Barbary.

"O do not haul the red flag down,"
Blow high, blow low, and so sailed we ;
"O keep all fast until we drown,"
On the bonny coasts of Barbary.

They called for cans of wine, and drank,
  Blow high, blow low, and so sailed we ;
They sang their songs until she sank,
  On the bonny coasts of Barbary.

Now let us brew good cans of flip,
  Blow high, blow low, and so sailed we ;
And drink a bowl to the Salcombe ship,
  On the bonny coasts of Barbary.

And drink a bowl to the lad of fame,
  Blow high, blow low, and so sailed we ;
Who put the pirate ship to shame,
  On the bonny coasts of Barbary.

Teach the Rover

WILL you hear of a bloody Battle,
  Lately fought upon the Seas,
It will make your Ears to rattle,
  And your Admiration cease ;
Have you heard of *Teach* the Rover,
  And his Knavery on the Main ;
How of Gold he was a Lover,
  How he lov'd an ill-got Gain.

When the Act of Grace appeared,
  Captain *Teach* with all his men,
Unto *Carolina* steered,
  Where they kindly us'd him then ;
There he marry'd to a Lady,
  And gave her five hundred Pound,
But to her he prov'd unsteady,
  For he soon march'd off the Ground.

And returned, as I tell you,
  To his Robbery as before,
Burning, sinking Ships of value,
  Filling them with Purple Gore;
When he was at *Carolina*,
  There the Governor did send,
To the Governor of *Virginia*,
  That he might assistance lend.

Then the Man-of-War's Commander,
  Two small Sloops he fitted out,
Fifty Men he put on board, Sir,
  Who resolv'd to stand it out:
The Lieutenant he commanded
  Both the Sloops, and you shall hear,
How before he landed,
  He suppress'd them without fear.

Valiant *Maynard* as he sailed,
  Soon the Pirate did espy,
With his Trumpet he then hailed,
  And to him they did reply:
"Captain *Teach* is our Commander."
  Maynard said, "He is the Man,
Whom I am resolv'd to hang, Sir,
  Let him do the best he can."

Teach replyed unto *Maynard*,
  "Sir, no Quarter you shall see,
But be hang'd on the Mainyard,
  You and all your Company."
Maynard said, "I none desire,
  Of such knaves as thee and thine,
None I'll give." *Teach* replied,
  "My boys, give me a Glass of Wine."

TEACH THE ROVER

He took the glass and drank Damnation,
  Unto *Maynard* and his Crew,
To himself and Generation,
  Then the Glass away he threw;
Brave *Maynard* was resolv'd to have him,
  Tho' he'd Cannons nine or ten;
Teach a broadside quickly gave him,
  Killing sixteen valiant Men.

Maynard boarded him, and to it
  They fell with Sword and Pistol too;
They had courage, and did show it,
  Killing of the Pirate's Crew.
Teach and *Maynard* on the Quarter,
  Fought it out most manfully,
Maynard's Sword did cut him shorter,
  Losing his head, he there did die.

Every sailor fought while he, Sir,
  Power had to wield the Sword,
Not a coward could you see, Sir,
  Fear was driven from aboard;
Wounded Men on both Sides fell, Sir,
  'Twas a doleful Sight to see,
Nothing could their Courage quell, Sir,
  O, they fought courageously.

When the bloody Fight was over,
  We're informed by a Letter writ,
Teach's Head was made a Cover,
  To the Jack Staff of the Ship:
Thus they sailed to *Virginia*,
  And when they the Story told,
How they kill'd the Pirates many,
  They'd Applause from young and old.

The Last Buccaneer

OH England is a pleasant place for them that's
    rich and high,
But England is a cruel place for such poor folks
    as I ;
And such a port for mariners I ne'er shall see again
As the pleasant Isle of Avès, beside the Spanish
    Main.

There were forty craft in Avès that were both
    swift and stout,
All furnished well with small arms and cannons
    round about ;
And a thousand men in Avès made laws so fair
    and free,
To choose their valiant captains and obey them
    loyally.

Thence we sailed against the Spaniard with his
    hoards of plate and gold,
Which he wrung with cruel tortures from Indian
    folk of old ;
Likewise the merchant captains, with hearts as
    hard as stone,
Who flog men and keel-haul them, and starve
    them to the bone.

Oh, the palms grew high in Avès, and fruits that
    shone like gold,
And the colibris and parrots they were gorgeous
    to behold ;
And the negro maids to Avès from bondage fast
    did flee,
To welcome gallant sailors, a-sweeping in from sea.

THE LAST BUCCANEER

Oh, sweet it was in Avès to hear the landward breeze,
A-swing with good tobacco in a net between the trees,
With a negro lass to fan you, while you listened to the roar
Of the breakers on the reef outside, that never touched the shore.

But Scripture saith, an ending to all fine things must be ;
So the King's ships sailed on Avès, and quite put down were we.
All day we fought like bull-dogs, but they burst the booms at night ;
And I fled in a piragua, sore wounded, from the fight.

Nine days I floated starving, and a negro lass beside,
Till for all I tried to cheer her, the poor young thing she died ;
But as I lay a-gasping, a Bristol sail came by,
And brought me home to England here, to beg until I die.

And now I'm old and going—I'm sure I can't tell where ;
One comfort is, this world's so hard, I can't be worse off there :
If I might but be a sea dove, I'd fly across the main
To the pleasant Isle of Avès, to look at it once again.

CHARLES KINGSLEY

The Last Buccaneer

The winds were yelling, the waves were swelling,
    The sky was black and drear,
When the crew with eyes of flame brought the
    ship without a name
    Alongside the last Buccaneer.

" Whence flies your sloop full sail before so fierce
    a gale,
    When all others drive bare on the seas ?
Say, come ye from the shore of the holy Salvador,
    Or the gulf of the rich Caribbees ? "

" From a shore no search hath found, from a gulf
    no line can sound,
    Without rudder or needle we steer ;
Above, below our bark dies the sea-fowl and the
    shark,
    As we fly by the last Buccaneer.

" To-night there shall be heard on the rocks of
    Cape de Verde
    A loud crash and a louder roar ;
And to-morrow shall the deep with a heavy
    moaning sweep
    The corpses and wreck to the shore."

The stately ship of Clyde securely now may ride
    In the breadth of the citron shades ;
And Severn's towering mast securely now hies fast,
    Through the seas of the balmy Trades.

From St. Jago's wealthy port, from Havannah's
    royal fort,
  The seaman goes forth without fear ;
For since that stormy night not a mortal hath
    had sight
  Of the flag of the last Buccaneer.

LORD MACAULAY

The Smuggler

(Air : " White Cockade ")

O MY true love's a smuggler and sails upon the sea,
And I would I were a seaman to go along with he;
To go along with he for the satins and the wine,
And run the tubs at Slapton when the stars do
    shine.

O Hollands is a good drink when the nights are
    cold,
And Brandy is a good drink for them as grows old.
There is lights in the cliff-top when the boats are
    home-bound,
And we run the tubs at Slapton when the word
    goes round.

The King he is a proud man in his grand red coat,
But I do love a smuggler in a little fishing-boat ;
For he runs the Mallins lace and he spends his
    money free,
And I would I were a seaman to go along with he.

CHANTIES

A CHANTY is a song sung by sailors when engaged in the severest of their labours. The word chanty is generally mispronounced by landsmen. It is not pronounced as spelt, like the word chant with an added *y* final. It is pronounced shanty, to rhyme with scanty, the *ch* soft and the *a* narrow. The verb to chanty is frequently used, as in the order "Chanty it up, now," or the injunction "Heave and chanty."

There are three varieties of chanty, each kind adapted to its special labour. There is the capstan chanty, sung at the capstan when warping, or weighing anchor, or hoisting topsails with the watch. There is the halliard chanty, sung at the topsail and top-gallant halliards, when the topsails and top-gallant sails are being mast-headed. And there is the sheet, tack, and bowline chanty, used when the fore, main, and crossjack sheets are hauled aft, and when the tacks are boarded and the bowlines tautened. Formerly, in the days when ships were built of wood, and leaked from an inch or two to two or three feet a day, there used to be pumping chanties, sung by the pumpers as they hove the brakes round. Now that ships are built of steel or iron, which either leak not at all or go to the bottom, there is no pumping to be done aboard, save the pumping of fresh water from the tanks in the hold for the use of the crew, and the daily pumping of salt water for the washing down of the decks. I have passed many miserable hours pumping out the leaks from a wooden ship, but I was never so fortunate as to hear a pumping chanty.

Strictly speaking, there is a fourth variety of chanty, but it is a bastard variety, very seldom used. The true chanty, of the kinds I have mentioned, is a song with a solo part and one or two choruses. The solo part consists of a line of rhyme which is repeated by the solo man after the first chorus has been shouted. The bastard variety which I have just mentioned has no solo part. It is a runaway chorus, sung by all hands as they race along the deck with the rope. You hear it in tacking ship. It is a good song to sing when the main and mizzen yards are being swung simultaneously. All hands are at the braces straining taut, and at the order they burst into song and " run away with it," bringing the great yards round with a crash. It is a most cheery kind of chanty, and the excitement of the moment, and the sight of the great yards spinning round, and the noise of the stamping feet impress it on the mind. The favourite runaway chorus is:

" What shall we do with a drunken sailor ?
What shall we do with a drunken sailor ?
What shall we do with a drunken sailor,
   Early in the morning ?
Way, hay, there she rises,
Way, hay, there she rises,
Way, hay, there she rises,
   Early in the morning.

" Chuck him in the long-boat till he gets sober,
Chuck him in the long-boat till he gets sober,
Chuck him in the long-boat till he gets sober,
   Early in the morning.
Way, hay, there she rises,
Way, hay, there she rises,
Way, hay, there she rises,
   Early in the morning.

It is sung to a vigorous tune in quick time. It is the custom among sailors to stamp with their feet at each "Way, hay." The effect is very spirited.

Of the chanties proper, the capstan chanties are the most beautiful, the halliard chanties the most commonly heard, and the sheet, tack, and bowline chanties the most ancient. In a capstan chanty the solo man begins with his single line of verse. Before he has spoken the last word of it the other men heaving at the bars break out with the first chorus. Immediately before the chorus has come to an end the solo man repeats his line of verse, to be interrupted at the last word by the second chorus, which is generally considerably longer than the first. It is a glorious thing to be on a forecastle-head, heaving at a capstan bar, hearing the chain coming clanking in below you to the music of a noisy chanty sung by a score of sailors.

The Solo, or Chanty-man. In Amsterdam there dwelt a maid.
The Sailors. Mark well what I do say:
The Solo, or Chanty-man. In Amsterdam there dwelt a maid,
In Amsterdam there dwelt a maid.
The Sailors. And I'll go no more a-ro-o-ving
With you, fair maid.
A-roving, a-roving.
Since roving's been my ru-in,
I'll go no more a-ro-o-ving with you, fair maid.

That is the most beautiful of all the chanties. It is sung to an old Elizabethan tune which stirs one's blood like a drum-tap. The song, or solo of it, is strangely like the song in one of Thomas Heywood's plays. Several of the couplets are identical. The curious will find the song in "Lucrece," in the fifth act. I cannot quote it here.

A halliard chanty is begun by the solo-man in the manner described above. It has generally two choruses, but they are of the same length— not short and long, as in the case of the anchor chanty. The solo man is always a person of some authority among the crowd. He begins his song after the first two or three pulls upon the halliards. There are countless halliard chanties, and new ones come into use each year. Those which one hears occasionally ashore are nearly always old ones, little used at sea. The sailors have grown tired of them. I do not know what chanties are most used now at sea. In my time we used to get the yards up to—

The Chanty-man. A long, long time and a long time ago,
The Sailors. To me *way* hay, o-*hi*-o ;
The Chanty-man. A long, long time and a long time ago,
The Sailors. A *long* time *ago.*
The Chanty-man. A smart Yankee packet lay out in the bay,
The Sailors. To me *way* hay, o-*hi*-o ;
The Chanty-man. A smart Yankee packet lay out in the bay,
The Sailors. A *long* time *ago* (etc.).

The pulls upon the rope are delivered during the choruses upon the words I have italicised. Another very popular chanty was :

The Chanty-man. Come all you little nigger-boys,
The Sailors. And roll the cotton down ;
The Chanty-man. O come all you little nigger-boys,
The Sailors. And roll the cotton down (etc.).

The tune to this is bright and merry. It puts you in a good temper to be singing it. Another strangely beautiful chanty is that known as "Hanging Johnny." It has a melancholy tune that is one of the saddest things I have ever heard. I heard it for the first time off the Horn, in a snowstorm, when we were hoisting topsails after heavy weather. There was a heavy, grey sea running and the decks were awash. The skies were sodden and oily, shutting in the sea about a quarter of a mile away. Some birds were flying about us, screaming.

> *The Chanty-man* began. They call me Hanging Johnny,
> *The Sailors.* Away-i-oh ;
> *The Chanty-man.* They call me Hanging Johnny,
> *The Sailors.* So hang, boys, hang.

I thought at the time that it was the whole scene set to music. I cannot repeat those words to their melancholy wavering music without seeing the line of yellow oilskins, the wet deck, the frozen ropes, and the great grey seas running up into the sky.

Of the sheet, tack, and bowline chanties the oldest is "Haul the Bowline," which was certainly in use in the reign of Henry VIII. It is still very popular, though the bowline is no longer the rope it was. It is a slow, stately melody, ending with a jerk as the men fall back with the rope.

> *The Chanty-man.* Haul on the bowline, the fore and maintop bowline. Haul on the bowline.
> *The Sailors.* The bowline *haul.*

Another excellent chanty in this kind is the following :

> *The Chanty-man.* Louis was the King of France afore the Revoluti-on.
> *The Sailors.* Away, haul away, boys; haul away toge-e-ther ;
> *The Chanty-man.* But Louis got his head cut off, which spoiled his consti-tu-ti-on.
> *The Sailors.* Away, haul away, boys; haul away *O.*

CHANTIES

The chanty is the invention of the merchant service. In the navy they have what is called the silent routine, and the men fall back upon their ropes in silence, "like a lot of soldiers," when the boatswain pipes. It must be very horrible to witness. In the merchant service, where the ships are invariably undermanned, one sings whenever a rope is cast off the pin. You haul a brace to the cry of "O, bunt him a bo," "O rouse him, boys," "Oho, Jew," "O ho ro, my boys," and similar phrases. You clew up a sail to the quick "Lee-ay," "Lee-ay," "Ho ro," "Ho," "Aha," uttered in a tone of disquiet or alarm. You furl a course to the chant of "Paddy Doyle and his Boots." Without these cries and without the chanties you would never get the work done. "A song is ten men on the rope." In foul weather off the Horn it is as comforting as a pot of hot drink. A wash and a song are the sailor's two luxuries.

Those who wish to obtain the music of the commoner chanties will find Miss Laura Smith's "Music of the Waters" and the anthology of Dr. Ferris Tozer of use to them. Several may be found in the songbook of the Guild of Handicraft. I have also seen a collection of them published (I believe) by Messrs. Metzler. The files of the "Boy's Own Paper," "The Cadet," and the publications of the Folk Song Society may also be consulted with advantage.

In the following pages I have included only a few of the chanties in general use. Many familiar chanties have been excluded owing to lack of space.

Lowlands

(HALLIARD CHANTY)

I DREAMT a dream the other night,
 Lowlands, Lowlands, hurrah, my John;
I dreamt a dream the other night,
 My Lowlands a-ray.

I dreamt I saw my own true love,
 Lowlands, Lowlands, hurrah, my John;
I dreamt I saw my own true love.
 My Lowlands a-ray.

He was green and wet with weeds so cold,
 Lowlands, Lowlands, hurrah, my John;
He was green and wet with weeds so cold,
 My Lowlands a-ray.

" I am drowned in the Lowland seas," he said,
 Lowlands, Lowlands, hurrah, my John;
" I am drowned in the Lowland seas," he said,
 My Lowlands a-ray.

" I shall never kiss you again," he said,
 Lowlands, Lowlands, hurrah, my John;
" I shall never kiss you again," he said,
 My Lowlands a-ray.

I will cut my breasts until they bleed,
 Lowlands, Lowlands, hurrah, my John;
I will cut my breasts until they bleed,
 My Lowlands a-ray.

I will cut away my bonny hair,
 Lowlands, Lowlands, hurrah, my John;
I will cut away my bonny hair,
 My Lowlands a-ray.

No other man shall think me fair,
  Lowlands, Lowlands, hurrah, my John;
No other man shall think me fair,
  My Lowlands a-ray.

O my love lies drowned in the windy Lowlands,
  Lowlands, Lowlands, hurrah, my John;
O my love lies drowned in the windy Lowlands,
  My Lowlands a-ray.

Storm Along
(HALLIARDS)

OLD STORMY he was a good old man,
  To me way hay; storm along, John;
Old Stormy he was a good old man,
  Come along, get along. Storm along, John.

Old Stormy he is dead and gone,
  To me way hay; storm along, John;
Old Stormy he is dead and gone,
  Come along, get along. Storm along, John.

Old Stormy died, and we dug his grave,
  To me way hay; storm along, John;
Old Stormy died, and we dug his grave,
  Come along, get along. Storm along, John.

In sailor town up Mobile Bay,
  To me way hay; storm along, John;
In sailor town up Mobile Bay,
  Come along, get along. Storm along, John.

Whiskey! Johnny!
(HALLIARDS)

O WHISKEY is the life of man,
  Whiskey! Johnny!

O whiskey is the life of man,
Whiskey for my Johnny.

I drink it out of an old tin can,
Whiskey ! Johnny !
I drink it out of an old tin can,
Whiskey for my Johnny.

I drink whiskey when I can,
Whiskey ! Johnny !
I drink whiskey when I can,
Whiskey for my Johnny.

I drink it hot, I drink it cold,
Whiskey ! Johnny !
I drink it hot, I drink it cold,
Whiskey for my Johnny.

I drink it new, I drink it old,
Whiskey ! Johnny !
I drink it new, I drink it old,
Whiskey for my Johnny.

Whiskey killed my poor old dad,
Whiskey ! Johnny !
Whiskey killed my poor old dad,
Whiskey for my Johnny.

Whiskey makes me pawn my clothes,
Whiskey ! Johnny !
Whiskey makes me pawn my clothes,
Whiskey for my Johnny.

Whiskey makes me scratch my toes (gout ?),
Whiskey ! Johnny !

Whiskey makes me scratch my toes,
Whiskey for my Johnny.

O fisherman, have you just come from sea?
Whiskey! Johnny!
O fisherman, have you just come from sea?
Whiskey for my Johnny.

O yes, sir, I have just come from sea,
Whiskey! Johnny!
O yes, sir, I have just come from sea,
Whiskey for my Johnny.

Then have you any crab-fish that you can sell to me?
Whiskey! Johnny!
Then have you any crab-fish that you can sell to me
Whiskey for my Johnny.

O yes, sir, I have crab-fish one, two, three,
Whiskey! Johnny!
O yes, sir, I have crab-fish one, two, three,
Whiskey for my Johnny.[1]

John François

(HALLIARDS)

BONEY was a warrior,
Away-i-oh;
Boney was a warrior,
John François.

---

[1] At this point the ballad becomes a little gross. The curious will find the remainder of the tale in a discreet little book published by the Percy Society, from the relics of Bishop Percy's collection. The ballad dates from the sixteenth century. It is still very popular at sea.

Boney fought the Proosh-i-ans,
Away-i-oh;
Boney fought the Proosh-i-ans,
John François.

Boney fought the Roosh-i-ans,
Away-i-oh;
Boney fought the Roosh-i-ans,
John François.

Drive her, captain, drive her,
Away-i-oh;
Drive her, captain, drive her,
John François.

Give her the top-gallant sails,
Away-i-oh;
Give her the top-gallant sails,
John François.

It's a weary way to Baltimore,
Away-i-oh;
It's a weary way to Baltimore,
John François.

Blow the Man Down

(Halliards)

Blow the man down, bullies, blow the man down,
Away-hay—blow the man down;
Blow the man down, bullies, blow him right down,
Give us a chance to blow the man down.

Blow him right down from the top of his crown,
Away-hay—blow the man down;
Blow him right down from the top of his crown,
Give us a chance to blow the man down.

BLOW THE MAN DOWN

As I was a-walking down Paradise Street,
  Away-hay—blow the man down ;
As I was a-walking down Paradise Street,
  Give us a chance to blow the man down.

A pretty young girl I chanced for to meet,
  Away-hay—blow the man down ;
A pretty young girl I chanced for to meet,
  Give us a chance to blow the man down.

This pretty young girl she said unto me,
  Away-hay—blow the man down ;
This pretty young girl she said unto me,
  Give us a chance to blow the man down.

"There's a fine full-rigged clipper just ready for sea,"
  Away-hay—blow the man down ;
"There's a fine full-rigged clipper just ready for sea,"
  Give us a chance to blow the man down.

The fine full-rigged clipper to Sydney was bound,
  Away-hay—blow the man down ;
The fine full-rigged clipper to Sydney was bound,
  Give us a chance to blow the man down.

She was very well manned and very well found,
  Away-hay—blow the man down ;
She was very well manned and very well found,
  Give us a chance to blow the man down.

As soon as the clipper was clear of the bar,
  Away-hay—blow the man down ;
As soon as the clipper was clear of the bar,
  Give us a chance to blow the man down.

The mate knocked me down with the end of a spar,
  Away-hay—blow the man down ;

The mate knocked me down with the end of a spar,
Give us a chance to blow the man down.

As soon as the clipper had got out to sea,
Away-hay—blow the man down;
As soon as the clipper had got out to sea,
Give us a chance to blow the man down.

I'd cruel hard treatment of every degree,
Away-hay—blow the man down;
I'd cruel hard treatment of every degree,
Give us a chance to blow the man down.

I'll give you a warning afore we belay,
Away-hay—blow the man down;
I'll give you a warning afore we belay,
Give us a chance to blow the man down.

Don't ever take heed of what pretty girls say,
Away-hay—blow the man down;
Don't ever take heed of what pretty girls say,
Give us a chance to blow the man down.

Roll the Cotton Down

(HALLIARDS)

COME roll the cotton down, my boys,
Roll the cotton down;
Come roll the cotton down, my boys,
O roll the cotton down.

Come hither, all you nigger boys,
Roll the cotton down;
Come hither, all you bigger boys,
O roll the cotton down.

A dollar a day is a white man's pay,
   Roll the cotton down ;
A dollar a day is a white man's pay,
   O roll the cotton down.

Ten dollars a day is a black man's pay,
   Roll the cotton down ;
Ten dollars a day is a black man's pay,
   O roll the cotton down.

The white man's pay is rather high,
   Roll the cotton down ;
The white man's pay is rather high,
   O roll the cotton down.

The black man's pay is rather low,
   Roll the cotton down ;
The black man's pay is rather low,
   O roll the cotton down.

Around Cape Horn we're bound to go,
   Roll the cotton down ;
Around Cape Horn we're bound to go,
   O roll the cotton down.

So stretch it aft and start a song,
   Roll the cotton down ;
So stretch it aft and start a song,
   O roll the cotton down.

Reuben Ranzo

(HALLIARDS)

O DO you know old Reuben Ranzo ?
   Ranzo, boys, Ranzo ;
O do you know old Reuben Ranzo ?
   Ranzo, boys, Ranzo.

Old Ranzo was a tailor,
   Ranzo, boys, Ranzo ;
Old Ranzo was a tailor,
   Ranzo, boys, Ranzo.

Old Ranzo was no sailor,
   Ranzo, boys, Ranzo ;
Old Ranzo was no sailor,
   Ranzo, boys, Ranzo.

So he shipped aboard of a whaler,
   Ranzo, boys, Ranzo ;
So he shipped aboard of a whaler,
   Ranzo, boys, Ranzo.

But he could not do his duty,
   Ranzo, boys, Ranzo ;
No, he could not do his duty,
   Ranzo, boys, Ranzo.

Roll and Go

(HALLIARDS)

THERE was a ship—she sailed to Spain.
   O. Roll and go ;
There was a ship—she sailed to Spain,
   O Tommy's on the topsail yard.

There was a ship came home again,
   O. Roll and go ;
There was a ship came home again,
   O Tommy's on the topsail yard.

What d'ye think was in her hold ?
   O. Roll and go ;

What d'ye think was in her hold?
  O Tommy's on the topsail yard.

There was diamonds, there was gold,
    O. Roll and go;
There was diamonds, there was gold,
  O Tommy's on the topsail yard.

And what was in her lazareet?
    O. Roll and go;
And what was in her lazareet?
  O Tommy's on the topsail yard.

Good split peas and bad bull meat,
    O. Roll and go;
Good split peas and bad bull meat,
  O Tommy's on the topsail yard.

Many sailormen gets drowned,
    O. Roll and go;
Many sailormen gets drowned,
  O Tommy's on the topsail yard.

Come Roll Him Over
(Halliards)

Oho, why don't you blow?
  Aha. Come roll him over;
Oho, why don't you blow?
  Aha. Come roll him over.

One man. To strike the bell,
  Aha. Come roll him over;
One man. To strike the bell,
  Aha. Come roll him over.

Two men.   To take the wheel,
  Aha.   Come roll him over ;
Two men.   To take the wheel,
  Aha.   Come roll him over.

Three men.   Top-gallant braces,
  Aha.   Come roll him over ;
Three men.   Top-gallant braces,
  Aha.   Come roll him over.

Hanging Johnny
(Halliards)

They call me Hanging Johnny,
  Away-i-oh ;
They call me Hanging Johnny,
  So hang, boys, hang.

First I hung my mother,
  Away-i-oh ;
First I hung my mother,
  So hang, boys, hang.

Then I hung my brother,
  Away-i-oh ;
Then I hung my brother,
  So hang, boys, hang.

A rope, a beam, and a ladder,
  Away-i-oh ;
A rope, a beam, and a ladder,
  So hang, boys, hang.

I'll hang you all together,
  Away-i-oh ;

I'll hang you all together,
  So hang, boys, hang.

Sally Brown

(HALLIARDS)

O SALLY BROWN of New York City,
  Ay ay, roll and go ;
O Sally Brown of New York City,
  I'll spend my money on Sally Brown.

O Sally Brown, you are very pretty,
  Ay ay, roll and go ;
O Sally Brown, you are very pretty,
  I'll spend my money on Sally Brown.

Your cheeks are red, your hair is golden,
  Ay ay, roll and go ;
Your cheeks are red, your hair is golden,
  I'll spend my money on Sally Brown.

Poor Old Joe

(HALLIARDS)

OLD JOE is dead, and gone to hell,
  O we say so and we hope so ;
Old Joe is dead, and gone to hell,
  O poor old Joe.

The ship did sail, the winds did roar,
  O we say so, and we hope so ;
The ship did sail, the winds did roar,
  O poor old Joe.

He's as dead as a nail in the lamp-room door,
  O we say so, and we hope so ;
He's as dead as a nail in the lamp-room door,
  O poor old Joe.

He won't come hazing us no more,
  O we say so, and we hope so ;
He won't come hazing us no more,
  O poor old Joe.

Tommy's Gone to Hilo

(HALLIARDS)

TOMMY's gone, what shall I do ?
  Tommy's gone to Hilo ;
Tommy's gone, what shall I do ?
  Tommy's gone to Hilo.

Hilo town is in Peru,
  Tommy's gone to Hilo ;
Hilo town is in Peru,
  Tommy's gone to Hilo.

He never kissed his girl good-bye,
  Tommy's gone to Hilo ;
He never kissed his girl good-bye,
  Tommy's gone to Hilo.

He signed for three pound ten a month
  Tommy's gone to Hilo ;
He signed for three pound ten a month,
  Tommy's gone to Hilo.

A Long Time Ago

(HALLIARDS)

A LONG, long time, and a long time ago,
    To me way hay, ohio ;
A long, long time, and a long time ago,
    A long time ago.

A smart Yankee packet lay out in the bay,
    To me way hay, ohio ;
A-waiting for a fair wind to get under way,
    A long time ago.

With all her poor sailors all sick and all sore,
    To me way hay, ohio ;
For they'd drunk all their lime-juice, and could get no more,
    A long time ago.

With all her poor sailors all sick and all sad,
    To me way, hay, ohio ;
For they'd drunk all their lime-juice, and no more could be had,
    A long time ago.

She was waiting for a fair wind to get under way,
    To me way hay, ohio ;
She was waiting for a fair wind to get under way,
    A long time ago.

If she hasn't had a fair wind she's lying there still,
    To me way hay, ohio ;
If she hasn't had a fair wind she's lying there still,
    A long time ago.

Blow, Bullies, Blow

(HALLIARDS)

THERE's a Black Ball barque coming down the river,
    Blow, bullies, blow;
There's a Black Ball barque coming down the river,
    Blow, my bully boys, blow.

And who d'ye think is Captain of her?
    Blow, bullies, blow;
O who d'ye think is Captain of her?
    Blow, my bully boys, blow.

Why, bully Hains is the Captain of her,
    Blow, bullies, blow;
Why, bully Hains is the Captain of her,
    Blow, my bully boys, blow.

He'll make you wish you was dead and buried,
    Blow, bullies, blow:
He'll make you wish you was dead and buried,
    Blow, my bully boys, blow.

You'll brighten brass, and you'll scrape the cable,
    Blow, bullies, blow;
You'll brighten brass, and you'll scrape the cable,
    Blow, my bully boys, blow.

And who d'ye think is mate aboard her?
    Blow, bullies, blow;
O who d'ye think is mate aboard her?
    Blow, my bully boys, blow.

Santander James is the mate aboard her,
    Blow, bullies, blow;
Santander James is the mate aboard her,
    Blow, my bully boys, blow.

He'll ride you down like you ride the spanker,
    Blow, bullies blow;
He'll ride you down like you ride the spanker,
    Blow, my bully boys, blow.

And who d'ye think is the second mate of her?
    Blow, bullies, blow;
O who d'ye think is the second mate of her?
    Blow, my bully boys, blow.

Some ugly case what hates poor sailors,
    Blow, bullies, blow;
Some ugly case what hates poor sailors,
    Blow, my bully boys, blow.

The Rio Grande

(CAPSTAN)

WHERE are you going to, my pretty maid?
    O away Rio;
Where are you going to, my pretty maid?
    We are bound to the Rio Grande.
    O away Rio,
    O away Rio,
O fare you well, my bonny young girl,
We are bound to the Rio Grande.

Have you a sweetheart, my pretty maid?
    O away Rio;

Have you a sweetheart, my pretty maid ?
We are bound to the Rio Grande.
O away Rio,
O away Rio,
O fare you well, my bonny young girl,
We are bound to the Rio Grande.

May I go with you, my pretty maid ?
O away Rio ;
May I go with you, my pretty maid
We are bound to the Rio Grande.
O away Rio,
O away Rio,
O fare you well, my bonny young girl,
We are bound to the Rio Grande.

I'm afraid you're a bad one, kind sir, she replied,
O away Rio ;
I'm afraid you're a bad one, kind sir, she replied,
We are bound to the Rio Grande.
O away Rio,
O away Rio,
O fare you well, my bonny young girl,
We are bound to the Rio Grande.

Sebastopol

(Capstan)

The Crimean war is over now,
  Sebastopol is taken ;
The Crimean war is over now,
  Sebastopol is taken.

So sing cheer, boys, cheer,
  Sebastopol is taken ;
And sing cheer, boys, cheer,
  Old England gained the day.

The Russians they was put to flight,
  Sebastopol is taken ;
The Russians they was put to flight,
  Sebastopol is taken.
So sing cheer, boys, cheer,
  Sebastopol is taken ;
And sing cheer, boys, cheer,
  Old England gained the day.

Our soldiers they are homeward bound,
  Sebastopol is taken ;
Our soldiers they are homeward bound,
  Sebastopol is taken.
So sing cheer, boys, cheer,
  Sebastopol is taken ;
And sing cheer, boys, cheer,
  Old England gained the day.

The Banks of the Sacramento
(CAPSTAN)

IN the Black Ball Line I served my time,
  To me hoodah. To me hoodah ;
In the Black Ball Line I served my time,
  So hurrah for the Black Ball Line.
    Blow, my bullies, blow,
    For California O.
    There's plenty of gold,
    So I've been told,
  On the banks of the Sacramento.

From Limehouse Docks to Sydney Heads,
  To me hoodah.   To me hoodah ;
From Limehouse Docks to Sydney Heads,
  So hurrah for the Black Ball Line.
    Blow, my bullies, blow,
    For California O.
    There's plenty of gold,
    So I've been told,
  On the banks of the Sacramento.

We were never more than seventy days,
  To me hoodah.   To me hoodah ;
We were never more than seventy days,
  So hurrah for the Black Ball Line.
    Blow, my bullies, blow,
    For California O.
    There's plenty of gold,
    So I've been told,
  On the banks of the Sacramento.

We cracked it on, on a big skiute,
  To me hoodah.   To me hoodah ;
We cracked it on, on a big skiute,
  So hurrah for the Black Ball Line
    Blow, my bullies, blow,
    For California O,
    There's plenty of gold,
    So I've been told,
  On the banks of the Sacramento.

The Maid of Amsterdam

(CAPSTAN)

IN Amsterdam there dwelt a maid
  Mark well what I do say ;

In Amsterdam there dwelt a maid,
And she was mistress of her trade.
> *And I'll go no more a-roving*
> *With you, fair maid.*
> *A-roving, a-roving,*
> *Since roving's been my ru-i-n,*
> *I'll go no more a-roving*
> *With you, fair maid.*

Her cheeks was red, her eyes was brown,
> *Mark well what I do say;*

Her cheeks was red, her eyes was brown,
Her hair like glow-worms hanging down.
> *And I'll go no more a-roving*
> *With you, fair maid.*
> *A-roving, a-roving,*
> *Since roving's been my ru-i-n,*
> *I'll go no more a-roving*
> *With you, fair maid.*[1]

Hand Over Hand

(HAND OVER HAND)

A HANDY ship, and a handy crew,
> *Handy, my boys, so handy;*

A handy ship, and a handy crew,
> *Handy, my boys, away oh.*

A handy skipper and second mate, too,
> *Handy, my boys, so handy;*

A handy skipper and second mate too,
> *Handy, my boys, away oh.*

[1] For the rest of the solo, see the song in "The Rape of Lucrece," by Thomas Heywood, Act IV, Scene vi.

A handy Bose[1] and a handy Sails,[2]
Handy, my boys, so handy;
A handy Bose and a handy Sails,
Handy, my boys, away oh.

Haul Away O

(Sheet, Tack, and Bowline)

Away, haul away, boys, haul away together,
Away, haul away, boys, haul away O;
Away, haul away, boys, haul away together,
Away, haul away, boys, haul away O.

Louis was the King of France afore the Revolu-ti-on,
Away, haul away, boys, haul away O;
Louis was the King of France afore the Revolu-ti-on,
Away, haul away, boys, haul away O.

But Louis got his head cut off, which spoiled his con-stitu-ti-on,
Away, haul away, boys, haul away O;
But Louis got his head cut off, which spoiled his con-sti-tu-tion,
Away, haul away, boys, haul away O.

Haul the Bowline

(Sheet, Tack, and Bowline)

Haul upon the bowline, the fore and main top bowline,
Haul the bowline, the bowline haul;

---

[1] Boatswain. [2] Sailmaker.

HAUL THE BOWLINE

Haul upon the bowline, the fore and main top bowline,
Haul the bowline, the bowline haul.

Haul upon the bowline, so early in the morning,
Haul the bowline, the bowline haul;
Haul upon the bowline, so early in the morning,
Haul the bowline, the bowline haul.

Haul upon the bowline, the bonny ship's a-sailing,
Haul the bowline, the bowline haul;
Haul upon the bowline, the bonny ship's a-sailing,
Haul the bowline, the bowline haul.

Haul upon the bowline, Kitty is my darling,
Haul the bowline, the bowline haul;
Haul upon the bowline, Kitty is my darling,
Haul the bowline, the bowline haul.

Haul upon the bowline, Kitty lives at Liverpool,
Haul the bowline, the bowline haul;
Haul upon the bowline, Kitty lives at Liverpool,
Haul the bowline, the bowline haul.

Haul upon the bowline, Liverpool's a fine town,
Haul the bowline, the bowline haul;
Haul upon the bowline, Liverpool's a fine town,
Haul the bowline, the bowline haul.

Haul upon the bowline, it's a far cry to pay-day,
Haul the bowline, the bowline haul;
Haul upon the bowline, it's a far cry to pay-day,
Haul the bowline, the bowline haul.

A Runaway Chorus

WHAT shall we do with a drunken sailor?
What shall we do with a drunken sailor?
What shall we do with a drunken sailor?
    Early in the morning.
  Way, hay, there she rises,
  Way, hay, there she rises,
  Way, hay, there she rises,
    Early in the morning.

Chuck him in the long-boat till he gets sober,
Chuck him in the long-boat till he gets sober,
Chuck him in the long-boat till he gets sober,
    Early in the morning.
  Way, hay, there she rises,
  Way, hay, there she rises,
  O boy, there she rises,
    Early in the morning.

What shall we do with a drunken soldier?
What shall we do with a drunken soldier?
What shall we do with a drunken soldier?
    Early in the morning.
  Way, hay, there she rises,
  Way, hay, there she rises,
  Way, hay, there she rises,
    Early in the morning.

Lock him in the guardroom till he gets sober,
Lock him in the guardroom till he gets sober,
Lock him in the guardroom till he gets sober,
    Early in the morning.

Way, hay, there she rises,
Way, hay, there she rises,
Way, hay, there she rises,
　　Early in the morning.

Paddy Doyle

(Furling)

To *my*,
　　Ay,
And we'll *furl*,
　　Ay,
And pay Paddy Doyle for his boots.

We'll *sing*,
　　Ay,
And we'll *heave*,
　　Ay,
And pay Paddy Doyle for his boots.

We'll *heave*,
　　Ay,
With a *swing*,
　　Ay,
And pay Paddy Doyle for his boots.

L'Envoi—Leave Her Johnny

(For Pumping and Halliards)

I thought I heard the captain say,
　　Leave her, Johnny, leave her ;
You may go ashore and touch your pay,
　　It's time for us to leave her.

A SAILOR'S GARLAND

You may make her fast, and pack your gear,
Leave her, Johnny, leave her ;
And leave her moored to the West Street Pier
It's time for us to leave her.

The winds were foul, the work was hard,
Leave her, Johnny, leave her ;
From Liverpool Docks to Brooklyn Yard,
It's time for us to leave her.

She would neither steer, nor stay, nor wear,
Leave her, Johnny, leave her ;
She shipped it green and she made us swear,
It's time for us to leave her.

She would neither wear, nor steer, nor stay,
Leave her, Johnny, leave her ;
Her running rigging carried away,
It's time for us to leave her.

The winds were foul, the trip was long,
Leave her, Johnny, leave her ;
Before we go we'll sing a song,
It's time for us to leave her.

We'll sing, Oh, may we never be,
Leave her, Johnny, leave her ;
On a hungry ship the like of she,
It's time for us to leave her.

Coil down.

So Long.